Do Not Avenge Us

Testimonies about the Sufferings of the Romanians Deported from Bessarabia to Siberia

Testimonies collected by Monk Moise

Translation, Notes, and Introduction to the English edition by
Octavian Gabor

Title: Do Not Avenge Us: Testimonies about the Suffering of the Romanians Deported from Bessarabia to Siberia
Testimonies collected by Monk Moise
Introduction to the Romanian edition by Monk Moise
Translation, Notes, and Introduction to the English edition by Octavian Gabor
Cover: Iulian Gherstoaga
Contributing Editor: David Dulceany
Editor: Ioana Onica and Ruxandra Vidu

ISBN: 978-1-936629-48-0

Printed in the United States of America

Published by Reflection Publishing
P.O. Box 2182, Citrus Heights, California 95611-2182
email: info@reflectionbooks.com
www.reflectionbooks.com

Table of Contents

Between Justice and Mercy

> "Mercy and justice in the same
> soul is like the man who worships God
> and idols in the same temple"
> (St. Isaac of Syria)

A while ago, I had a conversation with a gentleman. The discussion took place online, in the presence of others, as many of our conversations these days. We had a common friend, but we did not know one another. Someone had praised Marx, and I confessed that for me, after living in a communist country and after being exposed to a multitude of testimonies about the sufferings inflicted by a regime that considered Marx a spiritual father, it was difficult to accept that communism can work otherwise than it "worked" wherever it gained power. The gentleman pressed me further, talking about the beauty stemming out of the socialist doctrines' interest in the poor. I still confessed that the interest in "the poor" made no sense to me, as I could find no meaning in loving masses of people that have a particular quality which distinguish them from others. I could rather understand the interest in someone, a particular individual, say a Johnny or a Mary, the persons who may be, in different or all moments of their lives, poor. This interest in a Johnny and a Mary would not generate a slogan and would not be the attribute of the state, but rather of anyone who acts humanely. True care and sacrifice for another, whoever he or she may be, could not be imposed from above, from the state. I do acknowledge that the discussion was weak on both sides, as many of our "online communications" tend to be. None of us may have had the time to express clearly his views. Here, I am certainly biased, since I am narrating the story. But this is not about whether one of us "won" the battle, since dialogues, if they truly are dialogues, are not about wars. What I think, however, is telling for what falling in love with an idea can do to an inherently good person is the gentleman's final reply: "People like you are the reasons why things are wrong in this country! The world would be better without such individuals!" I could not help but think that this gentleman could have easily been a young man with good intentions who would want to cleanse the world of its problems by sending the "troublemakers," those who are just blind to "truth," to concentration camps.

I do not mention this story to paint unfavorably those who believe in socialist ideas or any other people, for that matter. Instead, I think this story reminds us that anyone, and especially those of us who may believe that they are the manifestation of beauty in the world, can become so blinded by our ideas that we can murder in their name. The moment when we see ourselves as potential saviors of the world is a dreadful one, for this is when we have already lost the world and ourselves: we become judges of beauty instead of having communion with it. It is a temptation that we all face. Some people believe that their lives are better without Jews; others, without Christians; still others, without Muslims. Some of us may just want a "beautiful" world with people who would have only one color, whichever that may be. Further, we hear today how the world would be a better place if homosexuals were to disappear, or, the reverse, if those who disagree with gay marriage would just be thrown away on a lost island. If we do not recognize ourselves in any of these situations, we may still remember a moment in our lives when we may have thought that our family would have been just fine if that distanced uncle did not belong to it.

The readers of *Do Not Avenge Us!* may find themselves in the middle of the same temptation: if just these communists did not exist, life in Bessarabia and Romania may have been better. When you witness the terrible sufferings experienced by the people of this volume, your anger and resentment toward the persecutors will be difficult to contain. This failing is "normal." To be tempted by justice, by paying back the one who harmed you with the same evil that you have received from him or her is what the majority, if not all, of us do. The people from this book have done it too. But they also remembered that it is difficult to remain a person when you reduce the people around you to the actions they have done.

While this book reveals how individuals faced the wrath brought upon them by a murderous regime, it is also about how one relates to another person. Fr. Moise, the monk who put together the testimonies of those persecuted by the Bolsheviks in Bessarabia, told me once that the people in this book are revivers, not survivors - and this phrase may not fully capture the beauty of his words. In Romanian, it sounds quite poetical: "învietori, nu învingători," that is people who revive, who rise again, as if from death, and not people who conquer, who simply win or are successful. Fr. Moise was referring especially to the education from these days, when, from an early age, children are taught to compete with others and do everything necessary to win. We are taught that we can be either tigers or gazelles in life.[1] We either eat from the flesh of another, or we are eaten. Both cases are found in *Do Not Avenge Us!* There are indeed tigers and gazelles in these stories. The book you have in your hands is written from the perspective of the gazelles. The darkness that transpires from those pages is overwhelming, and the suffering is unbearable, even for those who, after years, only read about these people's lives. The lack of humanity, the inability to perceive a human being in the presence of another, and the viciousness that a human being can manifest are as many reasons to say that the world would have been a better place without the Bolsheviks. How could the book then be beautiful? Who would want to read a text full of darkness, of death, and of destruction?

The answer may be found in Fr. Moise's phrase that I mentioned above. Indeed, the idea that we are to be revivers, not survivors, captures the essence of this book and witnesses to its beauty. You will encounter in these pages people who have lost everything: they lost their families, their homes, their country, their goods, and, at times, even their hopes. Nevertheless, they somehow break back to the surface once again[2] and do not lose precisely that which the Bolsheviks wanted to destroy: themselves. This recovery is achieved in

---

[1] I heard in the past a president of a college delivering a speech to the new freshman class telling students that the school would teach them to be tigers and not gazelles, so they could feed themselves with others.

[2] This does not mean that all people could revive; many did not.

connection: a son who reminds a mom of who she used to be, a good word from a fellow prisoner, or an embrace that reminds someone of his or her humanity.

This is not a book about morality. People do not give lessons and do not encourage others to only act in certain ways. In fact, many deal honestly with the temptation of being a "tiger." In those times, being a tiger meant to betray your neighbor or to arrange things with authorities so that someone else would be sent to Siberia in your place. It meant to become the head of the village and take everything from other people, trespass their properties, and threaten them with rape. After all, it also could have meant just a "small" thing, such as giving up your faith. I do not know how many of us can say, without a doubt, that we would choose the life of a beggar for our children if this were the only option that would allow them to maintain their human dignity.

The people in this book do not claim such a heroic thing. They go even as far as acknowledging that, as luck has it, they could have been on the other side. Nicolae Istrate, one of the narrators, actually says, "I may have been like them. If they did not take me to Siberia, I may have been like them." When he says this, Istrate acknowledges that life is not about being better than someone else, be it morally or socially. Suffering does not make one good; having powers over others does not make one evil. In fact, from the lines of this book we see once again - this testimony is recurrent among many of the survivors from communist persecution[3] - that there is nothing about human beings that make them good or bad.[4] There is, however, something, in which they express the meaning of being-human: the love for another person. Fr. Moise's revivers do not love concepts; they do not love equality, the poor, or freedom. They love a person in anyone of their neighbors.

*

---

[3] See also Aspazia Otel Petrescu's *With Christ in Prison*, also published by Reflection Publishing.

[4] I emphasize here that the phrase claims something about human beings, about persons, and not about actions.

A few more words about Bessarabia. The people you'll find in this book loved their country. For them, Bessarabia is Romania. The separation between brothers and sisters, which took place once the Soviet Union occupied Bessarabia toward the end of WWII, is a wound that remains open and that needs healing. Thus, I think it is appropriate to end this introduction with the words of one of the heroes of this book, Ion Moraru:

"By now, I have lived my life, and I thank God for everything that He has given me. My soul has only one more desire. I rose to fight for Romania, and the beatings that I have received everywhere were because I said that I was Romanian. It is true that, back then, when I established this organization, I did not have in mind to do something for history. I had my head in the clouds. Back then it was the romanticism of the age! I established "The Sword of Justice" as the burning bush of Romanianism, just as the Burning Bush movement in the Sovietized Romania. This is why I desire to receive back, before I die, my documents that attest my Romanian ethnic origin. I want to deposit my bones at the foundation of the country of Romania, and I would like to go to the Judgment of the nations with my papers in order, stating that I am Romanian."

*

A few words about the translation. The six narrators have different literary styles, and I tried to maintain this here. Some of them had little formal education, since they spent their childhood and youth in concentration camps in Siberia. The beauty of the book stems, however, from the honesty of the verb.

I maintained some words in Romanian, such as *bunica* and *bunelul*, and I explained them when I did so. I was inspired in doing so by Carmen Bugan's *Burying the Typewriter: A Memoir* (Graywolf Press, 2012).

All the footnotes are mine, except when noted.

Octavian Gabor

A Word for the Reader

Introduction to the Romanian Edition

In 1919, the world powers of the time gathered for peace talks in Versailles. The purpose of the meeting was to discuss and redraw the map of the European space after WWI. On this occasion, there were voices that challenged the union of Transylvania with Romania. The pretext invoked? Transylvania would be too civilized (today it would be *too European*) in comparison with a primitive and wild Romania.

In place of an answer, the Romanian representative, Ionel Brătianu, put on the table the ten-volume collection of *The Proverbs of Romanians*.[5] The effect was just as powerful. No European country could boast with such an accomplishment.

The reader has in his hands the first volume from a series, *Do Not Avenge Us!*[6] which brings under the same name, books and DVDs with documentaries. This series wants to reiterate, symbolically, the gesture from Versailles. You will find here what can be called "a lesson of spirituality" given by the anticommunist resistance.

I include here the saints of prisons who are waiting for their canonization and the fighters from the mountains; those who went through the hell of reeducation, and those who suffered in icy Siberia, deportees or prisoners of war. The women who were behind bars are also here, but also those often forgotten: the mothers, wives, and sisters of those imprisoned - patient martyrs who, year after year, bore the cross of anticipation and uncertainty at the gates of prisons.

Without gratuitous idealizations or accusations, with necessary selections, but also with inevitable glitches, we will

---

[5] *Proverbele Românilor din România, Basarabia, Bucovina, Ungaria, Istria și Macedonia* (*The Proverbs of the Romanians from Romania, Bessarabia, Bucovina, Hungary, Istria, and Macedonia*), edited by Iuliu Zanne at the end of the 19th century. An anastatic edition was published in 2003 by Scara Publishing House. The episode from Versailles is told here. (*Footnote in the Romanian Edition*)

[6] The second volume has not yet been published in Romanian.

bring them one by one before the reader. They will come with their torments and the horrors they experienced, but also with God's care for them, many times demonstrated by miracles. They will come with their troubles and spiritual falls, but especially with their victories in the spirit. As one of the sufferers said, "you see God better through your tears." In one word, we propose a fresco as vivid as possible of what Răzvan Codrescu, a Christian publicist, called "our only certificate of historical honor during half a century of national disaster." The most suitable title I could find for these testimonies was the message the Christian philosopher Mircea Vulcănescu sent from prison: "Do not avenge us!" Considered literally, this message has no relevance today. The risk is no longer to avenge them, but to forget them. Its spiritual force, however, remains. Is it a small matter to think in this way, when you are on the cross? Uttered at the moment of crucifixion, during the highest tension, these words reveal the essence of an attitude before people and before God that is not at all singular among the political detainees.

"It is dreadful to learn first-hand that there is no resurrection without crucifixion," Aspazia Oțel Petrescu, one of the sufferers, said.[7] "However, at the end of sufferings, the martyrs received the power to love and forgive. Without even realizing, the executioners polished a generation able to forgive."[8] The same lady Aspazia recounts how she fasted for forty days in prison in order to forgive the one who tortured her.[9]

Of course, not all former detainees think in the same way. I did not try to show them more forgiving than they actually are. We have things to learn even from those who confess that it is very hard for them to forgive. We understand from them how terrible their experiences were and how deep their wounds are. As for us, we must ask for ourselves how we stand in our

---

[7] Reflection Publishing has published one volume by Aspazia Oțel Petrescu, *With Christ in Prison* (2014).

[8] Testimony given to monk Moise in August 2010. (*Footnote in the Romanian Edition*)

[9] See *With Christ in Prison*. Reflection Publishing, 2014, p. 58.

relation with forgiveness, we who, most often, have a much easier cross.

A few words about the history of this audacious project. Years ago, I contemplated the idea of putting together a Patericon [10] with people and their special experiences in communist prisons. I read the memories of those who went through prisons, I talked to former political detainees, and I researched the files from CNSAS[11] for weeks.

I thought that the only thing that remained was to put everything in order. But then, while in a group of generous people, [12] the idea was born to create a video archive with former political detainees, with professional videos.

Being under time pressure, since the detainees die one by one, we began filming, first in Bucharest, then throughout the country. Just a few of those interviewed were under 80 years old. The eldest was 103 years old!

After almost one year and a half, we produced a video archive with very interesting testimonies. I was part of all the recordings. The vision of the *Patericon* was substantially changed, and we arrived at the series *Do Not Avenge Us!*

Last summer, I went to Bessarabia together with Bogdan Pîrlea. Bogdan was the one who filmed a large part of the testimonies in Romania and then worked on the documentaries that accompany this book. I was very surprised to encounter beyond the river Prut[13] another Romanian world of which, to my shame, I did not know much.

Stolen in 1812 by the Tsarist Empire, Bessarabia was subjected to a harsh policy of uprooting until 1917. Russian

---

[10] A Patericon is a collection of stories about the lives of saints, which often includes their sayings.

[11] The National Council for the Study of the Archives of the Securitate.

[12] The idea belonged to Dan Puric and doctor Pavel Chirilă. A very important support came from director Nicolae Mărgineanu, who is the son of a political detainee, Father Arsenie Boca Christian Foundation, the Saints of Prisons Foundation, and Carter Films. In various forms, many others helped to bring this project to an end. (*Footnote in the Romanian Edition*)

[13] The Prut is the river that runs between the present day Republic of Moldova and Romania.

became the official language in administration and schools, and the religious services were in Slavonic. People know well the story of a Russian bishop who, around 1870, was building a fire in his stove with religious books in Romanian gathered from his parishes.

Having in the background the fall of the Empire, which followed the Bolshevik revolution, Bessarabia was united to Romania in 1918. A more peaceful period followed until 1940, when the Soviet Union occupied Bessarabia.[14]

In 1941, the Romanian armies, which joined the war on the side of Germany, liberated Bessarabia. It was not for long. In 1944, it was again occupied by the Soviets. The communist period (which began by the terror of the one year of occupation, 1940-1941) is more than dramatic.

If we compare the communism in Romania to the one in Bessarabia, it was much more terrible there. The sovietization of Bessarabia implied in part its Russification. The regime fought fiercely against anything that meant Romanian identity: the Romanian language, the Latin alphabet, or Romanian national history. Beginning with the first year of occupation, the Romanian elite - priests, civil officers, politicians, and professors - were arrested and persecuted. Tens of thousands were assassinated or sent in the Soviet gulag or prisons.

In 1946-1947, during the organized famine, 10% of the population died (around 150,000 victims in less than 1,500,000 people). The regime prepared the collectivization of agriculture, and the peasants were forced to give to the state very large shares of their production. The year was extremely dry, the shares were very large, and the people remained without food.

From the 1,200 churches, only around 200 remained open. The others were either destroyed during the war by the soviets, were closed, or were given a different use. The cathedral in

---

[14] The Soviet Union occupied Bessarabia as a consequence of the German-Soviet Pact of 1939 (also known as Ribbentrop-Molotov Pact), which had a secret protocol dividing Eastern Europe in spheres of influence between Germany and the Soviet Union.

Chişinău,[15] for example, was transformed into a museum of atheism. There was only one priest for ten to twenty villages. In some cases, when the soviets came, they forced the priest to renounce Christ and, when he refused, they murdered him after terrible torments. Other priests were murdered because they opposed the profanation of churches.

While we filmed, we talked to survivors of the soviet camps and prisons and with people who, when they were children, were deported to Siberia. Many times having tears in their eyes, they described, simply and movingly, the unbelievable trials they had experienced. When I returned to Romania, I decided to begin the series of *Do Not Avenge Us!* with testimonies about the sufferings of the most tried part of the Romanian land, Bessarabia.

I was getting ready to end these thoughts, when, by chance (someone once said that chance is God's way to choose to remain anonymous) I found some thoughts of Grigore Vieru:

"I saw a documentary about a child who was born with his heart outside her body; some golden hands of some surgeons managed to put the heart in its place. This is how Bessarabia is, a child with her heart outside of her chest. Her place is with Romanian language, in Romanian history, and in the ancestral faith. This we can accomplish only together, first of all, with the Romanians from there, and then with the Romanians from here."[16]

Monk Moise

---

[15] Chişinău is the largest city in Moldova, presently the capital of the Republic.

[16] *My Poetry comes from great solitude and heavy suffering*—interview with Grigore Vieru by Stelian Gomboş, Chişinău, 2002. (*Footnote in the Romanian Edition*)

The Bird Without Wings

Margareta Cemârtan-Spânu

The village where I was born...

The village where I was born, the village of my grandparents and my great-grandparents, is Mihăilenii Vechi, in the Răşcani district of Bălţi county. Before the soviet communists came, people used to live there as they had learned from tradition, peacefully and beautifully. The greatest wealth was the land - not money or gold, but the land. If a man had land, he did not die of hunger, and he lived according to how he worked.

People were working hard, and God blessed them with all they needed. There was no household without plentiful grains, corn, beans, eggs, cheese, milk, and sweets. They were so well off that on the Saturday of the Souls, at the time of giving of alms, people could not find others who were poorer than them, and that is because all lived well.[17]

People feared God and sin. They knew that all evil brings punishment from above, so everyone strove to do good things. If it happened that some began a quarrel, it did not last. If one said, for example, "look, your pumpkin fell on my land, so it is my pumpkin now," and then the other replied, "no, it is mine, because I planted it on my land," then the wives or some of the neighbors immediately brought the priest and made peace between them. Each asked for forgiveness from the other, and that was it, because they knew that it was a sin to keep anger against your brother and that if you do not forgive your brother, you will not be forgiven either. The entire village came to church. Rarely would you find one person or the other who would not come, but even they still feared God. This is why there was no theft, drunkenness, or lechery among people. If anyone did this, he was the shame of the village, and everyone knew about him. The thieves, especially, were very shamed.

---

[17] In Orthodox Christianity, there are specific Saturdays assigned during the Liturgical year for memorial services for the dead. For example, there are the three such Saturdays at the beginning of Great Lent.

People hung a board around their neck, on which was written, "don't do as I did so that you do not become like me." They were taken in a carriage with this board around their neck on all the streets of the village. Every rose has its thorns.

The feasts were sacred. People prepared everything the night before, so that they would not work at all the following day, no cutting, no cooking. The only allowed thing was to feed and water the cattle. The moment vespers began,[18] there was only prayer and nothing else.

The elders' word had weight in the household. The young went to them to ask for advice about everything: how to plow, seed, or act. Whoever did not have an elder at home went to the neighbor to look for one. This is how the young people were educated: if you live with the elders in the house, even if you do not always like it, you must respect them and listen to them. Everyone had his own role. During the day, when all were going to the hill, to work, the elders remained at home, gave water to the chickens, fed them, whatever they could. They were not put to work: "Do this, do that, whether you can or not!" No! There was understanding and peace among them.

Separation[19] was a rarity; it took place only when one of the spouses could no longer endure it and left home. Otherwise, the effort was to reconcile them. First, the parents came in: "You embarrass us! How can we live after something like this? Are we Gypsies?"[20] They advised them to find the middle path, to each give up something, and thus to make peace.

In short, people lived wisely and had everything they needed.

---

[18] The liturgical day begins in the evening, with the vespers service.

[19] The narrator refers to divorce.

[20] In those times, the Gypsies were not integrated in villages, living on the outskirts. Both parties were prejudiced against one another, placing on the other group the worst human characteristics. For more details about the life of Gypsies in Eastern Europe see Elena Zamfir and Catalin Zamfir, eds., *Țiganii: între ignorare și îngrijorare*, Alternative, 1993, Elena Gabor, "Gipsy Stereotypes and Ideology Levels in Two European Feature Films, " *Intercultural Communication Studies* XVI:2, 2007, and Michael Stewart, *The Time of the Gypsies*, Westview Press, 1997.

My parents: Nicolae and Dochiţa Spânu

My grandparents were among the leaders of the village.

On my father's side, Grigore and Sofia Spânu met on a feast day,[21] liked each other, married, and had eleven children, of which five survived. Since they were well-off, *bunicul*[22] decided to sent all of them to school, except Anastasia, the eldest daughter, who remained to help in the household. Vladimir and Alexandru went to the School for Officers in Iaşi, while Maria and Nicolae, my father, studied for five years.

The grandparents on my mother's side, Ioan and Nadejda Scutaru, were also well-off, but less than my other *bunei*.[23] However, they had three beautiful daughters, and you could not take your eyes off them: Vera, Măriuţa, and Eudochia. Later, they also had a boy, Gheorghe.

The most wonderful of the girls was the little one, Dochiţa,[24] and she was the one with whom my father fell in love. He was not a very handsome young man, but he had a quick mind, sweet talk, and was stylish, with clothing made in Iaşi.[25] When they fell in love, my dad went to her parents to reach an agreement. Her parents did not give her anything, except her usual dowry: carpets, pillows, blankets, things like that. The grandparents on my father side wanted their daughter-in-law to also have some land and cattle, so they told my dad, "Colea, if they don't give her anything, go and find another, for there are as many girls as there are leaves and grass!"

But my dad did not listen to them. He went to my mom in secret, and they continued to see each other, until one day when

---

[21] The Romanian word, "hram," indicates the feast connected with the patron saint of a church. In Orthodoxy, every church has a patron saint. The day dedicated to that saint is a feast day for the community.

[22] Whenever the text referred to "grandpa" (*bunicul* or *bunelul*) or "grandma" (*bunica*), I kept the Romanian word. The idea came from reading Carmen Bugan's *Burying the Typewriter: A Memoir* (Graywolf Press, 2012). The word *bunelul* in Romanian is the diminutive or the word *bunul*, "the good one." Addressing an old man, the grandfather, with the diminutive of "the good one" is poetic in itself.

[23] Grandparents.

[24] Diminutive from Eudochia.

[25] Iaşi is the cultural capital of the province of Moldova in Romania.

they decided to elope. In those days, it still happened that girls chose to elope if the parents were against the marriage. So my dad took Dochiţa to his older sister Anastasia's house.

Since he had stolen her away from her parents, he also had to make an arrangement with them, because what other solution was there? This was the mentality in the village: if the girl left home and was shamed, then she had to marry the boy who stole her away; if not, another groom could accuse her later, "Woman, you ran away with that guy; how do I know what you did with him?!"

So my *bunei* had no other solution, and my parents married. They had a rich and beautiful wedding on the Holy Sunday[26] of 1937. One year later, Emil, my older brother, was born, and everything went well until the war came.

It's not Tamara, it's Margareta!

Beginning with 1940, people's peace and well-being were shattered. The Russians gave an ultimatum to Romania to withdraw its army and administration from Bessarabia.[27] Many people fled to the country,[28] leaving behind their lands and lifetime's savings.

In 1941, the war began and the Romanian Army crossed the river Prut to free Bessarabia.

All the lads of *bunelul* Grigore were called to arms. The eldest, Vladimir and Alexandru, were officers by profession and were taken directly to the front, but my dad was sent to training to learn to shoot the cannon. One night, when they were doing the exercises on the field, dad went to sleep under the cannon to avoid the mosquitoes. He placed a big rock under the wheel, because the land was a bit slanting, then he covered himself with his mantle and went to sleep. While sleeping, he pushed the rock to the side, and the cannon started downhill and

---

[26] The Holy Sunday is the Sunday of Pascha (Easter).

[27] See the introduction to the Romanian edition written by Fr. Moise.

[28] They fled to Romania. I could have simply translated with "they fled to Romania," but I wanted to leave the idea in the original: they still considered Romania to be their own country.

crushed his leg from knee to heel. They took him immediately to Bucharest, and he stayed in the hospital around four months, until he got better. Then, they discharged him because he was no longer good for war! How much he suffered in Siberia because of that leg … it's frightening!

In 1942, on November 19th, I came into the world, after a difficult birth. It so happened that *mama*[29] could not go to the Town Hall to get my birth certificate, so she sent *bunelul* Grigore to register me with the name of Tamara, because that's what she liked. There were two students in training at the Town Hall, two young girls from Bucharest. They took *bunelul* aside and slowly said:

"Father Grigore, what do you need Tamara for? Choose Margareta! Look how beautifully it sounds! It's a flower's name, and it is international and modern! Forget Tamara!"

Bunelul did not give up:

"Well, Dochiţa said to call her Tamara. She gave birth to her, she suffered, so she has all the right to choose!"

"Father Grigore, don't worry, she will like it as well! She just doesn't know that there is such a name, Margareta!"

The young girls convinced my *bunelul*.

When he came home, *mama* asked him, "Well, how is it with my Tamara?"

And *bunelul* said, "Well, it's not Tamara, it's Margareta!"

"Oh dear! Your tongue will roll around in your mouth before you get to say Margareta! And when she's old the kids will have to call her aunt Margareta, and the children won't be able to…"

But *mama* did not reproach him much. If this is what it was to be, it remained this way. They gave me this name at baptism too, because every name on earth is given by the Lord.

Mama went to sleep for good…

Two years after my birth, the typhus epidemic came into the village, and people began dying one after the other.

---

[29] As in the case with the grandparents, I kept the Romanian word for "mother" as well.

Mǎriuţa, my mother's sister-in-law, got sick as well. Her relatives did not go to visit her, because they were afraid, but mom, who was very compassionate, went to stay with her from time to time, brought her what she needed, or arranged her hair... My *mama* caught the typhus as well. Mǎriuţa got well, and *mama* went to sleep forever. She was twenty-six when she died, and dad was thirty.

The entire village came to the funeral, and all mourned her, for she was so unassuming, beautiful, and good. In our region, the custom is that only women mourn the dead, but now dad was the one who cried the most. He was chocking in tears, holding me in his arms. No man has cried as hard as him. He really missed *mama* because he loved her so much.

One year before this, when he was in Romania, his brother from Sibiu had advised him to remain there, for difficult times would be coming to Bessarabia. Dad did not want to: "No, no! I will go home, to my Dochiţa, to my children!"

Much did he endure after this, poor man! A widower with two small children, during war and famine! If *mama* were alive, perhaps things would have come to be different...

Bunica Nadejda's exile

Our family's troubles had just started.

Mama's middle sister, Mǎriuţa, was married with Dumitru Agafiţei, the chief policeman in Rǎdoaia. He was from Botoşani.[30] When the war started, he was taken in the army, as an officer; his wife with two small children, four years old and four months old, remained home. In 1944, when it was already known that the Russians would be lords over Bessarabia again, he sent a telegram to the village: "Maria, take the children, find a carriage, load it with as much stuff as you can, and cross the border. I will send someone to wait for you and take you to a host."

She did so. She got a carriage, took the children, some things from the house, and came to Mihǎileni, to her parents:

"Dad, mom, Dumitru sent me a telegram and asked me to

---

[30] Botoşani is a city in the north-east of Romania.

leave. Here, I leave, but I am afraid to go on the road by myself with the children. Come with me at least to the border!"

She was afraid, because there was pounding everywhere, planes, tanks, and she was a young woman with two small children. They took counsel together, and *bunelul* decided that *bunica* Nadejda would accompany Mǎriuţa to her host, and then she would come back in a hurry.

They arrived at the border with difficulty, because there was shooting from below and from above with cannons and planes. They crossed the Prut[31] and began wondering where Ialomiţa was. Dumitru had sent her there, where he had received a position and where he had found a host. But Ialomiţa was far from the border, toward Bulgaria.[32] Finally, they found the place, and *bunica* helped her daughter with her new house, paid a woman to come and help her, bathe the child, or buy food from the store. Then, she left to go back home. When she reached the border, in Botoşani, the Russian soldiers were already in charge:

"Nazdad! Nazdad!"[33]

She did not understand anything, and she tried to convince them, crying:

"My house, my children, my husband, everything is there!"

They said nothing:

"Niznai, nicevo!"[34]

And that was it!

She had stayed there for three days, crying, to reason with the soldiers to let her go home. On the third day, someone higher in rank came in a car. He knew Romanian, so he told her:

"The border is closed; it is the state's border, and you are not allowed to cross it! How do we know who you are? You have no paper, no passport, nothing! How do we know whether you are not a spy sent here on purpose?"

The poor woman was crying:

---

[31] The Prut is the river that separates Bessarabia from Romania.

[32] Ialomita is in the south of Romania, probably around 400 km from where they crossed the Prut from Bessarabia.

[33] Russian for: "Back! Back!" (*Footnote in the Romanian Edition*)

[34] Russian for "I don't know anything!" (*Footnote in the Romanian Edition*)

"Look, I took my daughter to Ialomița, and now I came back!"

"Go to your Ialomița, stay there, and be done! If you stay here longer, we'll shoot you! These soldiers say that you have terrorized them for three days!"

She had no choice. She asked someone to take her by car and went back, but she no longer knew exactly where. She spent two days looking for the place where she had left her daughter.

She stayed in Ialomița for sixteen years, until they allowed people to cross the border. She came home, but she found havoc: my mom, her younger daughter, had died, and she had no idea about it; her son banished her from home, and *bunelul* was now with another woman. At the end, she remained to live there, but they no longer had good days until the moment they died, first *bunica* and then *bunelul*.

The death of bunelul Grigore

The grandparents on my father's side were not free from calamities either.

They were working people, and few were like them in the village. This is why they had a beautiful household, with lands, cows, sheep, and horses; the children had their own homes. They had toiled their entire life; this is how they were: they wanted to have everything they needed so that they would not need to beg, to be a laughingstock, but rather an example for the children...

In 1940, when the Russians came for the first time, they recruited a giant of a man from the village to make him an activist.[35] He was a nobody, the type that could betray even his own mother. He was uneducated, having nothing to show for himself. He was nicknamed Grisha the Gipsy. He believed that the Russian occupation would last forever, and he started to wreak havoc in the village, especially against the hardworking

---

[35] The communists applied this method everywhere: they destroyed the leaders of the communities and replaced them with people who had no expertise for their positions and were ready to do anything to keep these positions.

people. He also came to *bunelul* Grigore, stole what he liked from him, and then removed all of the icons from the house by force, threw them in the yard, trampled on them, and set them on fire.

In 1941, when the Romanian army came, the people complained that their icons were taken, that they were being threatened at gunpoint and robbed. Everyone testified, and Grisha the Gipsy was tried and sent to prison for one year. They did not deport him to Siberia, did not torment him, did not torture him, did not shoot him, and did not take his house, as the Bolsheviks did to the Romanians. They only put him in prison for one year. He did not stay even that whole year because, after a few months, the Russians returned and liberated him. Then, Grisha the Gipsy denounced the people to the Soviets[36] because "they testified against me and I was in prison because of them."

Bunelul Grigore was arrested and condemned for 10 years. After the trial, they took him to Briceva, a small village in the vicinity, where they had built a special prison for old people, because, unlike the young, the old could not be sent to Siberia to work. *Bunelul* was 75 years old. They also arrested his in-law, Grigore Musteață, and took him there as well.

At Briceva, the conditions were so that they would all die. They kicked them and hit them with various weapons. They mocked them. When they asked for food, the guards called them "enemies of the people": they had to remain hungry. They managed to survive as they could until fall, but when winter came it began to freeze. Then, the soldiers allowed them to go on the hills to gather sunflower strains, vine ropes, sticks, and whatever else had not already been gathered.

While gathering this way, today from a *nedel*,[37] tomorrow from another one, *bunelul* arrived to his own *nedel* on the hill of Mihăileni. When he saw his land untilled, with the sunflower strains not gathered, a great sorrow came over him, and he

---

[36] The Soviets were local organizations that represented the central Soviet power.
[37] *Nedel* is a regionalism that designates a plot of land (according to the Romanian edition). I chose to leave it in Romanian, as I also did with other words, to retain some of the color of the book.

began to cry. He began to remember everything, how he used to live there, in that big house, with his dear wife, how he used to sleep under the cherry tree in the afternoon, how he used to go with the cows on the plain in the vicinity. It was there that he used to reap the golden grains, it was there that he used to make wine in the fall, it was there that two of his children were born. Now, there was nothing left: everything was robed, cut, and destroyed forever.

As he was staying there, crying, his in-law told him:

"You know how to write. Take some paper and write something!"

Someone gave him a piece of a newspaper, and he wrote with the chemical pencil: "Sofica, I will die soon, because they torment us terribly, they beat us, and they keep us hungry and cold. You take care of the grandchildren and of Colea, because he is widowed, and support one another. If I have wronged you in any way, forgive me! I also forgive you." Forgiveness was the most important thing, back then. God forbid if anyone died without being forgiven by the others and without forgiving them! Even if they had had no problems with one another, even if they had not quarreled, they absolutely had to die forgiven.

After he wrote this note, *bunelul* stuck it into a sunflower strain that he left standing on the field, and he left. From that day, he no longer came out of bed and he died after a short time.

After some time, someone was looking for firewood, and he got to *bunelu*'s lot. He found the strain with the note, he read it, because he knew how to read, came to *bunica* and told her. *Bunica* called the girls immediately, because they were now living in their own homes. They made *sarmale*,[38] baked bread, and cooked all kinds of things to take food to him, so that he would not be hungry.

---

[38] *Sarmale* are a traditional Romanian meal, also found in other East European countries. They are stuffed cabbage rolls, with meat (usually pork, but also beef). In Romania, the *sarmale* are made for the majority of the feasts around the year, especially for Christmas, but also for the meals after memorial services. Each region has its own tradition. In Moldova, they are very small and look similar to the Greek *dolmades*. In Transylvania, they are much larger, the size of 4-5 Moldavian *sarmale* put together.

Then, *bunica* put everything into a basket and went to prison alone, 15 kilometers on foot. When she arrived, the guard soldier yelled at her:

"Go home; he has been dead a long time!"

Bunica did not event want to hear.

"Go home! I will shoot you if you linger here!"

"Shoot me, but I won't go; I want to know for sure! Call for a commander,[39] a chief, do something, so I can talk to him. I don't believe he is dead!"

They called his in-law, Grigore Musteață, and they allowed them to speak over the gate. He told her everything in detail, how they went on the hill, how he wrote the note, and how he died. *Bunica* left all the food at the prison, as alms for his soul. Then she came home and made him a memorial and everything according to custom. It was 1945.

The famine

After the death of *mama* and *bunelu*, dad had to lead two households, *bunica*'s and ours'. She had three hectares of land, and we had four; then there were the cattle and the house. He had to work seven hectares of land, to sustain us growing and to help *bunica*.

My brother Emil had grown and was going to school by now. He studied well, and dad was full of joy when the teacher praised him, saying that he studied well and wrote beautiful poems. However, he was not only studying, for dad could not take care of all things by himself, and he put us at work at times.

Most of the times, he was sending us to shepherd the sheep, but for us this was not work; it was rest! We were leaving the sheep on the meadow, and then we were swinging, because dad had made for us a swing from ropes that were hung on a branch. Then we were sleeping or playing with the other children. We

---

[39] The Romanian word used here is *nacealnic*, another regionalism, originating from Russian.

had some *mămăliguţă cu branză*[40] in our bag from home, we climbed trees to pick cherries, and so we ate plentifully.

Our land was right on the bank of Răut River, and the grass was very lush, green, and rich. The cattle were well fed, and they went to drink water on their own. We used to leave our feet in the river and fall asleep, and the little fish would tickle our soles. It was like being in heaven, such beautiful memories, the likes of which I haven't had since. This happiness did not last long, because in 1946 the plague of famine came over Bessarabia; it was created artificially by the Bolsheviks to force the people to enter the kolkhoz.[41] That year, it was a terrible drought, and the people were organizing their crops, so they would have sufficient until next year. It was right then when the activists began to go from house to house to fumble in all corners to get the *postavca*.[42] They mercilessly swept clean the attics of the last grain of wheat, so that people would have nothing to live on.

They only knew this, "The share, pay the share!"

When they came to us, dad told them:

"But I have already paid! I myself took the share by carriage to Drochia, at the train station. Here is the bill, with the signature, showing that they received it. Why did you come a second time?"

"We came for supplement!"

That's how they said, in Russian, *dopolnitina*, "supplement."

"But I do not have supplement. Look, I have children. Where would I get the supplement?"

"You have it! You have it!"

---

[40] This is another traditional meal in Romania. *Mămăliga* is similar to corn mush, and could be mixed with cheese (*brânză*). Polenta is another name for it. *Mămăliga* was considered the bread of poor people, because it was often used in the peasants' household instead of wheat.

[41] The Bolsheviks wanted to convince people to give their land to the state. It was not the first time they used the famine method. In 1932-33, they had allegedly used the same approach in Ukraine: the Holodomor. See the documentary *The Soviet Story* directed by Edvins Snore, 2008.

[42] The share of products that people were required to give to the state.

They pushed dad to the side and swept everything from the attic. If they saw that they did not find anything, they came with a big spear and gored every meter of the household, to find out hiding-places. The peasants had begun to hide food in the earth, in the manger, in the cellar, wherever they could. The activists stabbed with the spear any place where they thought something would be hidden, and they took everything they found, without mercy. The poor people were shouting, crying. We were only four mouths total, but some had eight-ten children; with what could they feed them? The activists did not take anything into consideration; they swept everything, to the last grain.

After this, people had to take everything they had at home - carpets, earrings, golden rings - and went North, in Poland or Ukraine, to sell them for a bit[43] of food to save their children. They came home with half a bag of potatoes, *macuc* or *jom*,[44] and rarely with a bag of wheat. They were greatly lucky if they could get home with it because the trains were filled with people who robbed the weak and threw them down from the train-car - people traveled even on the roofs because there was no space in the train - and then took their bags. Some even died there. It was a disaster.

We were lucky with *bunica* Sofia, who was a very wise and provident woman. It was due to her that we escaped from famine and none of us died. When she salted the cheese in the barrel, she did not cut it to put it in brine, as it is usually done, but she shredded it all, smashed it into small pieces, put salt in it twice, and beat it until even a needle could not enter in it. The cheese stayed like this for years, without being spoiled. That cheese, the weeds growing in the shadow, plus the preserves *bunica* had made the previous years saved us. The others, if their attics were swept clean, as it was in our case, had nothing else to live on.

When the sheep began to die, dad cut one, to boil it so that

---

[43] "Tabultoc"—another regionalism.

[44] Both words are regionalisms with which I am not familiar. According to a friend of mine, Adrian Olteanu, the *macuc* are the remains of sunflower seeds when oil is made from them. *Jom* is made out of the remains of sugar beets.

we could eat it. I remember one time a sick sheep had died, and dad took the large pot in the yard to make soap out of it. People smelled it, and they began to come one by one, dressed only in tights, without a shirt, with nothing on them, because they had exchanged everything for food. They stayed at our fence and said:

"Neculai, give me please a piece of meat!"

"But the sheep was dead, you'll die as well!"

"I'll die, one way or the other…"

They ate the entire pot.

Since he was a bit stronger (we had that cheese, the preserves, and, at times, mutton), dad was often called to dig the graves for the dead, because there was no one else to do it. And he went because *bunica* always used to tell him, "It is a shame to say no, Neculai, it is a shame!"

He dug the hole, working with all his powers, and in the morning, when it was time to take the dead, he found the grave filled with other dead bodies, that's how many were dying. When he was coming back from the cemetery, he saw another six-seven swollen people lying on the ground, barely breathing.

It was a true genocide. The others, when they saw how people were falling like chickens, asked to be received in the "*colectiv*,"[45] out of fear. That's what the Bolsheviks wanted: in order to make the kolkhoz, so collectivization, you need to frighten man, so that he would say it himself: "Receive me in your *colectiv*, just so that I do not die!" And this is how it was done. When they saw what happened, all the others wrote requests to enter into the *colectiv*.

The deportation

After the famine passed, the terror of deportation took hold of the village.

People knew that they took the intellectuals to Siberia in 1940: mayors, doctors, or notaries. Dad was not among any of

---

[45] The word refers to the kolkhoz. The communists *collectivized* the land and formed *collectives*—large farms owned by the state, holding the land taken from the peasants.

them, and he was certain that he would not be deported. He was not a landlord, nor a noble man, and he had nothing to do with politics, so there were no reasons to take him. I found out what they concocted in his case only recently, when I took his file from the archives. After the death of *mama* and *bunelu*, dad had to take care of seven hectares of land by himself, so he took someone to help him. Because of this, they accused him of being a great landowner and that he "exploited foreign work."[46] Also, after he came home with his leg broken, he opened, together with a neighbor, a manufacturing store, in that man's yard, so that he could support his family.

When the Russians came, they robbed them of everything, they took the store, all the merchandise, and nothing remained. For this, they wrote in his file that he was a "great merchant," and so they took him to Siberia.

From our family, the most watched was *bunelul*. He had told the Romanians that Grisha the Gipsy had burned the icons and robbed people, so *bunelul* became the greatest enemy of the regime, especially because two of his children were officers in the Romanian army. But *bunelul* had been judged and had died in prison, so only *bunica* remained. Being *bunelu*'s wife, they considered that she must have been an accomplice in his deeds, and she had to be taken because of this.

The deportation took place on July 6. It was around noon, and we were all working outside. I was sweeping the yard, and dad was mounting some hay with Emil. All of a sudden, we heard a rumble, and we saw a big car coming toward us. It stopped at the gate, and four soldiers and the chief of the village's Soviet came out of it. They commanded dad to take a few things and get in the car with us. Dad froze because he did

---

[46] In the first years when they came into power, the communists framed many people, especially the leaders of communities, to get rid of them and be thus able to restructure the fabric of society. See Fr. George Calciu's *Interviews, Talks, and Homilies* (St. Herman of Alaska Brotherhood, 2010), who discusses this method. He also emphasizes that the communists wanted to break the connection between generations so that the traditional values could no longer be transmitted. At the same time, to be an owner was a capital sin, for it "demonstrated" that you took advantage of the poor.

not expect it. Then he began to oppose them:

"Why are you taking me? Where are you taking me? What did I do to you?!..."

And the activist told him:

"You deserve it! I asked you to be a teacher at the school, why didn't you want to do it? Now you'll teach the wolves in the forest!"

Indeed, the Bolsheviks had proposed to dad to be a teacher in the village. But how could you teach the Antichrist to children? Even *bunica* was against it: "What can you teach the children, if these people burn the icons and say that God does not exist!?"...

In the meantime, neighbors gathered at the fence and watched, but they did not say anything because they were afraid. If the Bolsheviks had the gun on the hip, could you do or say anything? They had put fear into people, so people feared even their own shadows. Whatever the activists said, they did, and all people lived like on needles![47]

However, a woman came close to me and told me:

"Run! Go to my yard; they will not look there for you! Go to the cellar, hide!"

I was six years old. I looked at her but did not understand anything: why should I run, why should I be without a dad, without a brother, with a stranger? And I did well that I did not run! If I ran, what? Wasn't I remaining a stranger? And who needs a stranger as a child? But now, whatever we suffered, we suffered together, and that's it!

So those soldiers were yelling at us:

"Come, faster, faster, come, up, up!"

The people from the fence started to yell at dad:

"Neculai, don't sit, take clothes! They take you to the glacier, take some warm clothes, take for the children!"

By now, people knew what Siberia meant.

Dad went in the house, took a suitcase with his groom suit, the shirt, some clothes for us, tossed it in the car, and then went back. We were clinging on his pants and kept going after him

---

[47] A Romanian expression similar to "walking on eggshells."

crying. He took two other blankets, an old and a new one, and came out with them under his arm. Then, Grisha the Gipsy, who had come with the soldiers, snatched the new blanket, which had a beautiful glow, and told my dad:

"You don't need it; we take you as food for the wolves, and you don't need to be warm there!"

My poor dad began to cry, and we were clinging to his pants, crying as well. My brother could already understand everything, because he was older, but I could not understand what was happening; I was crying because of his crying.

Dad looked at the house and the garden crying, but that one, Grisha the Gipsy, did not give him any moment of peace:

"Come, come, faster, come, get up!"

The people began to shout:

"But he hasn't taken anything! These children are naked!"

Since it was summer, we were barefoot; I was in a small dress, and my brother in a little shirt and shorts.

But they had no reaction:

"Up, up, come, come! We've already lost time with you! Up!" We were already next to the car, and Grisha the Gipsy came to dad and told him:

"Colea, I regret so much that your woman is not alive! I would do her really hard (forgive my expression, but he really said that!), and I would have given her to others too, because she was really beautiful!"

Dad got really dark, with an ugly look, and spitted at him, right in his face. The Gipsy - I remember this with fear - jumped at my dad to hit him, but the soldier who was to close the door told him something in Russian and pushed him aside. We went in the car, he closed the door, and we left.

We were alone in the car, and we did not know where they were taking us. All of a sudden, we stopped in the middle of the village, right at *bunica*'s fence. There was already a mountain of things at her gate, clothes, pillows, blankets, pots... All the relatives were there - the daughters, the sons-in-law, the grandsons - and all carried things out of the house.

Grisha the Gipsy started to shout:

"What does she need all this for? Why does she need it?

She doesn't need it! Don't take things out, in the street!"

But they did not look at him, and when the door of the car opened, they all began to throw those things inside.

Then, they helped *bunica* in the car. She was not crying like dad; she was not crying at all. She was peaceful and calm. When she was in the car - it feels as if I see her right now - she turned toward people, like a statue, she made a cross in the air, and she said:

"Good people, if I harmed you in any way, forgive me!"

All the others were crying, all the relatives, dad, us, but not her! She was calm, peaceful. Even now, when I tell the story, I feel like crying, but not her. She did not cry at all! I was so amazed...

Then, all of a sudden, she told the girl:

"Masha, go fast to the kitchen and bring me the small icon with the Mother of the Lord! It is hidden in a corner, behind the cardboard!"

She kept it hidden, because the Bolsheviks had destroyed everything.

Tanti[48] Maria ran fast, found it, and brought it to her. *Bunica* kissed it, made the sign of the cross one more time, and said:

"God be with us!"

Then, turning to Grisha, she told him:

"But you, Grisha the Gipsy, if you are not cursed by the people, then you will be cursed by God! You won't have good days!" That's what she said, then she turned, and the car left.

And this is how it happened. This Gipsy man was sturdy, vigorous, and he had some black moustache twisted upward. After seven years, when I returned from Siberia, I found him an old man - an old man, in seven years! - weak, with a white moustache, and completely blind. He had a stick with him, and a girl led him by the hand. God's justice! He was cursed by so many curses, by so many innocent people! What fault did these people have? Whom did they kill, whom did they rob, so to make them food for wolves and to take everything they earned

---

[48] Aunt Maria.

from father to son, for years and years? What did the children and the old people do to be deported?

He did not even have many more years to live, just a few. During this time, the communists made sure he did not lack anything, because he had served them: how many people he murdered, how many people he took to prisons or destroyed in beatings! And now, these devils were taking care of their own.[49] After seven years or so, he died, and his grandson was laughing next to the coffin; he was laughing so much that people were making the sign of the cross. That's how his end came!

The road to Siberia

After they loaded other people from the village, the truck came to the road. There were fourteen-fifteen other trucks waiting there, and the entire convoy started toward Bălți.[50]

Oh, Lord, how it was on the road! People were crying, the women, and especially those seeing their lots in passing, plucked their hair out from their heads. Poor people! They were leaving behind their houses, their gardens, the wealth they gathered, and they went without knowing where to be "food for the wolves," as the activists said. They did not give any explanation; they did not say, look, we will take you over there to work, or something like this. No! "Food for the wolves! You'll freeze there; the wolves will eat you!" That's all they said.

In Bălți, they unloaded us at the train station, and the cars left. At the train station, there were only deported people all around. They were brought in carriages, unloaded, and the carriages went back to pick up others; there was no longer place to put them. How many insults and all kinds of dirty things you could hear! There was no water. The children were shouting, "I want water, I want to go to the restroom!"

What restroom?!...

The soldiers were yelling, "Down, down, sit down!"

They were afraid that if anyone stood up, they would run.

---

[49] In Romanian, "Iar acuma cornorații aveau grijă de al lor michiduță."

[50] Bălți is an important city in Bessarabia. Literally, it means "swamps."

But how can you keep your children down? They, especially the little ones, like me, could not sit because they did not understand. I did not understand that it was a tragedy; for me, everything was new:

"Look what that one does; look at the other! But why does that one cry?"

And I suffered their suffering.

By now, dad was no longer crying. He sat down on the things we had. *Bunica* had not cried from the beginning. She sat there humbly and said:

"God's will be done, God's will be done!"

To anything, she only knew this: "The Lord and God, the Lord and God, may God's will be done," and that was it!

And she told us:

"Don't cry, because God is great; He will save us, and everything will be fine! We only have to pray!"

And this is how we calmed down a little.

But the others were crying and shouting; they looked for one another. Some of them had relatives from around Bălți who came to accompany them to the train, and they wanted to say a few words to them, but the soldiers did not allow them and pushed them with their guns, yelling. In short, it was a true nightmare.

They gathered all of us in the evening and pushed us into the train cars as if we were cattle: all around there was only dung, straws, and dirt. There was one shelf on each of the two sides and two small barred windows. A man could not go through the window, but they still had bars!

The people came in as they could, put their luggage down, and slept on the luggage. There was no air because the doors were immediately closed. When you were suffocating or could no longer bear the stench, you were going to the window to breathe a bit.

This is how we went toward Siberia. Once every three days, they stopped the train in a train station to supply it with water. Then, they allowed one person from each car to come out with a bucket to fill it. But what was a bucket of water for thirty-five people? It was only for one day, and we only had drops of it. Then, we were again thirsty and thirsty, especially because we received some salty fish for food, and even that only once every three days.

We had to relieve ourselves in a hole in the floor of the train car. We, children, were not very ashamed, but the young lads and girls were so ashamed! Especially the girls; they asked their parents to stay in front of them, to cover them. You could not even think about washing your hands or anything.

Next to me, on the shelf, there was a woman around seventy years old; she was tall, lean, and she would lie down all the time. She was lying there with her eyes open, staring at the ceiling. She fell asleep at times; she dreamt, but she was always silent; only from time to time, she would exchange a word with *bunica*.

One time, dad looked at her longer and told me:

"Hey, go and touch her,[51] is she cold or warm? She seems dead!"

"How dead?" I asked, because I did not even know what it meant back then.

I touched her, and she was cold. Looking at the white skin around her mouth, the people said that she had been dead for two days. We began knocking hard on the door, to make the soldiers open so that we could tell them. But they did not open; they only asked what the matter was. Cazacu Petre, who knew Russian, shouted:

"We have a dead woman here, she must be taken down because of the stench!"

"Harasho! Harasho!"[52]

They opened only the fourth day. Just imagine: 40 degrees outside, sweat, so many people unwashed in the car, the dead woman there, decomposing, and we were breathing this air.

The fourth day they took her out. And I remember how *bunica* was looking at her compassionately, saying:

"Why didn't she say that she was hurting? Look, I have a

---

[51] The word used here in Romanian is "a achipui," a regionalism.
[52] "Good! Good" in Russian. The meaning is better expressed by, "okay, okay."

candle, and I would have lit a candle for her if she said something…[53] But she was quiet, and look how she died, like the pagans! Where will they bury her, and who will know where her tomb is?!..."

Bunica was lamenting so. She did not cry, but she was lamenting terribly! And not only then, but later as well, whenever they stopped the train to throw out one of the dead, she lamented that there is no one to communicate home, to the relatives, to let them know where someone died and where that person is buried. What if the dogs will eat him? And she began to pray harder and more often so that it would not happen to her as well, that God would keep her alive until she goes back home, to die there.

After this, we went for another week or so, day and night, without stopping. By now we were really animals. We had scabies and lice all over, and everyone was whining about something. Someone was vomiting, another one could no longer move, another asked for water, but there was no water. We were thumping on the train cars for nothing. They did not open!

Finally, after one week, they stopped the train on a bridge, above a river. But the train was very long. I remember that, whenever there was a curve, Emil went to the window to count the cars: he could count until forty or so, and then he lost count. When they stopped the train, one part was before the bridge, one was on the bridge, and the other was after the bridge. They opened the doors. The people in the cars on the sides of the bridge started to come out. But we were over the water. Where could you get out, in the river? You had to cross all the cars to get out. Do it if you can, because the soldiers were shouting:

"Five minutes, you have five minutes! Go, wash, and take some water, each of you in whatever you have!"

But who had what? A bottle, a bucket, a flask… Dad took a pot, Emil a bottle, and we ran all those cars until we got to the bank. But it was already full. The people had put their heads into water, and they were drinking like cattle. Perhaps two-three

---

[53] In the Romanian Orthodox Christian tradition, people light a candle when someone is about to die.

cars out of the forty managed to string over that bank. We were waiting for our turn when, all of a sudden, a young guy jumped into the water and began swimming. When the soldiers saw it, they started to shoot in the river. He was going into the water, then coming out, then going back in, and the soldiers were shooting all the time. Then they began to shout at us, "Nazat! Nazat!" That is, go back to the cars; otherwise, they would shoot us. There was such an agitation because some people were just coming out of their cars and we were thronging back; there was shouting, cursing - a true hell. In that whirlpool, Emil got lost. A soldier hit his back with the gun, and Emil shouted aloud, "Daaaad!" Dad heard it, but how could he go back, when we were so crammed into one another? I was holding onto dad's pants, crying, and dad was calling Emil, without moving. Finally, we found him, barely walking and holding on to his back. He had a big large bruise for a long while after that moment.

With great difficulty, we arrived at the train car, and we sat down as we could. Some cursed that boy who ran because he created problems for us, and we could not get washed or take water. Others blessed him because at least he escaped and could tell the people how the Russians tormented us in the train cars. I remember that I was upset with him because he messed up everything, and I wanted to wash, to take water, to be full…

The train started and we went again until we arrived into a city, where we stopped. They allowed one man from each car to come out to take a bucket of water; even that man was flanked by guns. If they allowed at least ten men in each car to take a bucket, then maybe we would have each had a little. After we calmed down somewhat, we heard that in one of the cars, while the train was on the bridge, a woman threw her four-month old baby in the river through the hole in the floor and drowned him. When the people came back from the water, they asked her:

"Where is your child?"

And she answered honestly:

"I finished him! I could no longer endure to see how he was dying before my eyes, and I do not have milk in my breast! If I had water to drink, milk would come, but there is no water.

Look, I have three children here, what do I do with them? They took my man, and I do not know anything about him. What was I to do?!..."

Of course, many scolded her; others took her side, saying that the child was bound to die, one way or another, if she did not have anything to feed him. I remember that *bunica* condemned her, saying:

"It should not have been her to take his life, but God! She should have left him fade by himself; she should not have committed this sin! Great sin has fallen upon her head!..."

In the settlement of Orlovka

After three weeks on the road, we arrived at the gates of Siberia, in Urals. By now, the train stopped every few hours, and we could hear words outside. Cazacu Petre, who knew Russian, told us that there were "buyers." In the villages where we stopped, the leaders of collective farms came to see the "slaves" to get[54] them for work, to kolkhoz, for there was no one to take care of the land and the cattle. And they were asking, "How many are you? How are you? Who is a stronger man? Who is a stronger woman? We don't need old people, we don't need children..."

Cazacu Petre listened and listened, and then he was saying:

"No, it is not good here! They pay little and there are no conditions, no house, no nothing... We don't go down, perhaps later."

At the next stop, he said again:

"No, this is not for us either! There must be something better, we will get to something better!"

One day, the train stopped and the soldier who guarded us opened the door and said:

"That's it! You are the only ones left! You did not go anywhere, nobody asks for you anymore, you have nowhere to go, so do whatever you want! Sit here and die!"

We got scared: how's that? "Do whatever you want!" But what can you do alone in the forest, with no food, no water,

---

[54] In Romanian, "să-i nămească," another regionalism.

nothing, in unknown places? We stayed in that car by ourselves for a whole day. The people were saying now that it would have been better to go down earlier, that we may have been lucky to get in a good place. It was hard at the kolkhoz, because you were paid in "working days" at the end of the year - some wheat or who knows what. At the sovkhoz[55] it was better. There, there was a factory, a manufacturing plant, and you could work for money and thus buy something. But now it was over, we could not go back.

I do not know what the train conductor[56] did, to whom he talked, but as we were sitting in the wagon, we saw two big military trucks. They loaded us in them and took us through a long path in the forest that seemed never ending.

We looked from the window, and we saw all of a sudden a large deer, in plain daylight. We went another kilometer or so and we saw a wolf running before us. Then a wild boar, a moose, all kinds of brutes, in plain daylight. They were passing without fear of the cars! When they saw so many animals swarming here and there without fear, the women began to cry saying that they indeed were taking us as food for the wolves. And they said:

"Better if they had killed us back home, on the spot, in the village! At least we were buried next to our relatives! Now, look, they feed us to beasts!"

Late in the night, we arrived into a small village with around fifteen houses. Nothing could be seen, except the shadows of the houses and a small lake that scintillated. We rushed like the cattle into it, to drink water. When we had enough, they put all of us into a big house made out of beams, and we stayed there until the morning. When the dawn came, we rushed to the well! But there was no well! The only water was that lake. Everyone was going into that water, the horse, the cows... they had their dung in there, and still women washed their clothes in there and took water for drinking and food! We had no choice and we washed there.

---

[55] A state farm in the former USSR.
[56] Same word as before: *năcealnic*.

When it was already light, they arranged us at various houses, with the Russian women. They were all widows; there were only three men in the whole village, and even those were disabled from the war. The houses were small, with a kitchen and a room. They squeezed the Russians into the Kitchen, and they gave us the rooms, since we were many, and we were supposed to pay them in workdays.

After we each found a place wherever we could, we began to recover a little. First, we all rushed to find food, various kinds of mushroom that grew in the forest and fish from the pond. We got a little power, and our faces began to go back to pink. Then, the men dug a beautiful fountain with wooden enclosure, with a shadoof and bucket, as it was done back home.

The Russians were really amazed:

"Look, they are kulaks and they work."

The kulaks, or the nobles, did not work there. And they thought that we were kulaks, "enemies of the people," "white hands" who do not do anything.[57] After they drank and saw that the water was clean and good, they stopped taking from the pond and were coming to the fountain, even if it was at the outskirts of the village. They said,

"Oh, Moldavian, Moldavian! How *brava* you are, how *brava*[58] you are!"

And this is how we made peace with them.

We found out from them that the village's name was Orlovka and that it was the estate of a rich nobleman, Orlov. The Bolsheviks deported him and took his forests and lands. The school was in the large, tall manorial houses, covered with tin. The native, the nobleman's former servants, lived in the small houses around it, where they put us as well. They worked in the forest, cutting wood, taking care of the cattle, and they received some pay per workday, but they still did not have

---

[57] In the communist propaganda, the deportees were described as enemies of the people who used to take advantage of the working class.
[58] The narrator wants to imply that the Russians were using Romanian words incorrectly. "Bravo" is the word used to appreciate the work of another, something similar to "good job!"

enough bread and were always hungry. The earth did not give fruit there. This is why they cultivated only some wheat and sunflowers. [59] In order to be able to plant some tomatoes, cucumbers, or potatoes, they had to use a richer soil enriched with manure.

Almost everyone had a cow or at least a goat. The most difficult time was winter, when no one kept the animals outside because they feared the wolves. You had to live the whole winter in the house with the cow and the calf, who left their dung there. You cleaned it, of course, but you could not just stand next to the cow. The stench remained inside the whole winter.

When we were separated, we all got in the house with a Russian widow, Niura. She moved into the kitchen, and we had the large room, where there was no stove, no hob, no bed, nothing. Dad and Emil made a tall oven, quite large, so that we could all sleep on it and be warm. *Bunica* could not come up on the oven, [60] and dad made her a bed next to the wall, in the corner. I cannot imagine how she could stay there. We were all getting warm on the oven, but it was cold on that bed, and the wall was cold, but she came through. Only the Spirit of God gave her strength.

Then, dad and Emil made a separate entry for us and everything else that was needed in the house, because there was enough wood in the forest.

After that, dad began working. He did whatever they put him to do. He worked cutting wood in the forest, making hay, grazing the herd of wild horses, or gathering things behind the tractor.

The summer was bearable, but he suffered terribly during winter because of that crushed leg! *Bunica*, poor woman,

---

[59] The Romanian word used here is "răsărită," an old word for "floarea soarelui"—"sunflower."

[60] In Moldova, even to these days, older people used to sleep on the oven in the kitchen. The oven is made out of stone, and the "bed" is arranged on top of it. After being used during the day, the oven would provide heat for the cold nights.

changed his old felts[61] from his legs with some blankets, patched and re-patched, and then she put some straws in there too, but he was still freezing. When he came in from outside - I can see it now - his whole leg was livid, with sores and pus. We were lucky with *bunica*! She knew all the herbs: what is needed for that disease, what is needed for the other. She gathered the herbs over the summer and dried them for winter. With those herbs, she took care of dad the whole night. I remember he was asking her:

"Please, you will sleep during the day! Scratch me, rub me a little, perhaps I can fall asleep a little!"

He could not sleep because of the severe itch he had.

The second day, he showed his leg to the chief who watched him:

"Look at my leg, it hurts; I cannot work so much!"

And that one said:

"No! You are a *kulak* and you must suffer! Work, because you are rich! You came here to work, not to sleep…"

And dad went to work, because the guard had his pistol on him. Then *bunica* washed him again over night, lubricated him, rubbed him, and bandaged him well in the morning to go out in the frost. This is how dad suffered during the winter.

The frost was seven months long there. Usually, it was -20, -30 degrees,[62] but on some days it was even -50 degrees. At such moments, rarely was anyone coming out of the house. Only the people who lived closed to the farm went to water the cattle, to feed them. Having cows, the Russians made butter and lubricated their faces before going out in the frost. But how could we find any butter, when we had not even seen oil all those years? Then the Russians had sheepskins, thick felts with good soles, while our Moldavians had patched and re-patched clothes. When it snowed, the snow was one meter high or more. Then, we knew that the wolves would be coming to prey

---

[61] People did not have shoes or boots, but rather footwear made out of various felts. A traditional footwear is *opinca*, but the ones mentioned here are far from reaching the status of an *opinca*.

[62] Celsius degrees.

on the village! They could not hunt in such big snow, because they were sinking in it, and so they came to us by way of the paved path. If the Russians got drunk and forgot to take the cow or the pig into the house over night, then the wolves made a hole in the barn and ravaged everything. I was trembling with fear whenever I heard them outside howling! And I listened like this the entire night, because I was sleeping enough during the day, not having to go to work because I was too little, and I could no longer sleep overnight. I would have liked to go to school, because there was a school in the village, but I had nothing to put on. But Emil took *bunica*'s kerchiefs, filled them up with straws, and put them on his feet. This is how he was going out to learn, especially a little bit of Russian, because you could not manage without it. They spoke in Russian, and you could not understand anything. I stayed in the house all winter long, between four walls, like in a prison.

It was better during the summer. I was going around all day long finding some food for everyone, because Emil and dad were working and *bunica*, being old, preferred to stay in the house. It was not very warm; it was rather a bit cool. I was going through the forest or on the field, and I was gathering mushrooms, herbs, berries, or anything else I could find for food.

During the summer it was difficult rather because of the mosquitos, since they were destroying us. You had to always have a branch with you, to protect yourself; if you slacked just a bit, it was done and you were filled with bites. People used to say that the Russians, if they wanted to punish someone, left him naked tied to a tree, and he would be found dead the second day, eaten by mosquitos.

The first "encounter" with death

In the village, the most important moment over the year was "*The Feast of the Tripthyc*" that took place at the beginning of spring. When the time came, the natives lit a great bonfire on the lake and cooked the *bline*, something like our pancakes. Then they feasted there, on the lake's shore, until late in the night. Other than that, they feasted on May 1st,[63] November 7th,[64] New Year's Day... You could not even say what their faith was, because there was no church of any kind around.

I was most amazed by the fact that they did not have a cemetery in the village. If someone was sick and felt that his end was near, he told the family that he wanted to be buried under that fir tree, or that birch and so on. And thus, there were lots of graves all around the village. But what graves?! They did not even have a proper cross.[65] There was so much timber there, but they only cut two thin branches, tied them in a cross with a rope from tree bark, and that was it! During winter, that rope rotted, and the branches were taken by people who no longer had firewood, so nothing remained there. All this happened if they buried someone in the summer. But if someone died during winter, then all the men came with pickaxes and broke the frozen soil, which was as hard as a stone and would hardly break. In two days, they made a half a meter deep grave, just large enough so that the coffin could enter. Then they covered it with the same ice and snow. In the spring, they could find only the bones, because the wolves would take out the body and eat it. If we had died there, we would have truly been "food for wolves"! But the Russians did not fear this at all. In the summer, when we children were playing, you could hear a girl or a boy shouting all of a sudden:

"Look, these are my grandmother's bones! We buried her on this spot last winter!"

Now, that it was warm, they made a deeper hole, put the bones back into the earth, and there was the cemetery!

For any burial, the Russians had the custom to drink. They went by sleigh or carriage to a store in the neighboring village, brought back boxes filled with vodka, and began drinking and singing. After they had enough of singing, they began to fight. This was their tradition, all things ended in a fight. For feasts or for burials, if you did not fight someone, it meant that you did

---

[63] The International Day of Workers.
[64] The day of the Russian communist revolution.
[65] In Orthodox cemeteries, graves usually have a cross at the head.

not do anything. But they did not hold any grudge; when they came to themselves, they made peace.

This is how it was there, in the wild forest where we lived. Perhaps it was different in the city. I was small back then, and I did not understand many things, but some remained with me for life. I remember how one summer some people came to dad to ask him to dig a hole for an old woman who had died in their family. They were Tatars deported from Crimea.

I went with him and stayed there; I was all eyes and ears to see what would happen. Dad dug some seventy centimeters, until he got to ice; in those places, the earth remained icy underneath even during the summer. He also dug one meter in width, and they brought the Tatar woman to bury her. She had a large, white shirt on her. They put her in the grave without a coffin, without anything. They did not even lay her down, but rather propped her up as if she were sitting on a chair, her back leaning on the wall of the grave. They put a bowl of food in her arms and covered her.

I was very shocked by how they left her in that hole. Besides this, when he dug the grave, dad found some bones that belonged to the Tatar woman's man, who had been buried there seven years ago. I remember even dad was surprised:

"Look, in seven years, nothing remains from man, except the bones!"

I kept that in my mind, and by then I had some idea what death was.

After the burial, the family of the deceased called me at their place, because they also had children, six or seven. They did not have a table, as we normally had, but they sat on the floor. A girl next to me told me:

"Give me your hand!"

I gave it to her, and she looked and then told me:

"Look, your line shows that you must die soon!"

"Why die?"

"Just like this, you will die and that's it! If you do not believe me, ask my brother!"

He also said:

"If she says so, it means it is true. She knows about lines!"

Fear immediately overwhelmed me. I asked them:

"But what do you mean, die? You mean to bury me just like your grandma?"

"Yes, like grandma."

"I do not want to!"

I had a tantrum and ran home yelling:

"I don't want to die!"

Beginning with that moment, I began getting ready psychologically for death, to get used to the idea. That fear persisted until I was fifty years old. Afterwards, I returned to God, to faith, and the fear disappeared.

The "Spinner" and the "Scooter"

My brother, Emil, was like a spinner. This is how he was; he could not stay put for one minute. He was always moving and doing things. In order to have something to be able to go out to play, what did he concoct? He took two of *bunica*'s blouses, sewed them together, and put in between them brown cattails, from the lake. He dressed up with that and went to the frozen pond, for all the children of the natives played there. What did he invent? He made a "scooter": he broke a peace of ice one meter square and put it on the thick ice on the lake; then he took a stick from the forest, put a rusty nail in the tip, and when he pushed that stick in the ice on the lake, he could go from one end to the other of the lake, as if he were on a real scooter. All the boys looked at him from the brink and shouted after him:

"Give it to me too, give it to me too!"

I was following them from the window. I put my warm little palm on the frozen window, and I watched them with envy. I was a child as well, and, regardless of how things were, to stay in the house for seven months, as long as the frosts lasted... I would have gone outside to play too, but how do it if you have nothing to put in your shoes or to get dressed? I stayed at the window for a while and saw Emil going here and there on the pond, with the boys after him, shouting.

Then I turned from the window and began talking to *bunica*. I asked her who draws the flowers on the window so beautifully, and she told me that God does this, and the people do not know how.

As we were talking, all of a sudden the door opened, and a woman came in with a man who had Emil in his arms, all wet and frozen. They put him there on the bed and left immediately, as if they were afraid that we would blame them for something.

Emil was not moving at all. He lay there, livid, with his eyes closed. I was scared, but *bunica* shouted: "God and the Lord!" She took off everything he had on him and sent me to bring the gas lamp we had on the porch, for what else did we have? Herbs and gas! I woke up dad, who was sleeping on the oven, and we all began to rub him: his leg, hand, chest, back, we were turning him on all sides. After two-three hours, he opened his eyes:

"But where am I?"

"Eh... where are you..."

"I was in the hole in the pond. I yelled and yelled, and I can't remember anything else..."

Someone had broken the ice on the lake to take water or to water the cattle, and thin ice formed on that hole, which was then covered by snow. Emil did not see it, and he fell right in it, with his "scooter" and all.

Later, the woman who brought him told us:

"He was lucky with what he had on him, for his clothes were full of grease and grime from the tractor. Before they got wet, he was able to yell, and we heard him from the forest. The other kids got scared and ran away, and they left him by himself."

This is how Emil was born a second time. The great astonishment was that he did not get a cold, did not get frostbite, and did not have any problems. God gave wisdom to *bunica*, so that she took care of him with all kinds of teas, rubbed him with herbs and roots, and he did not get anything.

The "Beloved Leader's" Death

Bunica was our support the whole time, and we were saved from many things because of her. She was a very good, very faithful, and very wise woman. She raised me until I was ten years old, and she was like a mother to me. I spent much time with her, especially during winter, when we both remained in the house. Most of the time, she was lying down, praying. She put the small icon that she had taken at our departure on the wall, and she prayed before it and made us pray as well.

She spoke little, very little and in a reserved mode. She only told me a few stories from her youth and how *bunicul* died in Briceva, in prison. Other than that, I only remember her praying. Prayers, prayers, and prayers again!

"Three days, Lord, just give me three days, so that I can go back home, to die there, confessed and communed, with all my relatives. To be buried there, with a candle..."

This was her prayer. Day and night I heard it. At times, dad had enough of it and would tell her:

"Just be quiet, mom; it is for nothing; everything is for nothing!"

And she always replied:

"No, Colea, don't talk like that, it's not for nothing!"

And it was not for nothing. God gave her three months, not three days. He gave her three months to spend at home, with the relatives, to die at home, as a Christian.

Bunica was very faithful while we were there, in Siberia. Her prayers and wisdom saved us from many things. Dad was mindful of her and listened to her in all things. They would contradict each other, from time to time, only regarding faith because poor dad had despaired. He was faithful too at the beginning, even if not as much as *bunica*. But after the tragedy that happened to us, he began saying:

"Where is God? Why did He allow it? What was our mistake, what did we do? We didn't rob anyone, we didn't murder anyone... Why should these children suffer? Why does God allow something like this?"

At times, when he was very upset, I heard him say these words. But *bunica* used to come and say:

"No, this is a temptation. We must endure it and pass it well; if we resist, we will be God's; if not, it means we give ourselves to Satan..." She was like this, very calm, peaceful, and with a clear mind.

One week before Stalin died, I do not know what she dreamt, but she told us:

"It's done, we are saved! They will let us go home!"

"But what happened?"

"Look, the tyrant Stalin will soon perish!"

I laughed:

"This is Satan, how could he perish?"

After a week, they called all of us to school, young and old, to tell us that Stalin had died. The teacher began crying: "Our poor man, our beloved leader..." and so on. First, we could not believe it. Then, all of a sudden, we all burst:

"Hooray!!! Hooray!!!"

The natives looked at us and smiled, even though not openly, because they also wanted to be free of this regime. To work so much and to have no bread in the house?! Poor people, they were like cattle, because this is what the soviet system considered them.

When she saw that instead of crying we were rejoicing, the teacher called the director. The director was not really sound because of an explosion during the war. When anger took hold of him, we would run from his path. We immediately sat down and we waited. He came in and began yelling at us, Moldavians:

"You, the enemies of the people! Look, you have been staying here for so many years and to no end! You have not corrected yourselves; we cannot make anything out of you!"

But we could not care less. How long we had waited for this day! When we were there, it was on the lips of every Moldavian: when will Satan finally die,[66] when will he go, so we could return home?

The director shouted even louder:

"You must cry, not laugh and jump around! You must cry because our beloved leader died, and it will be very difficult for us without him from now on."

How come, difficult? However, to avoid contradicting him, two girls who were sisters, Dorica and Aurica, got an onion from a bag, bit from it, and started putting it around their eyes,

---

[66] In original, "să ghiberească," a regionalism.

to make themselves cry. But the boys, our Moldavians, all jumped around and shouted with joy.

This was the happiest day in Siberia!

The Apple with Scent from Home

One evening of a late autumn, as we were staying in the house, we heard someone knocking at the door. We opened, and a man around 50-60 years old came in, carrying a heavy suitcase with him. We recognized that he was one of our people, from Bessarabia, because he had a sheepskin hat.[67] He said "good evening," and then looked at us and said:

"There you go: I got to the wrong place again! If I do not know Russian, I cannot find my people. Do you know where Mândâcanu lives?"

His father had died there, in Siberia, and he came to see him. When we found out that he was from Mihăileni, we, of course, did not want to let him leave so soon, especially *bunica*. We all began to ask him to stay to tell us at least something about what was going on there. I remember he told us:

"The communists took everything for the kolkhoz! They took our horses, oxen, cows, plough, and earth... They go around carrying a gun at all times, menacing people, and they took everything from us..."

Bunica asked him:

"Are my girls alive, healthy?"

"Alive, but they work for masters. Russians from Chişinău, from the party, come to the village, and the women must feed them and take them to the hotel. If they refuse, when they no longer have turkeys or geese to feed them, then the Russians menace them, 'You'll go after your mother to Siberia!' They have no option; they must accept them. In short, the communists brought only disgust to the village, and no joy."

Bunica was content that at least they were healthy and had not died; they had not been imprisoned or taken some place.

The man was getting ready to leave to his relatives, and dad told him that he would accompany him to show him where they

---

[67] This is a traditional hat worn especially in the fall and winter.

lived. Of course, the man did not feel right to leave like this, and he opened his suitcase. He unlocked it, loosened the belts, and took out a ruddy-yellow apple, and he gave it to me, since I was the smallest. He said that it was for the soul of his father. I was confused, and I did not know what to do. I looked at *bunica*, I looked at dad, at the apple... But Emil jumped, grabbed it, and said "thank you."

Then dad put on some clothes and left with the man. We sat at the table and began passing around that ruddy-yellow apple among ourselves. *Bunica* was sitting, and her hands seemed to tremble because she wanted to hold it as well. Emil took it from me and put it under his nose, by his eyes...

No, I have no words; I cannot render what we felt because of that apple. For three days, we kept it as if it were God, as if it were gold. Gold was nothing compared to it. It was so dear to us because that apple, with its fragrance, took us back home. We saw again absolutely everything: the garden, the flowers, the fruit, the sheep, the horses, and the cow... everything was contained in it... We were home; it took us home completely, and we wanted to feel our home as much as possible. It did not even cross our minds to say, let's cut it, let's eat it, because I can no longer bear it. No word from anyone. Even during the night, when we went to sleep, we saw that apple in our dreams.

The third day was a Sunday. *Bunica* woke us up in the morning, washed us, and lined us before that small icon brought from home. Before that day, from time to time, dad refused to pray, for, if there were a God, why would He allow something like that. But that time even he prayed before that icon and said "Our Father." Then, *bunica* took the apple from the middle of the table and cut it exactly in four pieces; she gave it to each one of us as if it were communion... Even now I can see her old, dry hand, how she gave so beautifully that piece to each one of us. She made a cross over it before she cut it, just like she used to do with the bread back at home; that's what she did to that apple. She cut it and she gave each one of us a piece... But we did not eat it even then; we took it and licked it, smelled it and stared at it, as if we saw a miracle in it. I think it took an hour before we ate everything.

Today, when I walk on the street and see a bitten apple thrown someplace, I see immediately that apple from Siberia…

The Accident

After some time, dad was assigned to be a horse handler. No one wanted to do this work. There was a drove of around two hundred wild horses, and you had to take them grazing through the pastures and not allow them into the grains. If you lost them into the grains, you did not receive anything for that workday. There was so much grass everywhere, even in the forest, but the horses sensed where the grains were and were going there on purpose. Then, you had to run after them. I would run before them with a stick, and dad would do the same thing on the other side. Emil was riding an old horse that we had received from the brigade,[68] and we guided them where they had to be. And this is how we raised them.

One day, Emil took me from home on that old horse, to go to the brigade. Dad, as he saw us from a distance, left out the horses. The herd went directly toward the grains of wheat. Dad began to whistle and made signs to us to hurry. But how could we hurry, for our horse was old?! Emil hit him once, and the horse began running, but we heard him panting after five minutes. Emil knew him, and he told me:

"Jump down! Jump from the horse, because he will fall!"

I was afraid that I would fall under his hooves, and I did not jump immediately. When I finally jumped, it was too late: the horse fell as well. I was completely under the horse, only my head remained out. The horse was three-four hundred kilograms, but to me it seemed like a ton. I began hearing how my small bones were breaking, that's how heavy he was. When my brother saw that my eyes were beginning to come out of my head, he shouted:

"Kosogub, get up!... Get up, do you hear me?!"

He hit him with the whip on his head, where it hurt more, and the horse got up, but he could not get up fully. Only my legs remained underneath him. The air began to come back to

---

[68] Some state-own organization that was dealing with the animals.

my lungs. The legs could wait, because they were stronger. After around ten minutes, when the horse finally rested, Emil hit him again with the whip and he got up. I was no longer able to walk, to do anything. Dad took me to the brigade and lay me on a bed. My chest was crushed, the ribs were broken, and everything hurt when I breathed. Meanwhile the supervisor came to see what we were doing with the horses, if they escaped into the wheat. He was riding a young, healthy horse. He looked around and said:

"Look, the horses went into the wheat. You will not receive anything today!"

But dad replied:

"I am sick with fever, look what happened to the girl, the horse is old… We just cannot make it!"

He had asked for a young horse many times, so we could do our job properly, but they did not want to give him one. Then, finally, the supervisor said:

"Well, okay, take one and train it, whichever you want, and use it!"

Dad then found a carriage and sent me home, to *bunica*. *Bunica* treated me how she knew, with God and herbs, and this is how I was cured.

A Night in the Forest

After some time, while I was still healing, Emil took me one day on the new horse we received from the brigade. He had trained it for three days, to get it used to the bridle on its head. Now, he wanted me to ride it so that he could direct it with the whip.

I did not want to get on the horse, but he told me:

"Do you see this whip?"

I did not believe he would hit me, because he never did, and I was not afraid. Then he shouted:

"I'll take you in the forest and leave you there, to be eaten by wolves!"

I was most afraid of wolves, and so I listened and got up on the horse. When he felt me, the horse started to jump with his front legs and back legs, and I was bouncing on his back like a ball. Emil was standing there and was directing him. When he saw that the horse calmed down and was foaming at his mouth, Emil thought that the horse would listen to him. He gave me the reins and opened the gate of the enclosure.

Once he was out, the horse ran into the forest. I could not handle him, because he was not listening to me, and I had no power to hold him with the reins. My only purpose was this: to not fall under his hooves, because if I fell, it would have been over for me. I was holding as strong as I could. He went like this for quite a while (when dad found me, he said it was around 60 kilometers). He was running in the forest. On the one hand, I was afraid because I did not know where he was taking me; on the other hand, I was afraid to jump, because I thought that I would fall under his hooves for sure. I did not know what to do. A branch of a fir tree did the work. It hit me in the face and threw me off the horse.

It was already evening and I was scared: where was I? I knew the forest and the meadows where we usually took the horses, but I did not know anything there; I had never been to that place, because it was too far. Then I remembered what dad taught me: if you happen to be in the forest during night, get up into a tree! With great difficulty, because my chest was hurting, I climbed a tree. I did it more out of my fear of wolves. I waited to see: would Emil come, would dad come... but nobody came.

I did not close one eye the entire night. I was greatly afraid, because there were more animals than wolves; there were also lynxes, those big cats that stay in trees. I knew that they rarely attack humans, because they have their food, but I was still afraid. However, nothing happened. No wolf came, and I saw no other beast there; God spared me.

In the morning, with the dawn, dad and Emil came with the horse. They followed my tracks, because the forest was covered by a sponge of leaves, and everything could be seen there. This is how they found me. Dad told me that they had tried to look for me in the evening, but it was dark and they could not see anything, so they left me in the forest for a night. I felt like this was my second birth. I was very upset with Emil, but it did not last; what good would it have done? He was my brother, so we had to live together and reconcile. Then, he was not that evil. The Bolsheviks made him evil, with their inhuman regime. You cannot leave an animal without food or outside in the cold, but to do this with people, to leave them hungry and naked?! Need teaches you, it makes you tough... This is how it is!

The Temptation

A month had passed, I think, from this event, and one morning *bunica* prepared a satchel with food and clean clothes for dad and Emil, and she sent me to take these things to them to the horse brigade.

The brigade was twelve kilometers away from the village. Ten kilometers in the forest, and two in wheat fields. It was nothing for me, and it was not the first time I had gone there. But dear *bunica* seemed to sense something, and when she took me to the door she told me:

"Pay attention and don't count the crows on the road![69] Hurry up to come back home, so it does not get dark!"

And I went. Of course I counted the crows, and the insects, because I was very curious about all these creatures. I wanted to see them, to study them - this is how I filled my life. I do not know how long it took me to get there, but I arrived fast enough at the brigade, I gave them what *bunica* sent them, they ate, changed, put the dirty clothes back in the satchel, and dad told me:

"Let's go home; I will come with you until we get to the road!"

It was one kilometer to the road, and he began to tell me all sorts of things. *Bunica* talked very little with me, but dad, when I was with him, told me how he learned at school, how he went to theater classes, how he went to the dance, how he lived with mom, how they got married... I was listening amazed, with my mouth open, and I could not get enough of it.

Talking like this, we passed by the road on which I was supposed to go home to *bunica*, and we continued going ahead. I thought that if we went toward the village Kuzminovka, it

---

[69] An expression suggesting losing time with details.

meant that dad would not let me go home by myself and would come with me, so I continued ahead joyfully.

We arrived in that village, Kuzminovka, two kilometers from the horse farm, and we got close to a small store that had a window with bars where a shopwoman was staying. Dad bought a piece of chocolate, broke it in two, and gave me half. Long did I turn that chocolate in my hands, and I licked it until I swallowed it! Then, dad started talking to the shopwoman, and I went to the side, for that's how I was taught: when the adults discuss things, I am not supposed to mingle. I looked around for things to do, five-six steps away, in the grass. I found all kinds of creatures, and I studied them, waiting and waiting for dad to say something about the road. But he did not say anything. I was happy that I would remain with him and he would tell me many other things.

When it got dark, I heard him calling me, and he told me:

"Well, my dear, come, go home!"

I looked around, fearful:

"How? It is night by now!"

"What, don't tell me that you are afraid! Here, take a branch, and if a little mouse comes, you hit him with it and you're fine!"

Tears started coming from my eyes:

"Tăticuțule[70], I won't go, because I am afraid of wolves..."

"Well, I didn't know I had such a fearful daughter! Aren't you ashamed?"

I had received a good thrashing from him once, and I was afraid not to listen. He came with me to the road, he gave me that twig and the satchel with dirty clothes, and I left. While dad could still see me in the wheat field, I walked fast, but when he no longer saw me, I started to run strong. The moon was already out, a large, bright one. I was running, and it seemed like the moon also was running on the sky, and my soul was lighter because the moon was going with me, to light my way. The forest was closer and closer, dark as a black hole, and I had to sink into it. When this thought crossed my mind, I began

---

[70] *Tăticuțule* is the diminutive of *tata,* the Romanian word for *dad.*

shivering. If I had been older, it may have been different, but I was nine years old back then. I did not have much force to run either, because I was hungry and I had not eaten almost anything all day long.

When I sank into the forest, I began hearing screams, squeaks, and all kinds of noises, from all sides. I thought: the fox squeaks, the jackals and the owls scream; these animals do not attack; the main thing is to not run into wolves! I just finished this thought when I heard a wolf howling on my right side. Then, I heard another one on my left. That's it, I thought, they are surrounding me! I was so afraid! I was sweating and I felt my hair standing on my head. I remembered I had to climb a tree, but what tree, because I could not see anything, only bushes and shrubs that were scrapping my skin. I finally found a pine tree, but it had no branches, so I gave up. What could I do? Forward, forward, forward! I was running on that carriage road without seeing anything. And I ran, and I ran, and I ran, and they were howling, first one, then the other, then softer, then heavier, because there were three of them. Just imagine! Three wolves calling each other to go hunting, and I was the prey!

I ran until I could no longer, because out of fear, I felt like my soul was coming out of me, but I finally made it out of the forest. The wolves no longer howled, and, happy, I said to myself: it's done; if they are not howling, they must have gone to some other part of the forest. Then I thought: what other part? Now they see me better, and they can come after me. And I looked and looked behind me, to see whether I could see their eyes in that dark forest, their eyes like two bulbs, as I had seen them from the window at home.

I did not stop running, and I could already see the shadows of the houses from the village. When I got closer to the village, my Lord how the dogs were barking! I got scared: why do all dogs bark at the same time? I got to our door, and I began knocking, but nobody heard me. I wanted to shout, but I thought that the wolves would find me after my voice and would come to eat me. A child, what can I say... As if the wolves could not smell me? And I knocked and knocked, with my fists, legs, but nothing! I went around the house to the window, and I began knocking there as well. Still nothing! Another fear took hold of me: that *bunica* had died. If I knocked so much and she could not hear, it meant that she was dead and I would remain outside, and the wolves would eat me for sure. Something terrible took place in me at that moment, and I said: whatever happens, happens; I will yell, because I have no other choice now! And I began shouting:

"*Bunica!... Bunica!... Bunica!...*"

I hear it even now. The pond, the forest, everything around had an echo, and they shouted back from everywhere: "iiica!... iiica!... iiica!..."

"This is it," I said to myself; "the wolves now know where I am and they will come." And I yelled again:

"*Bunica!... Bunica!...*"

Finally, something shadowy showed itself at the window saying:

"Who's there?"

"Me, Margareta!"

And the echo, "reta!... reta!... reta!..." A painting of a nightmare, really.

When she heard that I said Margareta, she shouted:

"Come to the door faster!"

I went to the door, she let me in, and she immediately put the lock back. Once I crossed the threshold, I passed out, because I no longer had any powers. She did not turn the light on, and, not seeing me, she tripped and fell there. This is how we both remained until morning: I, because of that run - for it is terrible to run for 12 kilometers without stopping, with such huge terror; she, because she could not stand up being old. And she remained down there, waiting for me, saying:

"Colea, Colea, what have you done? What have you done?!..."

I no longer said anything. I was so happy that she was alive, that she was not dead and that I did not remain the entire night outside with the wolves. I do not know what she told dad afterward, because they did not talk in front of me. She only told me this:

"I told Colea a few things, I told him!..."

Something else is surprising, though: that night, twenty meters from our house, the wolves had devoured the neighbor's pig, because she had forgotten to take him in. Just twenty meters, think about it! I was there, and the wolves passed by me without doing anything to me, but they killed the pig! What does this mean? Man's destiny! If God does not will you to die on that day then you do not die, although the Bolsheviks had threatened us with death by wolves...look, I survived even until today!

What happened then, I do not know. I thought that dad either wanted to get rid of a mouth, or he tempted my destiny, or both. He had begun to doubt God, and perhaps he thought: if there is a God and she has days to live, she will survive; if not, I will get rid of a mouth to feed! Or perhaps he wanted to strengthen me to resist all difficulties that I might have to endure later, I do not know... Only God knows. But I, as a woman, as a mother, I would never have done such a thing...

Emil runs away to... Moldova!

One day, Emil came home from the horse farm to take a clean change of clothes and to see his comrades, the boys, because he missed them, being gone out in the wilderness. He left the satchel and went outside with them. After a short time, he came back with a Russian, one of his friends, and with a roll of something under his arm. We looked at them, and *bunica* asked:

"What's this?"

"Wool, *bunica*, so that you can make me some socks as you used to do in Moldova, long and thick, so I can walk with them in the snow!"

Bunica was happy because she knew how to knit all kinds of things. I remember how, when we were home, young women from the village used to come to her: "Aunt Sofia, how do you knit this, how do you make this?"... Skirts, blouses, dresses... she could knit anything! But in Siberia, she did not have anything for knitting. The Russians had no sheep, and nobody sold wool. The state took all of it and made felts and mantles for soldiers.

So when *bunica* saw that wool, she rejoiced and said:

"I'll spin it and knit it. I'll get three pairs of socks for sure…"

But the Russian boy shouted:

"I want some too, I want some too!"

The Russians did not knit anything like this.

And *bunica*:

"Fine, fine, it's enough for four…"

Then she suddenly came to her senses and said:

"Wait a moment! Where did you get it? Nobody sells this."

They avoided telling the truth at first, saying this and that, but had no choice in the end and Emil said:

"We were playing with the boys next to a storehouse; it was not closed, so we entered there to play; there was so much wool like this, soft, and I thought to take a little so that you can make me socks, to have something to wear. I'm sick of wearing these straws on my feet!"

"Was there any adult around? Did you ask for permission from anyone?"

"There was nobody!"

"If there was nobody, then it is stolen. Take it back immediately!"[71]

But they said, "no," that no one will notice, because there was so much of it there; but *bunica* also said "no" and that had to be it! To be sure that they would return the wool, she sent me with them. She did not trust Emil because he was somehow… perhaps not serious, but he was very smart. I was amazed how he concocted all sorts of things, like an inventor. This is

---

[71] The change in culture that communism brought is truly terrible. Adrian Olteanu, a friend of mine who helped me to understand many of the regionalisms in this book, told me once how, before collectivization, they were punished as children if they took one apple from the neighbor's tree. After the Bolsheviks took everything, one day he came home with an apple from their former orchard, which had been confiscated by the communists. It was the first time when his parents, instead of punishing him, began to cry. The reaction of *bunica* from this story is this much more significant. Although they did not have anything because it was taken away from them by the communists, she does not change her attitude: taking something that does not belong to you remains theft.

precisely why *bunica* was worried, that he would concoct a lie and would not take back the wool. And this is how it was. As we got further from the house, Emil told me:

"Come here, let's make it so that she believes that we went to the storehouse, but we'll take it to the horse farm instead, and I will speak to dad to see what he will say!"

But *bunica* came out to the road, because there were no fences, and she pointed at him, shouting:

"Pay attention; I can see you; go where I told you to go!"

This was the last time she would speak to Emil; the two of them have never seen each other from that moment on.

We went further, fought on the way, and Emil sent the Russian to take the roll back, but he did not want to do it.

"Weren't you the one who urged me to take it, saying that no one would know?"

The Russian did not say anything and went home. Emil did not want to go to the storehouse either, out of fear or because he did not want to leave the wool there. When I saw that he went toward the brigade, I told him:

"I cannot go back home; *bunica* will ask me and I must tell her the truth, because it is a sin to lie!"

"Well, come with me to the farm, and we'll see what dad says!"

When we arrived at the brigade, dad had left with the horses. Emil took the wool, loosened it, and placed it on the bed made out of boards, under the cover, saying that he would not even notice it; he knew that dad would not agree to it. When dad came back, I, being small - all small kids are honest - told him from the gate:

"We brought some wool and want to make socks, but *bunica* did not want to."

"From where did you get it?"

Emil quickly said:

"We were walking in the forest and found it!"

Now, since he spoke first, I was quiet. Dad was happy that the bed would be softer, and that was the end of it. In the morning, he left for the village, to sell some wild goose eggs and get some gas, and we stayed there to take care of the stud.

We made the fire, we ate a potato each, and Emil went out to put the saddle on the horse. All of a sudden I saw him looking down the road, and then he started toward the horse, jumped on it, and started riding away on it. He shouted back:

"They are coming after me because of the wool! Tell them I left yesterday, but you do not know where!"

I looked down the road too, and I saw two horsemen quickly riding by on their horses. I was scared: "if they come after Emil and he's not here, then they will take me! Where should I hide?" I went under the bed, where we kept the firewood. I took some pieces out, and I went in their place. Stupid kid, what can I say?... Of course they saw the fire outside, and they knew someone was in. They also saw the firewood, looked under the bed, and found me. They yelled at me in Russian to come out, but I was shaking all over and I did not budge. Then one of them grabbed my leg and pulled me out over the wood. He scratched my entire back, and my little dress was torn in a couple of places. It hurt badly, and I shouted:

"Leave me alone!"

They pulled me out, and one of them took me by my ears. I think they were policemen in civilian clothing, one younger and one older. They began to ask me:

"Where's your father?"

"He went to the market, to sell eggs."

"Aha, sabotage... He does not work, and the horses stay locked."

I almost said that he left Emil and me to take them out. I realized that was not good, and I was silent.

"Where's your brother?"

"He left."

"Where?"

"He didn't tell me."

"When did he leave?

"Yesterday."

They began with other questions too, but I was still crying, because my back hurt badly, and I could not get back to my senses. Meanwhile, dad came back. The moment I saw him, I jumped up and ran toward him! But the younger one caught me by my dress and pulled me back:

"Sit here!"

He made dad sit too and asked him:

"Where's your lad?"

Since he did not know anything, dad said:

"He was here this morning, I left both of them sleeping. I don't know where he is now…"

Then the young one came to me and slapped me so hard that he almost knocked me out.

"Liar! So little and you dare to lie to us?"

Dad jumped at them:

"Why do you hit the kid? What did she do to you?"

"You sit down! If not, we will arrest you and take you to prison! She should be shot here, on the spot, because she stole from the kolkhoz and did damage to their property… No more talking!"

They said other things as well, wrote everything into a notebook, and left. They did not arrest dad, but they now had information on him written down, on paper.

I was still crying, when dad looked at me and said:

"You deserve it! You should have told me where the wool came from! Why did you cover for Emil? You always cover for him!"

"I'm afraid of him because he beats me!"

"You should not be afraid. If he doesn't beat you, look, the KGB beats you instead… Where did Emil go?"

"He said he was leaving for Moldova!"

"Leaving for Moldova?! How childish…"

That's what he shouted to me when he ran on the horse, that he was leaving for Moldova. We found out his story later, because he wrote us a letter to Orlovka. After he ran from the brigade, he went for about sixty kilometers on the horse, to the big road. From there, the horse came back to the farm alone, and Emil found a driver who had mercy on him and took him without money to Kurgan, the capital of Ural.

In Kurgan, he went to the train station to jump on a train. His problem was that he asked someone working at the station

which train was going toward Moldova. That's what he needed!
This one turned him in to the police, and they sent him to a
correctional colony for children. This is how he ran to Moldova!
There, in the colony, he remained for five years, and perhaps he
had a better life than here. They guarded them all the time, but
they fed them three times per day and the children had warm
clothes, not how we were, hungry and naked all winter long!
They made them learn to read, write, count, and all kinds of
crafts in the factory.

Emil was smart. In three years, he caught up to the others,
even if they had had seven years of study. He was so good at
using all the tools in the plant, so much so that the supervisors
used him as example for others, remarking often: "Why don't
you all learn like this Moldavian?"...

Then, after five years, they allowed him to go back to
Bessarabia.

"We brought you here to die!"...

Some time had passed, and one evening, when dad had
gone to bed on the oven, someone knocked at the door. It was
tanti Galea,[72] the Russian. She sent me to wake up dad, and then
she told him:

"Let's go get some wheat! There are several of us, come
with us; you are dying of hunger; look, this kid is famished,
come!"

There were six Russian women and a Moldavian woman.
They wanted to steal from the field. It was late autumn, and the
wheat was going bad, under the snow, but they[73] still watched
it, as if they wanted to gather it and take it somewhere. The
guardian was drunk, and the moment they found this out, the
Russian women were ready! The Russians did not have bread
either, especially white bread, but only some dry, black bread if

---

[72] While the Romanian word "tanti" may be used for "aunt," it usually
designates a "Ms." A child calls every woman a "tanti."
[73] "They" refers to the communists. This impersonal "they" is often used by
the survivors of communist regimes when talking about the persecutors.

they gave it to them.[74] *Bunica* woke up as well and asked me what the Russian woman wanted; I translated, and she was against it:

"Don't go, Colea! God will punish you! They'll throw you in prison immediately, or they'll shoot you there, on the spot! They'll shoot all of us!"

But dad told her:

"We will die, one way or the other; I no longer have anything to feed you! Don't you see we are drying up?"

He did not listen to *bunica*, and he left.

He came back late, with half a sack, because his leg hurt and he could not carry more. He took out the wet wheat and put it on the oven to dry. We had there ten other kilograms of grain that we kept for difficult days. *Bunica* and I gathered them behind the harvester, on the field. Dad had worked there on the tractors, and he had seen that there were some grains remaining behind the car, so he told us:

"If you come and pick each one, grain by grain from the earth, you may be able to gather something, to have for the winter!"

One month and a half I toiled with *bunica* on the field; our fingers were red and stiff from the cold. We gathered those grains until snow came. Our fingers were already frozen completely, so I told *bunica*:

"Let's put everything in the sack, together with the soil, and we carry it home on our backs and sort it there! At least we can make the fire at home, but here we will stiffen up completely!"

I had a cold and was coughing, and I could no longer stay outside.

We filled up the sack, and we went home! She was already bent by the years, an old woman; I was small, with no power... We stumbled upon each other until we fell. Then, we would take a five-minute rest, and then go back to dragging the sack, because we could no longer carry it. But the sack could not hold

---

[74] In the West, many people think that white bread is not healthy. This is something unheard of in the East during communism, where you would see only bread made of rye, if even that.

and it broke. We endured so much pain getting those ten-fifteen kilograms of wheat! We kept it hidden behind the oven as if it were gold!

Just a few hours had passed since dad had returned, and the policeman came to our place. After the guard woke up from his drunkenness, he saw the tracks, asked some people about it, and found out. It was not difficult to find us; who could go stealing? The one most famished, the one who had nothing! For example, Axinia from Moşeni with her daughter Niusia, my friend, received help from Bessarabia, from her parents. Every week, they received a package with lard, cheese, preserves, and whatever else they had back there. They were not as weak and famished as we were!

So they found out who went to steal overnight, and they came to us in the morning. They arrested dad immediately, and they took all the wheat, including the one *bunica* and I had gathered on the field.

Bunica was always calm and fierce; she did not bend to anything, did not disgrace herself, did not cry, but this time, when she saw that they took absolutely the entire wheat, she threw herself to their feet and began begging them:

"Don't take it, because this one is ours, we gathered it with much difficulty, I gathered it with my granddaughter; we have witnesses! We did not steal it; we didn't do anything..."

But the commandant replied:

"Yes, I believe that you gathered it from the earth, and you did well, so it is not lost. But you had to take it to the state, because it belongs to the state! Why did you take it? If you gathered it, you had to deliver it to the state!"

"And what can we eat?"

"What, did you come here to eat? To live? We brought you here to die! You are condemned to death!"

I translated to *bunica* the commandant's words, and dad, being upset, told her:

"Mom, stand up from your knees! Hear what he says: he brought us here to die, not to live! Accept this: we have to die, and that's the end of it! We have no escape!"

Then they took dad to prison, and we remained alone,

bunica and I. It was winter and cold, the firewood ran out, and if there was no man in the house, it was very difficult for us. I would drag dry branches or even a thick bar at times from the forest and, being small, I would get tired and I would barely make it home. Then we had to cut those bars, but *bunica* was old and she no longer had much strength; I had even less strength than her, because if there was no food, we also had no strength.

After a while, *bunica* sent me to the cellar to count the potatoes, and she divided them into days, to have enough until the spring. That's what she was always saying, and I can still hear her:

"If God wills that we survive until we go out to get nettle, if God wills it…"

We went from three potatoes per day to two potatoes for both of us, and this is the food with which we survived. Sometimes, the Moldavians from the village brought us something. Especially Axinia from Moşeni, when she received something from home, she gave us a little piece of cheese. A Russian who was more merciful brought us a glass of milk every few days, and this was all our food. There was no way to resist for a long time, and *bunica*, especially after the commandant told her to her face that he brought us there to die, was preparing me to die, telling me that there is nothing terrible about it, that we will simply dry up, and that the angel of death will come and take us to heaven. This is how she would prepare me for death. I could not be at peace with the idea that I would die, but I did not tell her anything because I did not want to upset her. With great difficulty, we reached spring.

Dad's trial

In the spring, they told us that dad would be tried in Dolgovka, 25 kilometers away from the village. We could go see him one more time if we wanted. But who could go, *bunica*? She sent me:

"You go, Margareta, and see him! Maybe they will free him, maybe they will forgive him… Tell him to tell the truth, just as it happened!"

In the village, the rumor spread that dad was the organizer, because he was the only man. The women who were tried with him had relatives in the village, and they knew the truth so they were trying to somehow repair the damage. They made some gingerbread and some boiled potatoes, they tied them in a kerchief, and I left for Dolgovka with an older woman, the mother of one of the tried Russian women, and with Niusia Scobioala, who went to see her mom in the hospital.

The Russian woman, although older, was strong. If she had milk, cream, and butter, she did not hunger and could survive better. But I was weak, because I had nothing to eat, and so I fell after some walking. She waited for me to get up and yelled at me:

"Come! It will get dark because of you and the wolves will eat us in the forest!"

I will never forget this trip. I was very weak after winter, and to walk for 25 kilometers as weak as I was, a ten year old child, almost crippled…

Finally, with great difficulty and God's help, we arrived in the city and went straight to the Court. We slept there overnight, next to each other, and in the morning we waited for them to bring the inmates. They brought all eight of them into a large hall, and made them sit on some chairs, face to face with three fat judges. The trial was supposed to begin. The moment I saw dad, I began to cry and wanted to go to him, but a soldier pushed me back and told me that if I made another step, he would kick me out. Then they started to say various things, as in a trial. I did not understand much, until I heard *tanti* Galea, the Russian woman, say:

"Look, Spânu Neculai organized us. He called all of us to tell us to steal the wheat…"

When I heard this, I immediately stood up and said:

"*Tanti* Galea, how can you say such lies? You came to our window and knocked, and I woke up first and opened the door. How can you say such lies?!…"

But the judge, one of the three, yelled at me:

"Sit down, little brat! Nobody asked you anything. What, is this older woman lying? You are lying, because you are a small little brat!"

I began crying:

"How come… how come?"

"Be quiet, don't mingle!"

And I was quiet. But dad also said,

"The child cannot lie! It is true what she says: I did not organize it. These women called me, and I went, because we were dying of hunger. How could I take care of three souls if the wheat stays under the snow and rots?!..."

Two or three other people said something else, and then one of the judges said:

"We'll give him ten years, and eight to each woman!"

When he said ten years, I jumped from the chair and rushed to them, to their feet, crying and yelling:

"Don't take daddy!... Don't take him!..."

I knew that the communists in the village gave ten years to *bunelul* and murdered him, and I imagined that if they gave ten years to dad, that meant that they would kill him and I would no longer see him. I was staying there crying, and some women began crying too and shouting to the judges to not give him so many years because his family would die of hunger if they put him in prison for so many years, and also so unjustly.

But the judges shouted:

"Out, all of you out!"

A soldier grabbed me by the hand, took me out, and closed the door. I cried for some time and then I thought: "I will stay here, because it must be done by now, and I will see him when he comes out." Indeed, the women started to come out shortly, one by one, and then dad came out as well. I ran to him and gave him the little bundle with food. He managed to ask me about *bunica* and how we came out of winter. I told him that it was very hard and asked him crying:

"What will we do now without you?..."

He caressed me on my head and told me:

"Don't cry, because you cry to no avail! Look, I will try to do something for the two of you from there. I will work to do something!"

He took the bundle, they put him into a black car, and he

was gone. I remained there on a rock, and I did not know what to do. I could not be peaceful, especially with the thought that they had taken him from me forever, just like they did with *bunelul*. The woman who had come with me was crying as well. She grabbed me from the ground and said:

"Come! Let's go home!"

"I won't be able to get home!"

"You will be able to, because we are no longer hurrying; we have the whole day before us!"

We began to go back and we arrived home toward the night, with great difficulty. When I told *bunica* that they condemned dad for ten years, something terrible happened to her. She did not cry, she did not yell, but she refused everything: to eat, to wash, or to pray. She lied down, put a cover over her head, and that was it: she did not speak, she did not move, and she did not do anything. I let her alone for a day, thinking that she may get over it and she would get up. But she did not get up the second day, nor did she ask for food. Then I boiled two potatoes, made some berry tea, and went to her:

"*Bunica*, take, drink, and eat something!"

She said nothing. Absolutely nothing! She did not speak, not even a word, to tell me what her plan was, what I should do from then on. When I saw this, I felt lost as well.

On the third day, a Russian brought us a glass of milk. I divided it in two and added tea, so that I would make more of it. I came close to *bunica*, took the cover from her head, and told her:

"Please, drink this milk and tell me what to do! If you do not get up and don't eat anything, then I'll lie next to you, we'll both die, and it will end like this!"

Then she opened her eyes, moved a little, and said:

"Yes! I'll do it for you, because God is great and perhaps He would take care to save at least you!"

She got up with great difficulty, drank some tea, ate a potato, and recovered this way. We began sitting together again, talking, and praying, just like before. In order to get at least some food, I was going around all day long to find duck eggs, roots, and berries, and this is how summer passed.

Fall came upon us, and we had no firewood, no potatoes, nothing, and one day I went to the window and saw that snow was all over...

Departing from bunica

The frost barely came, and one day the Russian commandant who guarded the deported people came before our house, with a drayman and a sleigh.

He commanded me to get dressed immediately, because he would take me to the orphanage. It was a tragedy for me, because I did not want to be separated from *bunica*. What orphanage, what's that, where is that, where does he want to take me? The commandant told me that it was a place where they put together all orphan children, fed them, dressed them, and took them to school, so it would be good for me. I translated this to *bunica*, she thought about it a bit, and then she said:

"I think your dad wrote a complaint that we are alone and would die. Go, my dear, we have no choice! Go and be saved, at least you! If I die, I won't regret it because I lived my life, but you must live on!"

And she pleaded with me for a long time, because I did not want at all to be separated from her.

I had to finally listen to her, but then another problem came up: I had nothing to wear for the road! *Bunica* got undressed, taking off everything she had on her, really everything, and she put everything on me. She put dad's felts on my feet; they were broken and mended, terrible looking. They were so big that I was drowning in them. Then she made the sign of the cross over me, and she only said this at our parting:

"If you pray to God, you will get out of there! Do not forget to pray even for one day! If you forget, then God will also forget about you!"

Being an adult, she knew what an orphanage meant, especially a soviet one, but I could not understand at all; I could not imagine. The commandant had praised it, that they would feed you three times a day, give you clothes, and then you could go to school, so I believed it.

I was mourning *bunica*. How could I leave her there, with no one? I told her:

"What will you do? How will you live? How will you go after firewood if you gave me all your clothes?!..."

"Don't worry about me! You saw I have a cover on the bed; I'll make a vest out of it. If there is something, I'll ask for help from Axinia, and she won't give up on me. Have no worries, I will manage!"

She made the sign of the cross over me, then I sat next to the commandant in the sleigh, the drayman in front, and we left. She remained in front of the house - I can see her even now - almost naked, with a thin blouse on her, looking after me when the sleigh turned.

In that moment, I thought that she was getting ready to die, and I had no peace. How could she die? She was like a mother to me! That's how I saw her, as my mother, even if I called her *bunica*; she was the dearest person to me. For me, she was God! I don't remember her to have raised her voice one time, to blame me, or to say any bad words - there were no bad words in her house. Never! How could she die?

This is how the two of us parted forever.

The road to the orphanage

The first stop was in Dolgovka, where dad had been tried. The chiefs asked for my birth certificate. What birth certificate if we could not take anything with us when we left? Then they told me:

"Stay here until we send a letter to Mihăileni, in Bessarabia, so they can send you the certificate by mail!"

I got scared:

"But the letters can take one month! What do I do here for a month?!"

"Well, you'll stay with us, because we removed you from the records in the village. There is a stamp on your file, so you cannot go back."

I was ten years old, and I did not understand that I had a file as an enemy of the people, with an assigned number, and that I was under surveillance.

They forced me to live in prison, in custody, where all the delinquents stayed before trial. It was a large room, with bunk beds. They gave me one bed and sent me in, with eight-ten other men who waited to be tried.

It is true that when he took me in, the chief of the prison chose one of the inmates, the strongest, and told him:

"You watch over her; nobody should touch her! You answer for her, and we'll take this into consideration at your trial."

This is why they did not touch me, but the words I heard, the questions, what they were telling each other in my presence, this is something I cannot describe. They were murderers and thieves of all kinds, and they were speaking to me as if I were a man, only dirty words. I was shy and quiet, and I could no longer bear it.

One day, I went crying to the prison commandant and told him:

"Send me back to *bunica*; I can no longer listen to this trash, to all these dirty things I hear here!" But he told me:

"Look at that! Small, but with character, and she even comes to me with claims! Is it my fault that you do not have the certificate?"

"But what's my fault that they hurried us?"

"You should have been careful to take everything you needed with you ..."

"How, if they hurried us and beat us to get in the car? How could we get the papers and all? Did they tell us where they were taking us, for what, and what we will need? Nobody told us anything! Get in the car - that was all! And with their guns to our heads..."

He got upset:

"Look at her, she doesn't like it! What, you think the others here like it? They are waiting as well, and it is hard for them, but they endure it. You must endure it too!"

"But why shouldn't I endure it with *bunica*? I could go back there, and when this certificate comes, then I could come back!"

"No, because you are removed from the records. We must

supervise you, and that's it!"

When he saw that I was about to cry again, he told me:

"Well, let it be for now, go, and we'll think of something!"

Toward the evening, the chief came in the room and said:

"Spânu, get dressed!"

I took those large clothes, patched and repatched, from *bunica*. I was just a little child, small and wretched, skin and bones, and the clothes were hanging on me. I came out from the room, and a blonde, beautiful lady told me to follow her. I did not know where, but it was all the same to me; I just wanted to be free from those men. She was going ahead and, from time to time, looked back at me with evil eyes. I followed her, with those felts that I was barely dragging after me.

We arrived at a wooden Russian house. She opened the door and we came into a clean, warm room. She told me to get undressed. Everything was so clean and beautiful inside - where could I put my old and dirty clothes? I took them to the porch and I remained dressed only with a thin little dress. She went to the kitchen and warmed up some good food, and by that time the chief of the prison came as well. We stayed at the table all three of us, and I understood that she was his wife, and that this was his house, and that he had pity on me.

The Russians were compassionate too! This chief had understood how much I, an innocent child, was suffering, and he wanted to keep me with him until the certificate would come. But it was not to be! His wife could not stand me; she did not like me at all. She looked at me with contempt and did not say a word to me; I stayed in a corner, felt guilty, and did not know what to do. In the evening, they put me in bed in white, clean sheets; I felt like I was in heaven. But instead of sleeping, they talked until late into the night in their room. You could realize from their voices that they were quarreling, that they were upset.

In the morning, the Russian woman gave me tea, fed me, and took me back to prison. She dropped me there again, in that room, and those men laughed at me saying:

"Where did you go? Did you take a walk? Did you go with men?"

I heard all kinds of dirty words and stupid things from them, and I was getting sick just from hearing them.

The next day, early morning, the chief of the prison came and told me again:

"Get dressed and come with me!"

I went after him, barely walking with those felts, and we stopped at the outskirts of the city, at an old, shattered house. We entered, and he said in Russian:

"Good evening!"

"Good evening!"

"I would like you to take in this little girl, for she is one of yours!"

It was a Moldavian family with six children, among whom there was also a four month old toddler. When I heard my language, I melted with joy. I came in and immediately got connected with them!

"Have you eaten?"

"I have."

"Then let's go to work!"

"Gladly! Let's go! I'll do anything I can…"

I washed the child, cleaned the floor, and helped in the kitchen, basically, anything that was needed in the house. I was so happy… Of course, I missed *bunica* very much, but I was happy. It felt as if I were home, in Moldova!

But the devil brought me back into trouble. One day, the mistress gave me a jar and sent me to buy some jam as fast as possible, because the dough for the pie was fermenting. I went, the seller filled up the jar, and while I was going back I had the thought to touch it at least a bit, to feel the taste on my tongue. I was not hungry, because they fed me with whatever they could take from their children. It was not much, but I was happy with what they gave me, especially potatoes. I did not need anything else, because I was used to potatoes and hunger. But, in that moment, the devil pushed me to touch the jam. I took the jar out, and it was damp, because it was winter, and the jam was warm. I dropped it, but the jam did not go out of the jar, because it was not soft, but 100 grams fell on the road, in the snow. I gathered as much as I could and put it back. One brown stain remained on the snow. I looked around to see if anyone saw me, and I ate the entire stain. Of course, I was late, and the lady was upset. When she saw that two millimeters were missing from the jar, she asked me:

"What happened? Did you eat from the jar or the seller did not fill it?"

I did not understand that the dough got bad because of me being late and that was why she was upset. Instead of clarifying things, telling her that I dropped it, that it did not have a lid and fell into the snow, I got scared and went immediately outside in the yard. I sat there and waited. What was I waiting for? I do not know. I was a stupid child! I waited so that perhaps someone would come out and tell me:

"Come, let's go in; you'll freeze! Come, it's nothing terrible, it's fine!"

But no one came out after me, and then my pride played a farce on me and instead of going back to them humbly, I went to prison on my own will. When the chief saw me there, he told me astonished:

"What happened to you? Even your own people don't like you? Even your own people don't love you?..."

I remained in prison for another week after this. Then, the birth certificate came, and they called the drayman again with his sleigh, to take me further.

When we left, it was already November and a terrible cold, -30 degrees.[75] The drayman had a long sheepskin that touched the ground and a hat, but I only had those thin and patched clothes; I was wretched. I am amazed I survived.

We traveled for almost the entire day, and he said toward the evening:

"The orphanage may be near, but I do not risk it. I don't need to be eaten by wolves! Let's get a place overnight in a village!"

We stopped in the first village, in front of a meager house, and he knocked at the door. A Moldavian came out, because all of Siberia was full of Moldavians. The drayman told him:

---

[75] Celsius.

"Look, I'm taking this little girl to the orphanage, but we cannot go during the night. Could you host us here?"

He took us in with a glad heart. He took the horse in the stable, with the cow, and invited us in the house. I was stiff because of the frost. He put me up on the oven, where there were three other boys. When his wife found out I was Moldavian, she began speaking in Romanian with me. They gave us tea and they invited us to dinner. I began to feel well again: I forgot about the frost and the cold. As I was staying on the oven, the two of them, the man and his woman, were looking and looking at me. They both went in another room, came back after ten minutes, and told the drayman:

"We discussed it, and we decided to adopt this little girl. Don't take her to the orphanage, because it will be very hard for her there!"

But the Russian replied:

"No, I am not allowed! I have her file here, top secret. I have to take her there to get a signature."

"We'll sign! We will take her here and we will sign. In our place, in Bessarabia, if someone dies and a child remains an orphan, a relative takes him. We consider that she is our relative, because we like the girl and we pity her..."

"But ask her, does she want to stay?"

When they asked me, I remembered dad and my brother, and I said,

"No, I want to be with *bunica*, with dad, at our home in Mihăileni!"

And the Russian told them:

"You see?! If she did not have anyone, you could go with me to the orphanage and adopt her. But she has a father, a grandmother, a brother, and relatives who can take her. There is no way for her to stay with you!"

They were saddened, but they had no option.

We all went to sleep on the oven, because it was warm. I woke up a few times, and I saw that the woman was making pancakes. She took the flour from five mouths [76] to make

---

[76] There were five people in the family.

pancakes for an orphan, to have on the road! If they are still alive, they and their descendants, may God give them health; if they have passed, may they be with the righteous, for they were such good people! I am sorry that I do not know their names or the village where they were from, but maybe someone will find out now. Those boys were my age, and they must remember that an orphan slept at their place one night!

In the morning, the man woke up first. He gave water to the horse and loaded the sleigh with hay. The woman put the pancakes on some paper and gave them to me for the road. They would have given me clothes as well, but I think they had none. They looked after us with so much pity: the drayman with a padded coat, a sheepskin long to the ground, a hat, gloves, and felts with new soles, and me, wretched, broken, with those patched felts, filled with hay!

We went back on the road, and after a while the frost got even stronger. The drayman went down from the sleigh and began walking to warm up. He told me to do the same, but how could I go down since I was barely walking with those large, broken felts? I was afraid that I would remain behind the sleigh and the wolves would eat me, so I told him I would not get out. The frost had completely penetrated me, and my toes began having frostbite. He was always telling me to pay attention, in case of wolves, to see if anyone was coming, because I was facing the forest. But I was becoming more and more stiff, and I wanted to sleep.

It was getting dark and we were not finding the orphanage. The drayman asked a tractor driver who happened to be there, and he directed us. We traveled until it was completely dark, and the forest did not end. I felt pain in my entire body; I could not even move my head, and I only wanted to sleep. I thought that, if the driver said that it would not be much longer, I had to bear it. I don't know, but I think I inherited the genes from my grandmother on my mother's side, because she lived for one hundred years. Otherwise, I am amazed how I survived the entire road, at -45 degrees!

The orphanage in Zverinka

We finally found the orphanage. There was only one small light, in a service room. The drayman came down from the sleigh, knocked at the door, came back, and shouted at me:

"Come, get down; we finally arrived!"

I tried to move, but I could not. I forced myself: nothing! I was stiff, and that was the end of it!

He went in to talk to the director, and when he saw that I was not coming down, he came back:

"What, did you fall asleep? Come down, we arrived!"

I muttered something, but I no longer had any voice. He then came close to the sleigh and looked at me:

"Oh, but you got stiff! Come, comrade director,[77] help me; look, she is stiff, and we need two people to take her!"

The director came out, they took me as stiff as I was, and put me on a table inside. They asked the doctor to come urgently for a serious case, a frozen child. When the doctor came, she began treating me with rubbings and injections, but I did not feel anything. I only saw the syringe, but I did not feel the sting. This is how it went for the whole night. The director blamed the drayman and told him he would sue him:

"How could you get dressed this way and bring the child frozen? The orphanage is for healthy children, not for disabled ones. If she does not recover, you take her back, because we do not need such children!"

"But I asked her if she was cold. What's my fault?"

"What do you mean what's your fault? Didn't you see that she was not dressed? You got dressed; didn't you see that she didn't have anything? Did you think you could bring her here dead? Go and save the horse at least, put the sheepskin on him!"

They toiled with me the entire night, and they poured rubbing alcohol in my mouth toward the morning. I was getting hungry and sleepy, but they did not allow me to fall asleep. I finally felt when the doctor hit me. When she saw that I felt pain, she gave me some medicine, gave me another injection,

---

[77] In Communism, the appellative "comrade" was quite universal. The word replaced "mister" and "miss," which were considered too bourgeois.

and left. I could finally sleep. When I woke up, I was still on the table, covered, and the food was next to me, on a chair. This is how my life at the orphanage started.

There were around fifty children at that orphanage, boys and girls, all Russians. Only one of them was perhaps Ukrainian. There were two children from Bessarabia as well, a boy with his older sister, but they were not Moldavians, but Russian refugees from the time of the tsars. As long as I remembered my language, I tried to speak with that girl, but she was older and we did not meet often. When I no longer had anyone to talk to and I had nothing to read, I forgot Romanian. I stayed at the orphanage for three years, and I forgot my language in three years! When I had heard at home that soldiers went to the army in Russia and came back after some years forgetting the language, I could not believe it. But it is true! If you do not have anyone to talk to, you forget.

Life at the orphanage was rough. After the war, there were many orphaned, abandoned, and unattended children in Russia. They gathered them from the streets, from the garbage, from under the bridges, and locked them in orphanages. Poor children were like the wild horses, and you had to adapt to this wilderness.

The moment they found out I was Moldavian, they began calling me all sorts of names: jackal, parasite, or enemy of the people... Then, when they saw that I was making the sign of the cross, they called me *bogomolka*, that is, the "pious one," which was a way of mocking me.

I shed so many tears because I wanted to go back, to *bunica*! I wanted those two potatoes per day, but with *bunica*...

Here, it's true, they fed us three times a day. You would not feel full, but you would not die of hunger either. You could survive. We had an artificial pond next to the orphanage, and they bought fish from there. They gave us fish every day: fish soup and fried fish. The second year, I only had to get near the kitchen and smell fish, and I immediately vomited. My body could no longer take it. But of course it was better, if you compare it with two-three potatoes per day, as I had eaten with *bunica*! On the great feasts, November 7th, May 1st,[78] they gave us something better. We had some meat, a frozen apple, or some candies.

The majority of children were busy with stealing. This is why the orphanage was at the outskirts of the forest, separated from the village. When they could get to the village, during summer, they would go into houses through the windows and steal everything. The people came to the director to complain, but he used to tell them:

"What can you do, they are hungry!"

"But don't you feed them?"

"But what, is this nourishment?..."

And it went on like this.

How I became a pioneer[79]

For a month, I exchanged letters with *bunica*. I told her that no one made the sign of the cross there and that they wanted to make me a pioneer... She wrote me that I should avoid doing it at all costs because the pioneers belonged to a satanic sect, and then you would become a communist and like Satan; "don't you give yourself to them, because God will punish you!" She also told me that if I could not cross myself openly, I should wait for the children to fall asleep.

I fell asleep before them many times, because I was a child who did not know anything else other than work, work, and work. I did not know how to waste time. This is how my family was. In Orlovka, with *bunica*, we had no work because there was nothing, no thread, no cloth, and you had nothing to work with. But at the orphanage, when I got to the older group, the girls embroidered, crocheted, and sewed all kinds of things. I learned immediately to do it, because I resembled *bunica*, I was skilled. And I started to sew as well! But I needed more thread and material.

Thus, I started going with the children to gather bones. We

---

[78] The communist revolution and the international day of workers.

[79] During communism, the majority of children were made pioneers. It was their entrance into the youth organizations of the communist party.

went on the shore of Tobol, a very large and fast river that came from the mountains. There was sand on the shores, and the bones came out only if you hit the sand with your feet. I still do not know where all those bones came from. There must have been either a cemetery or a war in which many horses died...

I took those bones to a special place - they did something with them, made them into flour or glue - and I received some money in exchange. I would immediately buy some thread and material with the money, so that I could make a small pillow, a napkin, or a handkerchief. And I liked it. One day, all the Russians and the educators began telling me:

"Make one for me too! Make me one!"

"I'll do it, if you bring me thread and some cloth!"

They brought me those things, and I made things for all of them, but also for me. In three years, I filled a suitcase with all kinds of things - dowry, as *bunica* used to say; a girl must get married with a dowry. During summer, when all the children were having fun, stealing, or running in the forest or to the pond, I would stay bent, from morning until evening, sewing. After sewing, I went to school, then I did my homework, and back to work. I did everything with love, with joy, so that something would remain after me. That's what *bunica* used to say, that if you do not do anything, you lived for nothing.

When I was more rested[80] and could do it, I waited for the girls to go to sleep, and then I prayed, as *bunica* had taught me. One night, a girl saw that I woke up, knelt, made a cross, and whispered "Our Father." In the morning, everyone knew about it. There, at the orphanage, no one had faith. It was a shame to believe in God, a great shame. The management gathered everyone, all the educators, from all sections. They brought all of us together, made a square, and I was in the middle, the guiltiest child because I made the sign of the cross. And they began:

"What? Aren't you ashamed? Are you that stupid? You are no longer with *bunica*; forget what she told you! Now you are with us and you must listen to us!"

---

[80] *Hodinită* in original.

Three days in a row they continued with this. Then they decided: we must make her a pioneer, we must give her tasks, and then she will forget about God! They told me about making me a pioneer, but I refused, especially because *bunica* had written that I should absolutely not do it. So I said no and no, and they terrorized me for a few months. They did not expect me to be that stubborn regarding this. But *bunica* was God for me, and I had to listen to her, not to them. I had not yet realized that I was in different hands now, and I had to obey them, because *bunica* was far away.

However, they did not give up. The educator gave me a small book with the laws of the pioneers, to learn them for when they would accept me. So they made a square with the entire school, saying it was because we were receiving Spânu Rita among the pioneers. I ran to the forest and hid. The educator was embarrassed, because it was her task to make me a pioneer. As punishment, she threw me into a dark niche where they kept the brooms and the rags for the floor. She threw me there, hungry and cold, in late autumn. I was dressed - I was no longer going around like in Orlovka, only in the light dress, because they had given me a thick outfit with trousers and a blouse. However, it was cold, and during the night I felt the cold down to my bones, so I began knocking on the door. The girls passed by, but they did not open it, because the educator had threatened them severely.

The second day, she took me out and brought me to the director. He was not a harsh man, but kind and understanding. When the others spoke to me against God, they spoke harshly, as if I were a felon. He was not like that; one could see he was different. When the educator began to insult me in his presence, he said:

"Let's forget about it, because Rita will understand it after all! She understood now, and she will no longer make a cross. She will be like all the other children; what reason has she to be different from the others? We will feed her, dress her, educate her, and she needs to respond well. Isn't this so, Rita?"

I moved my head without saying anything, but I felt that he did not say these things with malice, that he did not really believe them. After we came out of the room, the educator opened the door of that niche and threw me back in, even if the director told her to leave me alone. I froze again, and my legs began to hurt. I remembered how I almost lost them when I came to the orphanage, because this was what the doctor told me: I could have lost my legs if I had stayed one or two more hours in that frost! They all knew about my case, and the educator told me:

"If you remain there, just think what will happen to your legs!"

Being a fragile child, I of course got scared and gave up after a while. I thought that if *bunica* and dad would see what pain I had to go through, they may agree if I did what these people asked me.

The teacher was also a great support. She did not show that she was Christian, but she took my side against everyone else. She told me:

"Stand against them, be smarter! If anyone throws dirt on you, throw dirt back! If they hit you, hit them back! If they see you crying and suffering, they will laugh at you even more."

This is how it was. The educator was not the only one who made fun of me; the children, especially the boys, did the same thing. You could not pass by them! They either tripped you so that you would fall on your face, or they hit you immediately. I was "the enemy of the people," the parasite! How could one live like this?!...

Today, I would not suffer that much if someone unjustly told me ugly words, but these words stuck with me so painfully back then! Why would they call me this, if I did not do anything? Why would they throw dirt on me?!... And I suffered terribly.

When the teacher saw me this way, she made me stay after class and told me:

"You must become a pioneer, and then they will leave you alone, they will not torture you that much. If you want to have faith, have faith in your soul; no one can take God out of your soul. Isn't it so?"

"It is!"

"You see?"

If she didn't put it this way, perhaps I would not have given in, but when she told me this, it seemed logical. Who could take God out of my soul? I have faith, and that's it! I will pray in my mind, as *bunica* taught me.

So I gave in. They took me out from confinement, because the children had begun to be indignant as well. When they heard that they were freezing me and not feeding me, the boys yelled at the educator directly:

"Why do you punish this Moldavian girl? Look, none of us, boys, is a pioneer!"

Indeed, only one of them was a pioneer and wore a red tie, but he would run away from the boys and kept in the company of girls, because they did not beat him. No other boy was a pioneer. They were wild and said:

"Why do I need this piece of cloth? To wipe my nose with it or what?"

The girls also told the educator:

"Leave this Moldavian girl alone, if she does not want to! She has a grandmother, a father, and a brother, why would she listen to you? She listens to her relatives…. Leave her alone!"

So they took me out from there. The teacher spoke to the educator, then she spoke with me, and they took me out. They made me a pioneer, and one boy burned my tie. He burned the tie the next day; but he also burned my hair!

After that, they also gave me a task: to be a teacher helper. They made a second catalog and if the child came to school, I marked him present; if he did not come, I marked him absent. After classes, I had to go to the director to give him the attendance, so he could take measures. What measures, if no one listened? The director called the child to the office, and the child went there laughing. The director asked him, the child promised he would come to school, but he did not come to school the following day either. And it went on this way.

But I thus became the guilty one. I was the "traitor," the "denouncer," and the beatings and tripping began. One of them hit me so hard in the ear that it hurts even today. They laughed at me and made fun of me in all possible ways.

But how could I refuse Lidia Vasilievna, the teacher? She asked me:

"Rita, I must do this, but I do not have time, so please help me!"

I accepted, because *bunica* taught me to never say no when someone asked for a favor.

I was sorry for her, because she had two small children and came to teach there from the village, three kilometers away. I sometimes called her "mother." I was eager to call someone "mama" my whole life, and, from time to time, I called her "mother." She had pity on me, invited me to her place, took from her own children, and fed me with a glass of milk, a candy... Much later I found out that she was deported as well, from Moscow. Her father, a lawyer, had been shot by the Russians, and they sent her mother and her to the furthest reaches of Siberia. They made her work in the most difficult places, where no one wanted to work. Here, at the orphanage, no teacher made it; all of them ran from the wild children, but she made it.

At the school of survival

The children's insults were the most difficult things to endure at the orphanage. The girls were also rough and would fight. I started fighting too, because this is what the teacher told me:

"If they hit you, hit back; otherwise they trample on you and no one will defend you! There is no one to protect you, no one to cry after you. Do you want to survive? Fight!"

And I fought.

One day, I was sitting calmly on the bed, reading. One of the girls, the worst and the nastiest, came to me and told me:

"You, Moldavian, why are you reading? Get up and wash the floor, because I am in charge!"

You had to wash the floor, to take the night bucket outside, to the closet, to wash it, to bring water and firewood, to make the fire... usual tasks for life. She told me to do all this in her place. I told her:

"I won't do it!"

"Why? You did it for others!"

"I did it because they were sick and could not do it. But you are healthy, so do it yourself!"

She grabbed my book and threw it as far as she could. I remained calm and did not give in. Then she grabbed my leg, pulled me from the bed, and banged my head on the wall. But I did not give up: I got up and threw her against the wall with all my strength.

I thought: if only *bunica* could see me now! How was I before, when I was with her? A docile lamb, with shame before people, with honesty and prayers to God... But need teaches you, makes you tough, and I was really embittered there; I had changed.

The greatest tragedy came because of my faith: I lost it. They continually told me that God did not exist. Imagine what a radical change that was in my soul! For ten years, I had only heard of God, God, and God, and all of a sudden, there was no God!

The teacher was the only one who told me differently, but I did not stay much with her. From time to time, she remained after classes and taught me to keep my faith in my soul, to not give up, to not allow them to trample me, to have dignity, and to not be ashamed to respond.

Day by day, they would say one thing and then the other, until they convinced me.

First, I began to blame God. If He existed, why did He accept something like this? Then, with time, after not hearing anything about Him or hearing only that he does not exist and that it is shameful to believe in Him, because only stupid old women believe, and that man is god, because man can do anything, I truly stopped believing.

I still had moments when I thought that He existed and watched everything. For example, I asked for some watermelon from two girls who were eating, and they did not want to give me any at all, not even to taste it. They told me:

"If you want some, come with us to steal it tomorrow!"

I went. I could not steal, because the watchman was vigilant, and he almost shot us. When we came back, the kitchen was closed, and we remained hungry: no melon and no food! Then I thought that God punished me because I wanted to steal. But it was not something profound.

The days passed this way, and slowly I forgot both my language and God. I was beginning to wonder why I got to this point, why I was changing so …

Lord, may no one ever enter through the doors of an orphanage! I do not know how it is now, but what I lived through was terrible. At times, we were so homesick, and we dreamed to be with our parents, dreamed of a normal life! We used to sing songs full of pain, about the tombs of our mothers and fathers, about death, or that we were nobody and nothing. We were not singing, we were screaming. The whole forest resounded with our pain.

On the brink of death

There was only one girl among those at the orphanage with whom I felt closer, Zoia Panamariova.

One day, when I was alone in the room embroidering, Zoia came to me and told me:

"Let's take a swim in the pond and break some water lilies!"

It was summer, and all children were having fun wherever they could. You had complete freedom; you could do what you wanted. The only forbidden thing was to run away or go stealing in the village, but even this still happened, of course.

I went to the pond with Zoia and got into the water. She knew how to swim and went to the water lilies, and I followed her. I even came across a water lily, and I almost drowned when I pulled it. Water lilies have some thin stems, thinner than a finger and as long as the depth of the water. When I pulled it, the stem did not break, because it was very resistant. I looked at Zoia and saw that she bit on the stem with her teeth. I did the same thing, and this gave me courage, because I had one water lily already and I wanted to go after a second one. The water was already reaching up to my mouth, and I shouted:

"Zoia, is it deep where you are?"

"It's not deep; don't be afraid, take one more step!"

I took one more step, and when I saw that I did not reach the bottom, I began to move my hand and legs frantically. The more I moved, the more I got entangled in the lilies' stems. I was so entangled that I could no longer come out. And so, peacefully and nicely, I lost all my breath and sunk to the bottom.

During all this, she turned her head, saw that I was not there and that bubbles were coming out from the water, and she realized I was drowning. As she was just two steps away from me, she swam, dived into the water, found my head, and pulled me out from my hair. I had already swallowed enough water, and it took some time before I recovered.

That moment strengthened my friendship with Zoia. I felt her closer and cherished her more. If she were not there to take me out, or if she were as scared as those boys who left Emil in the pond and ran away, I would have died.

Not long after this I did another one. One afternoon, I took my blanket, went in the weeds, and read there until I fell asleep. I did not even go to eat. The educator, who had read my file and knew what Emil did, was scared that I also ran away to Moldova. When they finally found me, she scolded me badly, saying that I could have been eaten by snakes, that there were beasts in those weeds, and that she did not want to go to prison because of me. She gave me a hard punishment, and I gave my word that I would never do something like that again.

A few days after this, I came out to the road and sat there to read. It was quiet; carriages or cars rarely passed by. That day, a man and a woman, both young, around thirty five years old, came toward me and asked me why I was so far away from the village and if I was not afraid to be there alone. I told them I was not afraid because I lived at the orphanage, three hundred meters from the road. We began talking, and I stayed very long with them. I do not know why; perhaps I had the desire to speak with other people as well...

After a week or so, the director called me. When I went in, I saw them. They were smiling and told me they came to adopt me, because they had no children and liked me very much. The director asked me:

"Do you know them?"

"Yes, I talked to them."

"Do you want them to adopt you?"

"What do you mean?"

"To be their girl with documents, so they would be responsible for you."

"What about dad?... What about *bunica*?..."

"It's over with dad and *bunica*! They will be your mother and father!"

"No, I don't want to! No, no, no!"

And I ran away.

How bunica Sofia died

One day, I received a letter from Niusia Scobioala who told me that *bunica* went home, to Bessarabia.

After I left for the orphanage, that village, Orlovka, was completely destroyed. If they took eight people to prison, no one remained to work, to take care of the farms. They moved all of them to Kuzminovka, where the horse brigade was. I do not know how *bunica* managed to survive there.

In the meantime, dad was writing complaints from prison to Moscow, saying that an old woman with no blame was dying because there was no one to take care of her. Just imagine, she was 78 years old, hungry and cold, and had no one to take care of her! The people from our village helped her from time to time, and this is how she survived for two more years. Then, they sent a committee of doctors to see if she indeed could not take care of herself, and they sent her home.

When she went back, the communists sent her to the district, in Rășcani, to see who she had in the village and who could take her in. Nasta, her eldest daughter, accepted to take her in, to take care of her. The communists left *bunica* there under Nasta's care. Both her girls took care of her, but they could no longer do anything, because she already was completely dystrophic and regardless of how you would feed her or take care of her, she could no longer recover.

She stayed at Nasta's around three months. Then, she called the priest at home, confessed, had communion, and when she felt that her last breath was close - she had a gift from the Lord, because she knew the moment - she went to her house. The daughters told her:

"Where are you going? You are weak. Where are you leaving?"

"I'm going to my house, so that I can die at home!"

She went to her house, which was then a policlinic, in the center of the village. She arrived at the well that she and *bunelul* Grigore dug. She tried to get water, but she instead spilled it on the ground, because she was very weak and had to use crutches. A young woman came to help her:

"What happened, are you sick? Are you going to the policlinic to get well?"

"I'm going to die in my house. Please, help me to get there!"

The woman helped her, and *bunica* went into the house. She opened a door, and a doctor was checking a woman. She opened another, and a nurse was giving an injection to a man. He yelled at her: "Why do you open the door without knocking? What are you doing here?"

Poor *bunica* did not say anything. If at least he would have been a young man, who would have not known her and would have not known that it was her house, but no, he was instead someone of her age and knew all these things. When he was done with the injection, the man came out. *Bunica*, being helpless, was sitting on the threshold. He wanted to pass, but she was in his way. And he yelled at her again:

"What are you doing here? Your daughter took you in, go and stay there! Why did you come here? Are you coming to get well? Your health is finished!"

She barely whispered to him:

"I came to my house…"

"It's no longer yours; it is the state's! It's not yours; nothing is yours here. Get up and leave, don't stay in people's way!"

Bunica went from the threshold to the porch and she suddenly stiffened up and gave up her soul there, next to her house. If not in her house, at least next to the house where she worked for so many years and gave birth to eleven children. This is how her prayer, that she had said every day and night in Siberia, was fulfilled. God gave her not only three days, as she asked, but three months. She spent three months at home, in her village, and she died with a candle, confessed and communed. They buried her beautifully, with three priests, a memorial service, alms, and everything as is the custom…

Thinking about home

I cannot describe my joy when dad came to see me at the orphanage!

After his condemnation, he barely did one full year, and then the amnesty came, after Stalin's death, and they liberated him. They liberated him from prison but did not allow him to go back to Bessarabia. He came to the orphanage to take me, to rent a room some place, and to find some work. However, the director did not agree to it:

"Where is your residence visa?"

"Nowhere!"

"Where do you work?"

"Nowhere!"

"How do you want to provide for her?... Go back, arrange things, and then come back and take her!"

When dad came, the children looked at him as to something they have never seen before. When I saw how much they desired to be with a civilian, with a father, I forgave them immediately for everything.

If they heard I was leaving, they began calling me by name, Rita. They were crying, especially the little ones, saying:

"Maybe someone will take us from here too!"

"Write to us, write to us!"

The children had no fault! Those times and that regime made them this way, wild. I realized that you could model anything for children, especially at the age of thirteen-fourteen years, if you have patience and if you care. But who cared there? The educator came in the morning and shouted: "Wake up!" In the evening, she came, counted us, and yelled again: "To bed!" And she left.

To stay and talk to us? No! Nobody cared about anything! But I did not leave from the orphanage so soon.

Dad went and found some work in Kurgan, at the factory. He worked there for about two years and a half, until 1956, when they let him go home. He did not visit me all this time, but he often wrote me that he would take me immediately when they would let him do it, and we would both leave. I was speaking in Russian with him, but he said that there was no problem, that we would go back and I would learn to speak Romanian again.

After a while, I received a letter from Niusia Scobioala that dad and Emil left for Bessarabia.

I panicked: they all went back and left me here?!... I began to terrorize them with letters. My letters were only cries, and I implored them: "Take me, take me from here!"...

The teacher tried to calm me:

"You can only go to your dad if he wants to take you. He will take you when he can... But do not lament, do not cry! You can study here seven years, and then you will go to a vocational school. You can become a teacher, because you are very fit for studying. If your dad does not take you now, it means that he has nowhere to take you..."

"How could he not have somewhere to take me? There are two houses in Mihăileni, *bunica*'s and ours, how could he not have somewhere to take me?!"

I could not understand it! I thought that if Stalin died, we could go back and live like before, in our house. How could she tell me that we did not have somewhere to live?...

A cousin or an old uncle answered my tearful letters from time to time. This is how I learned that *bunica* died and that they did not accept dad and Emil in the village. The relatives avoided them, because they were required to go to the Soviet to denounce anyone they met, what they said, and so on. They had so many troubles with the collectivization that no one cared anymore about dad or my brother. You came, they fed you, and good bye... What could they do? Dad went to the city, to Drochia, to find work, and Emil went back to the Soviet

Union, [81] because he could not stay anywhere without a residence visa. [82]

When I found out that everyone left and I was the only one who remained, I was overtaken by such grief that I cannot describe it. Before that time, when the children called me "bastard," "Moldavian bastard," I was very resentful. I was not abandoned; I had a father, a grandmother, a brother! After I found out that everyone left, that *bunica* died, and that there was no word from dad, I felt like I was abandoned. I was crying and wondering why I got to that point. How could I remain there?

The return to Bessarabia

I could not do anything else but write letters home. I terrorized all of them. When I saw that the closest relatives did not answer, I began writing to the second-degree relatives. I wrote to my uncle: "Take me from here, take me from here, because I can no longer bear it"…

Then, uncle[83] Gheorghe's wife, mom's brother, talked to dad in Drochia and told him:

"If you cannot take her, I'll take her because I need help. We are building a house, but I am a tailor and I have to give a rate to the kolkhoz; I have no one to help me. She will help me as long as we build the house, and then I will help her. I will teach her tailoring, and she will be well."

She convinced dad to write a request. Dad sent the request to the orphanage, to the director. He said there that he would take me, that he was working as a stoker at the sugar factory in Drochia, that he had a place to keep me and so on. They were all lies, because dad lived in a dorm, with eight other men in a

---

[81] The author means in the other parts of the Soviet Union. Moldova was already a part of the Soviet Union.

[82] People were not allowed to stay in any location without having a visa in their papers.

[83] The word used here is *moş*, a word used for older men in the same way one would say "Father Christmas." Another possible translation is "old man." In another example, Honoré de Balzac's *Le Père Goriot* has been translated as *Father Goriot* or *Old Man Goriot*. In our case, *Moş Gheorghe* also happens to be the narrator's uncle.

room, and he had no place to keep me. I had an indescribable joy when the director called me to tell me that dad wrote a request and called me home. I felt such great joy!

The second day, the director and his wife took me and the other two children from Moldova, together with our files, and we left by train to Bessarabia. When I heard about a train, I was scared. I thought that it would be just like how they had brought us seven years before, with those train cars for cattle. But what a difference! Now there were cabins, large windows, and they gave us tea. We received food for a week from the orphanage. It was not really enough, but we had the hope that we were going home and we would have plenty there.

When we arrived in Bălți, nobody was waiting for me. I went together with the other children to an apartment of an aunt of the director, in the city. The director was a kind man, and when he saw me so upset, seeing that no one had waited for me, he told me:

"Rita, don't be upset! If no one comes, we'll take you back. You will not die!"

But how could I go back to that hell, after I had dreamt for seven years to come back home? Of course I did not even consider it! But I did not say anything; I was not crying and I was quiet.

At one moment, someone knocked at the door. It was a young woman with a man. They looked over the other children and stopped at me:

"Are you Margareta?"

No one had called me Margareta for years, but Rita, and I had forgotten that name. I was silent for a while thinking, and I remembered as if in a fog that *bunica*, dad, and Emil called me Margareta. I did not know that woman who seemed to be a stranger, even if I had been very spoiled by her when I was a child, before deportation. She was a tailor and had sewed little dresses for me on feast days and had given me cords. It was my aunt, but I no longer knew it. They were foreigners for me! I could not understand what they were looking for.

When they saw that I did not react, she took dad's picture from her pocket:

"Do you know this man?"

I shook my head, because I did not really understand what she was saying. She used Romanian, and I was already Russian... Then, her younger brother, *badea*[84] Petre, started speaking with me in Russian, because he had been in the army with the Russians, and he made things clear:

"We came after you, because your dad cannot come to take you; he is busy."

The director told him:

"Someone needs to sign that I delivered her!"

Badea Petre signed, and the director said:

"It's done, I no longer have anything to do with her!"

But he sensed that if dad did not come, something was not in order and told me softly:

"If there is any problem, we can take you back!"

But I did not want to hear it; there was no way I would go back! I could not wait to meet dad.

The three of us took a car until the intersection Rășcani-Drochia, and we walked from there for around ten kilometers. I was looking all around, to see the places of my childhood. I did not recognize anything, neither the hills, nor the plains; I did not recognize anything. When we left, there used be orchards, fruits... it was beautiful everywhere; the earth was not naked; you could see green everywhere. Now, there were no huts on the hills, no wells, no furrows, no trees, nothing... The whole earth was out of order: there was corn everywhere, over thousands of acres, or sunflower, and the greenery was no longer there. I thought in my mind: but this is not Mihăileni; I knew how the road was supposed to be, in Rășcani! But I was ashamed to ask anything. My aunt and uncle were going before me and spoke in Romanian, and I, behind them, listened but could not understand anything, and I was very irritated by this.

We arrived at the outskirts of the village, on a hill, and I began looking for our house, because it was the tallest and could be seen from a distance.

---

[84] "Badea" is the name that younger children used to call their older brothers, friends, or relatives.

Badea Petre noticed it and told me:

"Margareta, don't look for anything! Your house no longer exists!"

"How come it no longer exists?"

"They brought it down and took all the materials to New Mihăileni, next to the road, and they made a school out of them."

"But where will I live?! At *bunica*'s?"

"At *bunica*'s there is no longer a house either!"

"How come? But who's is it?"

"It belongs to the kolkhoz, to the state. It is a policlinic now, and you are not allowed to live there!"

Then my morale collapsed so badly... I cannot even tell you. I came back, but where did I come back?!...

And I asked:

"But where is dad?"

"In Drochia."

"Where is Drochia?"

"One train station away..."

"Then, where am I going?!"

"You will live with your aunt and your uncle, as if you were their daughter, because they do not have children, and you will live with them!"

"But what about dad?!"

"He will come to visit and see you!"

All these things were such a blow for me, that I could not recover for a week or so. I could not understand how, if Stalin died and we could go back, they did not return all of it to us? Where could we live, in the air, where could we live?! Everyone has his own house. But us, where?!...

I asked my aunt to stop by *bunica*'s house. It was changed, with the walls modeled differently, and with a different entry. It was full of sick people, doctors, and nurses. Right next to it, there was a small house with two rooms, where we all crowded in the winter, at the stove. I wanted to go in, to see it one more time, because I remembered well how I used to stay and fall asleep on the oven on which *bunica* made pies and all kinds of goodies. When I tried to go in, the door was locked. My aunt told me that Russians lived there. I understood that it was not empty and that I could not go in, and I went to my aunt's house disgusted.

In place of a horse...

Aunt Maria was uncle Gheorghe's wife, mom's younger brother, and she had also suffered much because of the Russians. Uncle Gheorghe's eldest sister was married with a chief policeman who had run to Romania. Because of this, the communists terrorized their entire family. When they could not do what the communists wanted, they would be immediately threatened with deportation to Siberia.

In '44, my uncle left for the war and my aunt remained alone with her father in law. He was my *bunelul* on my mother's side; he feared the Russians as if they were fire, because they always threatened him:

"Aha, your daughter married a policeman... you'll see that you'll suffer on her account!"

The Bolsheviks persecuted you even if they had no reason, and if they had one it was even worse... *Bunelul* feared them; the moment they saw them at the gate, he took his hat from his head and bowed his head down before them. My poor aunt, being young, eighteen-nineteen years old, how could she defend herself? The Russians came in the house as if at a restaurant, made *bunelul* give them brandy, and then they told him:

"You, old man, get out!"

And they had fun with her. The chiefs here and those coming from Chişinău or Răşcani did what they wanted with her. If they knew that her man was at war, she was done for! After he came back, uncle Gheorghe scolded her much for this, because the whole village was talking. He reproached her, but she told him:

"What could I have done? Should I have let them kill me? Or take me to Siberia? What could I have done if there was no one to protect me?..."

After my uncle came home, they let her in peace, of course, and she repented. She went to the church, confessed, and asked the priest what she could do to wash her sins. My aunt could no longer have children because of these crazy Russians. My uncle could not stand the Russians especially because of this!

When I arrived at my aunt's house, I expected that *bunelul* and my uncle would rush to me and take me in their arms... Nothing! Uncle Gheorghe was sitting there, on the trunk of a tree, and was biting the scythe. My aunt led me to him:

"He is uncle Gheorghe!"

I got close to him, he looked at me, seemed to smile timidly, and mumbled something there that I did not understand, and that was it!

My aunt changed her clothes and began arranging the table, because I had not eaten for a whole day and I was starving. She fed me well, gave me an old dress of hers, and put me to work from the first day: to crush the clay, to bring in water, firewood, everything.

In fact, I replaced their horse. They had had a horse, cows, and sheep, but the state had taken everything from them. Now, I took the horse's place: run here, run there, run here, run there. I had to bring water from the valley, five hundred meters away. I was just a thin, small child; the buckets weighted twenty kilograms, and I had to bring them on the hill... If some water fell from them, I was yelled at for bringing them this way, and I really worked hard to bring them up the hill filled.

There were other hardships I was not used to, because we were not asked to do anything at the orphanage. They only made us hoe the potatoes and the carrots in the summer, but nothing else. We were not used to working in a household. Also, I was weak and powerless, being only thirteen and a half.

The months passed, and dad did not come, so I felt abandoned. When people are content, they do everything with love and willingly, but when I saw that dad was no longer coming and that I could not find out anything about him, I was very disappointed and did everything without joy. I was like the soldier, so to say: go, come, do this, bring that, clean here, boil this, and so on!

My aunt behaved coldly with me. I saw her playing with the small children, how she lured them and told them stories, but she did not do this with me. She never told me:

"Come, tell us, how did you live? How did you suffer? Was it good, bad?..."

She never caressed my head to tell me:

"Poor child, how did you live there, as an orphan!"

I expected to find the world from before the deportation, when all my relatives carried me on their arms as if I were a doll, giving me gifts... That's what I remembered, that Masha did things with me and gave me things, that aunt Mǎriuța kissed me, held me strongly in her arms, and stole me away to her place, and that aunt Nasta called me to her place and gave me gifts... Now, it was all over; it seemed as if they were not the same people! I did not expect such a sudden change. I only later understood that poor aunt Maria did not have time. There were things to do, crops to sow, to give the rate to the kolkhoz; they needed money for the house to build it. This is why she insisted to take me, because she needed help. My uncle obeyed, because my aunt was the man of the house. She moved all over like a squirrel; she worked, she did the shopping, and she went out to get things. Uncle Gheorghe went only once after some boards in Ukraine, and then he told her that he would never go again: you want a new house, you go! And that's what they did.

Finally, dad showed up one day. There could have been no greater happiness! I jumped on him from the gate, held him, and didn't allow him to move, this is how excited I was. I thought: this is it: he came to take me!

They received him well; they talked together for a long time. I was actually amazed that they spoke so kindly and beautifully with dad, but they still only scolded me: "this is not done, you didn't bring that yet, you didn't arrive on time"... But they were so nice and delicate with dad... I did not understand why!

That evening, I went with dad to visit his sisters. Nasta, the eldest, received us well, warmly, with an open heart. But aunt Masha, the youngest sister, received us very coldly. She had two boys, just a bit older than me, and she did not allow them to stay with us at the table. Dad asked her to let them talk to me, but she sent them away. I was very surprised. After many years,

I found out that she had signed up with the Securitate[85] and that she would have denounced us, dad and me, and that she would have told them everything that we did and said. She did not want to have the children present, so that they would not contradict each other if the kids were asked questions as well. May God forgive her! I do not condemn her, if they forced her... Her husband had been tried and murdered with *bunelul*, her mother-in-law was deported, and her mother lived with the fear that she would also be sent to Siberia, with the children. But I did not know anything about this back then, and I told dad:

"Aunt Masha seems to be upset!"

Dad scolded me:

"Regardless of how she is, you must respect her! When I came from Siberia, I had no place to go, and she took me in and fed me until I got a place in Drochia. You must respect her!"

This is what I did. Even after I left the village, I always stopped by her place and by Nasta's with a gift, something, to give them some joy.

They never told us what they suffered, but I found out from others that they were living as if they always had a gun pointed at their heads. There were even ten Russians per day coming over for dinner, to have steak and wine. It did not matter whether they had it or not; they had to put it on the table; if not, it was Siberia for them. "Siberia," the Russians would say, "we will take you to Siberia, just like your mom!" And they did what they were asked, out of fear.

After we left from dad's sisters, dad and I went to our house, to the place where our house once was. Now, it was the place of another man, and he had built there another house, not as beautiful and large as ours. We both stood at the fence and

---

[85] The Securitate recruited many people as informants. One of the consequences of this practice was the disappearance of trust among people. One could no longer know whether one's interlocutors were or not informants for the secret police - even one's closest friends or family members could be blackmailed or menaced with consequences if they did not become collaborators. It is one of the methods by which a totalitarian regime breaks apart the connection between people.

began crying: look, our house was there, there were flowers in that corner, the vineyard was there, the yard, the dog...

I began shouting over the fence:

"Tărcuț, Tărcuț, come over here!"

"Which Tărcuț, don't you see it's another dog?"

"I know, I'm just saying..."

We both cried and remembered mom. He told me how he built the house with her. In those times, it was very difficult and expensive to get materials; you had to work a lot to build a house. But they raised it up together, and it was beautiful and large, there was none like it in the whole village.

Then we went to the cemetery, to the tomb of *mama* and *bunica*, and we cried there as well.

Dad told them:

"Good day, my dears, forgive me for not having come for such a long time! You rest here and you are well, but we remain on this earth only for torment..."

From the cemetery, we went back to my aunt and we sat at the table. They sent me to bed, and they talked until late in the night. I could not fall asleep, out of happiness; I was anxious to see morning, to go with dad to Drochia. At dawn, I saw him getting dressed to leave.

"Where are you going? Wait for me to get dressed too!"

"But I'm leaving alone; you will stay."

Another tragedy in my soul.

"Why should I remain? I want to be with you; you are my dad..."

"I cannot take you because I live at the men's dorm, and I receive almost nothing as salary. Look, your aunt promised that after you help them to finish the house, they will also help you and give you a start in life, and all will be well."

I did not think about the future back then; I only wanted to be with him. I had had so many dreams, that we would be together, all three of us, with Emil and him, since *bunica* was no longer with us. I was blaming *bunica* as well; why did she die and why did she not wait for me, since she so wanted me to return home? This is what the women in the village told me, that with her last words, when she gave up her soul, she said:

"I will die, but bring Margareta back, don't leave her there among foreigners!"

The neighbor who last spoke with her told me the same thing:

"She only cared about you: bring Margareta back, bring her back from there, do not leave her in that wilderness!"

Why didn't she wait for me then?

I threw myself to dad's knees, grabbed his legs, and told him:

"Do not leave me here, my dear daddy! Take me with you; I will work, I will do everything that I must, I will make food, I will wash, I will iron, I will clean the house... I learned everything here, with my uncle."

"Which house? How could I take you if I do not have where?..."

He was full of sorrow as well, but he did not cry. But I cried so much, and I implored him and promised that I would find work some place and bring in money, just hoping that he would take me from there. He did not reject me, but remained tough.

When she saw that I cried loudly and that it was resounding in the neighborhood, my aunt could no longer stand it and told me:

"Get up from your knees and don't shame us; the whole village hears you and will say that we cut you here! You are grown up, you received love letters from the orphanage, and they ask you for marriage... Aren't you ashamed?"

Then, I seemed to recover, I shook it off, and told dad:

"So you leave me again!"

"I have no choice!"

And he left.

I ran to the ravine, under a tree, and I remained there a long time, crying until I got completely tired. When I went back in the evening, I said to myself: I will obey, because I am abandoned; whatever they say, I will do. This is how I began doing everything, like a robot. I was just upset because I could not do what was dear to me, what I liked, the things I got used to doing at the orphanage: to embroider, to knit, to create something, to read a book, to write… I had no paper, no pencil or pen, and there was no book in that house; I was ashamed to ask for anything.

I went like this for some months, until the day when my uncle slapped me. I thought that I would no longer be beaten in my country, as I was in that wild orphanage, but that's not what happened…

I was fourteen years old, and I had my first period; I got scared, because I did not know what it was. I was weak, and I could not sleep during the night because of pain. During the day, after I brought the water, I found a small break when they did not check what I was doing. I went to the house that was yet unfinished, where there were some chairs and an unfinished table for the carpenters. I sat on a chair in the fetus position, and I said: perhaps it will go away if I stay a bit! I fell asleep. I did not sleep much, perhaps just a few minutes, when I heard aunt Maria shouting:

"Gheorghe, come and see how your niece works!"

My uncle got scared and ran fast, not knowing what happened. She told him:

"Punish her; I do not feed her for nothing!"

Then he came to me and slapped me so hard that I saw stars! I did not say anything; I did not even cry. I thought: "they signed for me and I belong to them; they will do whatever they want with me." And I worked hard to make things well again.

But there is no good without bad and no bad without good. After a few months, I found in some carton boxes a piece of white material, made out of silk; I immediately saw how one could make a nice head kerchief, embroidered all around, crocheted… Since the seamstress had string everywhere, I picked up a thread and began to crochet. When my aunt called for me, I immediately hid my work under that box and quickly ran to her to ask her what she wanted me to do. I did my chore, and when I saw that there was a small break, I went back to crocheting.

Perhaps I did this many times, because aunt Maria guessed something, watched me, and when she saw that I was crocheting, she began shouting again:

"Gheorghe, come and see! We don't know where to begin with all the work that needs to be done, and look what she does!"

I said to myself: "he will not beat me now, because I did not fall asleep; I was working on something; I don't think he would beat me for something like this!"

My uncle came and stopped next to me. He did not hit me like last time, but he caught me by my neck and began knocking my head against that unfinished table. He scratched me all over, because he hit me on the table several times, until he saw that there was blood not only from my nose, but also from my lips, sprinkling the walls and his shirt. Then aunt Maria said:

"Gheorghe, enough! I think she learned her lesson!"

He let me go and left without saying one word. If he said at least one word, something... But no, he did everything she asked him to do, because he sensed that she was the mistress of the house. His heart was also rough; I did not see any kindness in him.

In any case, they bloodied me bad and they left. I used my hand to stop the blood, and I got all dirty on my hands and my dress. In a few minutes, I heard some noise, and I thought: they will come again, and they will beat me again! I was scared, and I ran outside. At the gate, I saw the bowl with water for the dog. I washed my face and hands with that water and I went on the road. I walked to the place where our land used to be. I stopped there, and I thought to myself:

"What should I do next? Where should I go?"

At that moment, I remembered I still had a father. Will he not wail for me, will he not protect me?!...

I decided to go toward Drochia.

"Servant" in Drochia

I stopped someone who was passing by on a cart and asked him to show me the direction toward Drochia. I began walking fast there, but the night came, regardless of how fast I went. I was happy because there was no forest and there were no wolves, as in Siberia. Finally, I saw the lights from the sugar factory at the horizon. When I arrived there, I saw some barracks, like those for the prisoners in the concentration camps, where the workers lived. I knocked at a door where there was some light, and a man came out:

"What do you need? Why do you walk around in the night?"

"I came to ask about dad, Spânu Nicolae!"

"He is not in this barrack. Go to another one, perhaps there!"

I went to another barrack, but there were no lights. However, I knocked at the door. An angry man came out, and he insulted me because I was going around in the night to wake up people.

I told him:

"I need dad, Spânu Nicolae!"

"Yes, he's here!"

He took me to his bed, woke him up, and told him:

"You have guests!"

When he saw me dirty with blood on my face and on the dress, he began crying and said:

"I knew you would not make it!"

I thought: "if you knew, why did you leave me?" But I didn't tell him. He gave me a piece of black bread and a glass of water, and we both slept on that narrow bed, my head at his feet and my feet at his head. We began looking for a landlord early the next morning. We walked all over Drochia, and we barely found a small room with an oven and a kitchenette. There was nothing there: no dishes, no sheets, no covers, nothing. We started living there, but I felt terrible. I was older, going on fifteen years old, and I knew I was a burden for dad. He often sighed, so I told him:

"I'll find some work!"

But he told me:

"It would be better if you went to school, because you received a nice evaluation and good grades from the orphanage!"

"But how can we live if you are the only one who works?"

He received thirty rubles as a stocker. What could you do with thirty rubles? It was just enough to not die, to eat something just to survive!

If he saw this, he did not insist. Of course he regretted that I could not study, because any parent wants what is good for his child, but if you have no resources, what can you do? He began looking for work for me, but it was hard to find any. The adults themselves could not find work, let alone the children! However, I do not know how, he talked to a chief and they took me during autumn to prepare pickled food for the winter for cafeterias. I cut cabbage and carrots, mixed them with salt, stuffed them in barrels, and put them in the cellar. This last part was the most difficult; it was the job for a man, but there were only young girls and I, a child. At times, we dropped the barrel and it flumped there, and we washed the cabbage again, and they insulted us and told us that we would not be paid. They gave us ten rubles per month, a small amount, but it was some help for dad and I. I worked like this until the season ended and there were no more vegetables.

When they sent me home, I had to go somewhere else!

Dad searched until he found another place. He came home happy and told me:

"Tomorrow you'll go to work, but please don't say that I am your dad; tell them I am one of your uncles."

He was ashamed to make his own child do such work.

I went to my new job in the morning, someplace at the periphery of Drochia. There was only a small house, where the boss lived, and I had to work outside, to process the dogs. They brought dead dogs in carriages, shot, and we had to take their skin, meat, and bones. We were four: three adult men and I, a child, each one with his own mission. My task was to salt the skins. Because of this, my hands remained only skin and bones, because the salt ate everything... The others, when they saw my hands, were amazed: "What happened to your hands?" Well, nothing... This is why they took me there, because no one wanted to do such a thing. There was a stench of carcasses, flies everywhere, worms... Lord, what a disaster!

I worked there for a long time: I salted the skins, formed them, put them in a trolley, and took them to a certain place. Besides this, I did whatever they asked me, anything that was needed. They gave me twenty-five rubles per month, so five rubles less than dad, and I was very proud because this is how much we had to pay monthly for the hole in which we lived. I was proud that I contributed to the household, so that dad would not be upset.

But one day the controlling officer came and said:

"Let's see the residence visa for this child! Where is her passport?"

This and that, look, I will soon bring it…

But where to bring it from, if I was not even fifteen years old!

Dad came home, and I do not know what he said, what lie he told, but they allowed me to stay there one more year. Then, they kicked me out, because they were not allowed to accept people from other villages; you had to have a residence visa for Drochia in your passport, and children were not allowed to work.

In the meantime, the mistress of the house where we lived lost twenty-five rubles from her purse; she accused us and claimed that we should give her the money. She sued us, and we were called to the court. The investigator asked us many questions, and then he told dad:

"Bring your daughter's file from the orphanage, to see her evaluation; we know how the people who come from there are!"

Dad brought my file, and when the investigator read it, he was shocked. He left us in peace and began to investigate the masters, because they had a fourteen year old boy and an older daughter. After some time, they called us again to trial, and it was proven that the mistress' boy had stolen the money. The woman asked for forgiveness, but dad did not want to remain there, so we looked for another landlord.

As we were asking all over the place, dad found out that someone was looking for a nanny for their children. It was a family with a three year old little girl, and the wife was pregnant again. The husband was an engineer, and he was often away for delegations. He wanted me to take care of the little girl, to help in the household, wash, make the fire, bring in coal, firewood, in short, everything that was needed. As payment, we could live for free in one of their rooms. The room was large, spacious, with two beds, a table, and a kitchenette. We felt like we were in heaven, and everything was good.

But dad was not content that I did not have a trade. Thus, in secret, he borrowed some money and got two large bags of wool. He took these two bags and went to a special store, added some money, and got a sewing machine in exchange. He came home with it and told me:

"A trade, my dear girl, is a golden bracelet. If you know to do something, you do not fail. So take this, sew,[86] and work... I think your aunt taught you how to do it!"

"No, I never worked on the sewing machine!"

"What? You stayed there for almost one year and you did not sew anything?"

"Nothing, ever!"

"But she promised..."

"I do not know what she promised, but I did not have time to learn anything!"

Thus, I had to learn by myself. Dad went to work, and I would stay at home all day long. I worked as needed for the landlord, did everything fast, clean, beautiful, then I went for a walk with the girl, and when I put her to sleep in the afternoon, I went quickly to the sewing machine, to learn to sew! The mistress gave me some patches, because I did not have any material to work with. The only things I had were the dress from the orphanage, which was a school uniform, and another summer dress. I began learning to sew on those patches.

One day, dad brought me some fabric and said:

"Come, my dear, sew me a shirt, for I have nothing to wear!"

I was surprised: how should I sew if I did not know how? I learned to use the machine, but for a shirt you needed to cut and sew, how could I do this? But dad urged me:

"Come, think, think, think..."

My whole life he taught me to think: think, think, use your mind, and you will find the solution!

---

[86] "A stroci" in the original—a regionalism.

He was going to work, and I remained home to learn, because I was ashamed. I had a sewing machine, but I did not know how to sew?... What could I have done? I took his old shirt and measured it. Fearing that I would make it too small, I put in two-three centimeters more, just in case. I cut with great fear, I tacked it, and then I began to sew it. In a week or so, I finally finished it. When dad put it on, something tremendous happened: it fit him as if it were made for one of the scarecrows that people put on the field... Instead of insulting me, he began laughing. I was glad and I almost could not believe it; if it were uncle Gheorghe, he would have immediately hit me! I began laughing too! It was the first and the last time I saw dad laughing with so much vigor and tears.

Then, slowly, slowly, I undid the shirt, I made it smaller, and I made it as it should have been. After a few months, dad came again with some other fabric:

"Come, sew a dress for yourself; you have nothing to wear!"

I looked at the one from the orphanage, so I would do it the same way, but I did not measured it well, so it was too short, I could not wear it. He then bought me some other fabric, still thin, and I sewed a dress not for a ten, but I could say for a seven.[87] I even took a picture with it, and I wore it for a long time, until it broke. This was my first experience with sewing.

Back to the village

After some time, my aunt came to Drochia.

After my departure, the whole village heard that they beat me. The people working to build the house, that came to do the windows, saw blood on the walls, so they asked her:

"Did you slaughter the chicken here or what?"

People found out they beat me badly, and then all the relatives shamed her, both from my mother and my father's sides:

"How could you do this? You brought the girl from the

---

[87] The notation system in schools was from 1 to 10, 10 being the maximum. A 7 is the equivalent to a C in American schools.

orphanage, and look what you did to her! You promised you would take care of her, and look what you did…"

So, to silence people, she came to us and asked dad:

"Please, brother-in-law, send her back; the house is almost done, and she will no longer have that much work…"

But dad answered:

"Look, I bought her a sewing machine, and she does not know how to use it, let alone to make something with it! You said you would make her a seamstress, you promised…"

"But I did not have time; I had the house. I will teach her over the winter, because she learns fast and I saw that she knows to do many things… I will teach her in the winter!"

It was not meant to be! I stayed there the whole winter and summer, and she did not have time to teach me sewing. Instead, she asked me to do things that I liked doing. I had to embroider for the new house, and she made me embroider *doroste*, some kind of narrow carpets, with beautiful models on them, that were to be hanged on the walls with thumbtacks. I sewed dozens of these things, until she said it was enough. During winter, she also made me teasel the wool, tack the clothes, but she never had time to teach me to sew at the machine. However, I still manage to learn something, because I would pass by the sewing machine when she worked there. But she would yell at me:

"Hurry, go and cook something; Gheorghe comes soon! Go weeding, go digging!"

I did so much: cleaning the vineyard, gathering fruit, seeding beets, setting the vine on strings, for many kilometers. Still, everything did me good. The hardest thing was when it froze and I had to harvest the beets. My hands were frozen and when the roots were large, I could not uproot them fully and they broke. This was the hardest thing; as for the other things, I did all of them.

Getting married

I was already grown, I was rounder, and had become a young lady. In those times, the lads asked the girls to go to balls. They went there, danced, and talked. When I began to go to balls, I did not even know how to dance. A younger uncle of mine took me there all the time, because my aunt told him to do so:

"Take her and teach her to dance; she's wild!"

But I went to no end; I did not want to dance with anyone because I was shy. When we came back, my uncle said:

"I took her, but she did not want to dance!"

My aunt lectured me, that she had enough of my Siberia, that I am wild... The truth is that I was withdrawn, closed, and I was at ease only with dad. With him I was happy and open; the two of us understood one another; he never yelled at me or anything like that.

Still, to take me out of my wilderness, my aunt tried to take me to church, but I told her:

"I do not go to church because I do not believe in God; there is no God!"

I repeated to her everything that the Russians told me at the orphanage, all the nonsense from Siberia, and I argued so well for them that it seemed that she began doubting too. But then she was saying:

"No, you will go! Even if you do not believe, you will go with me!"

And this is how she took me to church, by force, to learn chanting with her in the choir. We went once, we went twice, and slowly I stopped telling her that there was no God, even if I did not believe absolutely at all. I went like a sheep does: wherever they take you, that's where you go. But I did not believe.

If I began going to church, to dance, the boys saw me and started asking: Who is she, whose is she? My aunt and uncle had built a new house, and everyone thought that if I marry, they would give me the house and I would have a good dowry. The lads began coming to the window, to ask me to dance, for Easter, for the feasts at church, for all the feasts...

This is how I got married when I was sixteen, and my life as a child ended. They chose the groom as well. I did not want to marry him, but they told me:

"You are young, you do not know much; we know what

you need!"

If I was an orphan, without anything, I had to take the one they told me, because he had a house, he had a job, and he would not ask for anything from them.

I got married and left to my husband's house. We demolished his old house and we built a new one, so I went back to construction and work.

In 1960 I gave birth to our first child, Victor, and after moving into the new house, I said: let's learn to sew, since I have a sewing machine! I began sewing by myself, for me, for my husband, until I learned. I began receiving orders afterwards, because the women in the village said:

"Well, if you stayed at Maria's, she taught you, because she is a good seamstress!"

But they did not know that I learned by myself.

Then, in 1964, I moved with my family to Chişinău. In 1973 my second child was born, Romeo, and life continued gently on its course.

The Return to Christ

During this entire period, my connection with God was broken. From time to time, when I passed by a church, something seemed to tingle me, as if something did not allow me to pass with indifference. I surprised myself that I mentioned God when I was upset with someone, but only then:

"Be careful; God sees all!"

I would say this to whomever I was upset with, but I did not believe it; I did not believe in anything. The return to the Church, to Christ, was due to my youngest child, Romeo.

He went to the school of choreography in Kiev, in Ukraine, and, after he finished it, I wanted to bring him to work here, in Chişinău, but they did not accept him because I did not have any connections. They said that if he studied in Kiev, he would become Russianized and his dances would not be Moldavian.[88] My boy told them:

---

[88] This took place after 1990, when Moldova became an independent state, no longer under the Soviet Union.

"It is an excellent school in Kiev; I learned the dances of all peoples: Italians, Poles, French...."

"You only need to know our dances!"

And they did not accept him.

We went to the minister of culture, for an audience, and, being a great patriot, he told us:

"Why do you need him to go here? It's better to go to the mother country, Romania!"

He gave us a paper for the Minister of Culture in Bucharest, and we went to Romania. They received us beautifully, just like you would receive real brothers, and they called a lady to see what the boy knows. She examined him and said:

"Bravo! Where did you learn to dance?"

"In Kiev!"

"Well, they have an excellent school there! Choose where you want to work, because they need people everywhere."

"Where?"

"Wherever you want: Cluj, Timişoara, Suceava, Bucharest..."

We were lost! What should we choose? The route Suceava-Bălţi had just opened, and we said: let's go to Suceava, because it is easier for us! We chose the Folk Ensemble "Ciprian Porumbescu" in Suceava.

Even when he was a student in high school, in Kiev, Romeo began to go array. He was always telling me of religion. When he came home, I waited to find out what concerts he had, how he passed the exams, what grades he had, but he was speaking always of religion, as if he studied at the Seminary or at a Theology school.

This is how this change took place with him: in the dorm where he lived with the others, the boys quarreled and fought all the time. They were not wild children, like at the orphanage, but they were all lads from good, well-to-do families. He then began to read, to search for an answer to this turmoil in books. Why do people quarrel among themselves? Why do they find fault in others? Why do they fight? The teachers directed him toward psychology, psychology took him to philosophy, and philosophy to theology.

When he found theology, he studied all the religions, and he chose Krishna from all of them. He said that he understood it better, that it was logical. When he was coming home from high school, he put his plate on the table and started to chant. He was singing something, and then he ate. When it was only us, the family, I accepted it, because I am lenient by nature. One day, though, we went to have dinner with his godmother, and he put his plate before him, as always, and started chanting before everyone. My patience ended there, and I asked him nicely to stop. He listened to me and stopped. When we came home, I told him:

"Let's talk!"

I told him calmly, beautifully, and delicately:

"Look, we baptized you in the church, at Ciuflea. Your godparents, my in-laws, and I were present; you are baptized there, so you are Orthodox."

"Yes."

"Have you studied Orthodoxy?"

"I've read it!"

"Be good, then, and don't betray us; this is all I am asking, don't betray us! I pray you not to do it, using my right as a mom! I am not asking anything else: do not betray our entire people! Do you want to be Christian? Go ahead and have faith, nobody stops you, but be the way your great-grandfathers and your fathers were; be this way!"

He listened to me, and from that day forward, he took to reading the Bible, and he began studying it more closely, with more interest. He then left back to Kiev and did not say anything for a while. From time to time, he reproached us that we were not believers. I was already pleased; I had nothing against him being a Christian; I was rather happy that he would not do bad things, that he would be a correct child.

After he was hired as dancer in Suceava, he spent all his free time in the library. Once, when I visited him, the librarian told me:

"Madame, your son should not be an artist, but a scholar! Look, he read half of this library!"

"But how, because he does not know Romanian yet?"

"I don't know, but look here how I registered them: he reads all of them. He must study at the university; his place is not here!"

If she told me such a thing, I began to ask him if he did not want to go to the university. First, he hesitated, because he had a good job there, lived on his own, and he was no longer in our care. After all, he decided to try Theology, in Iaşi. I did not agree with Theology, for what use can you have with it, but I could not turn against him. They examined him in Chişinău, in Russian, he took the exams, and he was admitted as a student in Iaşi, in 1993. When my husband found out that he was accepted at the Department of Theology, he made a terrible scandal:

"I no longer want to know you! You won't receive one penny from us, nothing! You will live the way you want; let's see how you'll manage as a student at the university..."

But the boy did not give up:

"Don't you worry, I have made some money, and when there is no more, I will see, I will manage; I won't ask anything from you, ever. I have not asked anything so far either: if you give me some, fine, if not, that is fine as well..."

And he left. When he came home during breaks, he spoke to me only about religion, Orthodoxy, of course. He was going to monasteries, and he told me how the monks pray there. He bought me a small icon with the image of the Savior, photographed from the Torino shroud. But I was not moved at all; it did not make an impression on me. I was patient and understanding, so I listened to him. I did not want to upset him, because he was like a friend: he told me everything that happened to him, and we would talk much together.

Well, one day passed after another, and then he began to reproach me - nicely, diplomatically - and to argue that he was not allowed to study Theology if his parents were pagans, that they would kick him out. This is how he made me start thinking.

Then, one day, he told me:

"Have I ever asked you for anything in life?"

"No, nothing!"

It was true. As a child, he did not ask for anything. If he had torn clothes, he would go out like that; we patched them and he was fine. Other children were ashamed, but not him; he did not rebel; he believed us when we said that we could not afford it, that we did not have things.

"Well," he said, "I will ask something of you now!"

"What?"

"But promise that you will do it…"

"If I can!"

"You can, because it does not cost money… Look, I want you to read the Bible! I gave it to you when I was in Kiev, at the school. Have you ever opened it?"

"No."

"But I gave it to you so that you would read it!"

"Fine! I read so many books, I will read this one as well!"

I very much enjoyed reading; this was my spiritual nourishment. When I came back from Siberia, I did not have any books, but after I got married, I only knew this, the road to the village library. This was my passion, so to say.

My son went back to Iaşi, and I tried to read the Bible, the Old Testament. From the first page, it did not seem attractive at all. I went from Job to David, from David to Isaiah, from this to that. I was not interested. After a while, I gave up. When the boy came home, on vacation, he asked me:

"Have you read the Bible?"

"No!"

"Why?"

"I don't know, I don't understand it; my eyes just close when I read it!"

"Then begin with the New Testament!"

I began with the New Testament, but it did not attract me from the first page.

He had lost his patience, and he no longer talked to me calmly and gently, but roughly and irritated:

"You will read it, you will believe, you must know the truth!"

I got angry as well:

"How dare you talk to your mom like this? What is this

tone? I won't allow this any longer!"

"The parents must be Christian!"

"There you go, the egg teaches the chicken! You chose Christianity, very well, be a Christian! But leave me alone, let me be how I want to be!"

"I will not leave you alone!"

Then I really got angry, I threw myself on the carpet, facing up, and I said:

"Lord, if you exist, give me a sign, so that I will no longer quarrel that much with my son, whom I see so rarely!"

And I was crying with rivers of tears to impress him so that he would leave me alone and no longer nag me. I did not pray honestly, for I knew very well, not a hundred percent, but two hundred percent, that there would be no sign, because God did not exist and all things were just stories.

He said to me:

"Come, stand up, it's enough! I'll give you peace now, but know that I won't leave you! Please read the Bible! I do not want anything; I did not ask for anything in life; this is the only thing that I am asking from you, "read the Bible," and you cannot do it?!..."

And he left very upset. I remained home very grieved. My husband was in Siberia, for work. I took the Bible in the evening, the New Testament, and I thought: how is it possible that a whole world believes and I do not? Do I think I am smarter?! I do not know how this thought came to me, but I was amazed that an entire world believes, the whole earth has some faith, one in Allah, another one in God, another one in Krishna, but only me in nothing. I said to myself: this means I became a Russian from Siberia, an atheist, as they taught me there. But I am not a Russian, I am a Moldavian, and I must not be different from my nation. A child understood that he must be Christian, he must believe in something, but I did not. Well, I will take the Bible, I will read, I will understand, and I think I will be corrected!

I began to read the New Testament, and after half a page my eyes were closed again. I looked at the watch; it was fifteen minutes to midnight. I put the Bible next to me; I turned off the light, laid on the bed, and went to sleep. I felt immediately a weight coming on me. I was surprised: from where could it come? If anything fell on me, I should have felt something hard, but there was something soft and very heavy that pressed down on me. It caught my hands under me, and I could not move. It pressed me more and more, until I felt like all my bones were breaking. My head was the only free thing, but I could hear how all my joints were cracking. When I felt that my entrails were coming out of me, I thought: this is the end! But I was really struggling to understand who this was, what this thing was. I did not regret that I was dying, but I wanted to know who was doing it to me.

A terrible fear came over me, and I thought that only Satan could work in this way. I do not know how this thought came to me, since I did not believe either in God or Satan. So I said: aha, if it is Satan, he is afraid of the cross; let's make a cross! But how could I make a cross when my hands were caught under me? Let's say an "Our Father" in my mind! But I have not said it in forty-two years, and I no longer knew it. But at that moment it came immediately to my mind, as if I had had repeated it the whole time. When I saw that the weight did not diminish, I thought: Romeo said that you should say it three times. When I said the prayer the third time, I felt that the weight rose a bit and my blood rushed back to me.

I continued to say "Our Father" in my mind, and I thought that I must come down from the bed, to reach the switch to turn on the light, because the devil is afraid of the light and would disappear. Now that I felt that the air came back to my lungs, I used all my force and, crawling like a snake from under that weight, I let myself fall down from the bed. Next to the bed, on the wooden floor, I saw a red fire. I was amazed: why doesn't the house burn if there is a flame? And I thought, even if I had not heard this anywhere, that there is fire in hell, where Satan is.

I crawled like this, with that weight on me, up to the switch. When I turned on the light, the flame and the weight disappeared. I was very happy, and I did not know what to do, when I saw a big, red cat, with glassy eyes, coming from under the bed. It looked straight at me and came slowly toward me. I thought that Satan could transform himself into animals, even if no one had told me that either. I came out of the room and slammed the door behind me, so that the tomcat would not follow me.

When I arrived in the hallway, another amazing thing happened! To my left, there were the stairs. Why didn't I run that way, to escape? I went the other way, toward the kitchen, having in mind to jump from the window, from the fourth floor, so that the devil would not come after me to press me with the weight. I thought: "what do I need? Isn't it better to jump and die immediately, so that he would no longer torment me?"

With this thought, I opened the door from the kitchen. When I tried to go in, a tall man, dressed as a monk, with black clothes, pressed his back on the door and I could not pass. I was ashamed to touch him. I thought: "this is a monk; how can I put my hand on him... I will go slowly through here, on the left, for it seems larger!" But there was no way to pass. As I was trying to pass, the monk turned his face toward me all of a sudden and looked at me. When I saw Him, I recognized Him. He was the Savior, looking exactly as on the shroud. My son had brought me many icons, and all were painted differently, but I saw Him with that face! I fell to my knees and began crying and saying:

"Lord Jesus Christ, I recognized You, yes, I recognized You! I am guilty because I have not believed, I am very guilty... You know that I asked for a sign and You gave me the sign. I will believe from now on, and I will tell others too..."

I did not know what else to tell Him and what else to do. He seemed to know that I was confused, turned toward me, and gave me His hand. It was yellow, with long and thin fingers, only bones and skin. I felt flustered seeing such a hand. I kissed His hand, and He withdrew it and said, "Amen." He turned again with His back toward me, and at that moment I found myself awake on the bed. I was alone in the room, with no one around me. The Bible was there, open, and the clock showed midnight. I thought: I went through so many things in fifteen minutes! This is how the Lord Himself convinced me and brought me back to Him, me, the one completely lost.

"May it be as it once was"...

After this, I totally changed, and I came close to God, to the Church. My husband, who does not come from a faithful background, began to shout at me when he saw that I would bring home three-four icons here, three-four icons there:

"What is this, church? What does this mean? I no longer want to see them around!"

But I also told him:

"No, let them be, endure them, for this is not Stalin's or Lenin's portrait, but the image of Christ God, of the Mother of God, of the saints..."

He began to get used to it, but not fully. But I believe that God would bring him also to Him before the end, just as He brought me.

Long after that miracle, I remembered that I promised, "I will believe from now on, and I will tell others too!" Of course, I told some people around me, one or the other, but my conscience seemed to rebuke me that it was not enough. This is how I got the idea to write. I first sent a fragment to *Literatură și Artă*[89] in Chișinău. After some time, at a commemoration of the deported people, I met the editor in chief from the magazine. I asked him:

"I sent you an article... Do you know, was it good or not?"

"Wasn't it called 'The Apple'?"

"Yes, 'The Apple'!"

"I have it here, with me! I brought it to read it to all the people deported."

And he asked me:

"Do you have other stories like this?"

"I was deported; of course I do!"

"You write them extraordinarily! If you have many, make me a book!"

I finished the manuscript in three months. I wanted to name it *Amintiri din copilărie,*[90] but I thought that people would

---

[89] *Literature and Art*, a literary magazine in Chișinău.
[90] *Memories from Childhood*. In Romania, there is a very famous book with this name written by one of the most renowned authors for children, Ion

confuse it with Creangă! So I thought: since it had to do with the wolves, and because I was so afraid of them and it marked me for life, I would call it *The Wolves*! This is how the book came out.

I wrote it so that people would know what communism was, what it brought, especially to us, Bessarabians. Even today there are people who say that it brought much good, and for this good there had to be sacrifices... But what is the good done by communism, socialism? What did it bring? And where is it now, if it was built on sacrifices? Let's say that we were sacrificed and sixty other million together with us, because this is what the statistics say, that the Soviet Union sacrificed sixty million lives. What did they do with it? What did they accomplish? Can you build anything on terror? Can you build on bones and blood?!...

This is how Satan entered Lenin, and he began to ruin all harmony. Before, man was free: if you wanted to work, to have things, then you worked and had what you needed; if you did not want to have much, you were in the middle; if you wanted nothing at all, the others helped you, gave you alms. You did not have authority and honor in the village, but you did not die of hunger. You were free and did things according to your conscience. But the Bolsheviks brought terror, murder, and robbery, and this is how freedom died.

How many lives did the "humanitarian" Bolshevism destroy! The Russians themselves recognize this now when they write about what they did, what they lived, and what they witnessed. They were shocked as well. You, an innocent man, whether old or a child, had to suffer like this, for twenty years in Siberia? For what? If you know why you suffer, you don't get upset; if I murdered someone intentionally, then they must punish me! But if you did not do anything, why punish you? So many young people taken to mines in Siberia! They never returned from there! For what ideal?...

Creangă. Creangă lived in the 19th century, between 1837 and 1889, and he was a very good friend of the Romanian national poet, Mihai Eminescu.

A political candidate said recently at "Vocea Basarabiei"[91] that we should not condemn communism and that those deported were taken there justly, because they deserved it!... What did my *bunica*, Sofia, deserve? *Bunelul* at least did something: he denounced that Gipsy man who burned the icons and who robbed the Romanians... But what did *bunica* do? She did not even come out of the house! What did my brother and I do? What did dad do, to be condemned to such torments? If we came back, this is a great miracle, and this is only because *bunica* prayed very much. We resisted with the Spirit of the Lord, purely and simply, and we came back because of her prayers. But how many have never returned?!...

If I returned, I was no longer as before. Everything I saw and suffered in the seven years of Siberia is disastrous and irreparable. They truly maimed my tender soul; Satan implanted in me a hatred for my whole life, and I can never forgive him.

If I regret anything from all the things that I went through, I regret my childhood. The other things, no - this is how man must go through life and is allowed by God, so that he may be purified of sins. But I regret that wretched childhood! Thinking how my children grew up now and how I was back then, it seems as different as day and night! I don't even believe how much I spoiled my boys, allowing them to sleep more in the morning, giving them to eat better meals, and me, not eating so that I could give it to them. Who behaved this way with me? Or how I caressed them, how I cared for them as much as possible, how I took them to the hospital... Who did anything like this with me?...

Not only at the orphanage, in Siberia, but even at home, with the relatives, when I came back. For the Bolsheviks embittered people here as well. I got so sick at my uncles that I lost consciousness, but nobody took me to the hospital or gave me medicine. My aunt never caressed me or asked me what was hurting. No; if I was meant to live, fine, if not, no! I do not condemn her and I do not hate her. God forgive her, because I understood all things later. When could she ask me, if there

---

[91] The Voice of Bessarabia—a radio station in Chişinău.

were so many things to do: work on the field, give the rate for the kolkhoz, and build a house!

I did not even have time to talk in detail with my boys in the house, to tell them how I lived in Siberia! Only after I wrote the book, my boy raised his head:

"How, mom, and you were quiet all this time?!"

"But when could I have told you, my dear boy?..."

Sometimes when they were little and wanted a story before bed, I would tell them about wolves, about the forest, but they thought it was a story tale, not the truth.

This is how our communication was, because Soviet life was like this: you woke up early in the morning, took the children to kindergarten, from there you ran to work, came home in the evening to make some food, ran to bring the children back, washed them, put them to bed, and then had to start all over the next day. When could I tell them?!...

This is how it was with me, with my childhood... There were thousands like me, tormented and bitter, because an orphan child is only a bitter tear, an unfulfilled desire, a bird without wings...

This is why I pray to God for all my people and for the whole nation to turn His face toward us, in Bessarabia, to deliver us from this terrible Bolshevik plague, so that our children would no longer suffer, but that it may be again as it was before, when people lived as they learned from the old, beautifully and peacefully...

Chişinău, Bessarabia, July 5, 2011

Under the Sign of the "Sword of Justice"

Ion Moraru

The village of my childhood…

I was born on March 9, 1929, in the village Mândâc, near the city of Drochia, in Bessarabia. The village of my childhood was just like all the villages in Bessarabia before the war, set along a stream, with small houses made of twigs with roofs of rye straws. All houses were built quite similarly. Sometimes, people built them alone, but usually the whole village participated in raising them up. During the summer, they made clay. The men rolled up their sleeves, and some glued the clay with the straws, others smoothed the walls, and still others worked on the attic. The women prepared much food, and the house was raised up in a day! They waited for it to dry during August, and then put up its roof, and they could live in it.

In the heart of the village there was an old wooden church, where all the people would go on Sunday. The people were faithful, and it was a shameful thing to not go to church on feast days. Even at home, we prayed before everything. My *bunica*, Alexandra, had her own rule every morning and evening - even if the village were on fire, even if the house were on fire, she would have not given up on prayer! When she was finished, she sat down, combed her raven hair, put it in a bun,[92] and when this ritual was done, she began working! She went to the oven made out of stone and clay, just next to the house, and she did her work there the whole day: making two-three pots of polenta per day - polenta with scrambled eggs, polenta with fish, polenta with scraps, polenta with sheep cheese, just like every other Romanian. I don't know how the Bessarabians did not die from so much polenta!

During feast days, it was completely different, for feasts were sacred for us. On Saturday, toward evening, when the sun was going down, *bunicul* went to mow grass and brought back food for the horses and cattle, so that he would not have to mow

---

[92] "Foflic" in original, a regionalism.

on Sunday. *Bunica* cooked on Saturday too, as we would all go to church on Sunday morning. In those times, people were not very educated; their lives flowed naturally, according to what was given to them. They knew how to do many things naturally, following the nature of things. *Bunelul* for example, did not know much agronomy, but he knew with precision when to sow the corn. In the spring, he was just coming to me saying:

"Vaniusha, come, let's see if it is time to sow!"

On our land, on a small hill, there was a large cross made out of stone. *Bunelul* used to make a cigarette from corn, sit on a stone, and begin puffing that cigarette. After a while, he would stand up and say:

"Let's go home; it is not the time for sowing!"

I was wondering how he could know. Then I realized where his knowledge came from: the stone was cold. He did not need academic studies to understand that it was too cold for sowing.

The majority of the people in the village had good hearts, but there were also some who were different, as it is everywhere. There were small thieves but also bigger thieves. Spiritually speaking, the latter were condemned definitively: they were totally rejected by the village. They were not accepted anywhere; they were not invited to weddings and not even to the gatherings when people built the home of a villager.

However, the majority of the peasants were proper and followed the traditions. When the feasts of winter or the Holy Pascha came, it felt as if the Kingdom of Heaven descended in the village. How many beautiful carols were heard on Christmas, all connected with the Savior... How many customs... The feast of feasts was Pascha. The Savior's Resurrection was the miracle of miracles for all! People believed and hoped that this Resurrection would come for them as well. Nobody knew, however, how it would be, and this is why they feared death. As soon as it was heard that someone was about to die, either because of age or sickness, everyone went to him to ask for forgiveness and waited around to hold his candle, because it was considered a sin to die without a candle. The marriages were also done according to tradition. The youth married boys and girls from other villages as well, as long as they came from families with a good name. If the girl was not a virgin, on the second day, when people played the sheet,[93] it was a huge scandal; it could even lead to separation. There were things like this taking place as well, for man has been sinful since Eve, and the bodily passions fight within man's soul...

In the village, the priest's word was the law of the Gospel. The priest was well respected, even if he also had his own shortcomings. He could be as sinful as all the others, but he was clothed with the grace of priesthood, and through this he brought God's blessing on earth. Beside the services during feasts, the priest taught religion at school, one hour per week in every class. During the Great Lent and the Christmas lent, all children went to confession and communion, two by two, hand in hand.

The priest and the teacher were the most respected people in the village. The revenue officer and the sheriff followed them in importance, but the peasants did not love them. The revenue officer ripped them off with the taxes, and the policemen were, as people say in our parts, "jerked from baptism," so they were lost - they would beat people, swear, and things like that.

The mayor had the leadership of the village. There were political parties, but they were not very important, because people voted as they thought right. If someone liked the orator who came to tell him fables, then he voted for him. What did the peasant understand from the party's doctrine?!...

I grew up with bunelul...

When I was eight months old, dad left mom because of some misunderstandings about the dowry. He went to the Romanian army, and he never came back. I never knew him.

I grew up with *bunelul*, who was the pillar of wisdom that supported me my whole life, until he went to the world of the

---

[93] This is an old tradition that was related to the virginity of the young bride. After the new couple spent together their first night as a married couple, the mother of the bride came outside with the sheet that was supposed to have blood on it, to so prove the young woman's honor.

righteous. *Bunelul* Pintilie Oloinic had been in the Tsarist Russian Army for seven years. He learned Russian well from a petty officer, and he also learned to read in *glagorita*, an old alphabet of the Slavonic language from before the Christianization of Russians.

Bunelul was completely devoted to the Tsar. For him, the Tsar was in second place on earth, after the Heavenly Father. This admiration for the Tsar that *bunelul* and the old people had in our parts was not accidental. Immediately after they entered Bessarabia, in 1812, the Russians did everything in their power to denationalize it: they took out the Romanian language from the educational system and from the Church; they put Russian administration everywhere and did their best to cultivate a boundless love for the "father Tsar." Since Russia was an empire that always tried to get new lands and so needed soldiers for war, the leaders introduced the mandatory military service of 25 years in the Tsarist army.

The Socialist Revolution caught *bunelul* in his seventh year in the army, in the town of Tver. As they were liberated from the army, my good *bunelul* - young and sturdy back then - came home with a bag [94] with some bank-notes with the face of Empress Ekaterina, which were considered to be of great value. *Bunelul* cared a lot about them. Every Sunday, he took out the picture of the Tsar with his family and fixed it with some thumbtacks on the chimney. Then, he put the bag next to it and read to us from the Holy Gospel in *glagorita* from the book that he had brought together with an old Horologion from Russia. At the end, he said sighing:

"Well, my dear, the Tsar was a good man, but the vagabonds took him down! But God is great, and those times may come back..." And those times came back soon, but not how *bunelul* thought they would...

1940 - We came to liberate you!

It was the year 1940 when we heard the rumor that Bessarabia would be surrendered to Russia. The teacher from

---

[94] "Tobultoc" in the original, a regionalism.

the village ran to *bunelul*, called him in the back of the garden, and told him:

"*Bade*[95] Pintilie, the Russians are coming!"

The old man came in the house and told his old woman:

"Alixandra, the Russians are coming!"

Bunelul hurried and took out his bag with money. With tremendous joy, he put the picture of the Tsar on the chimney, so that it could be seen. He did not know what awaited him.

Not even three days had passed, and two men came to him:

"*Bade* Pintilie, you know Russian well; please come and let's receive the Russians with bread and salt!"[96]

"Then wait, men, so I can shave first!"

Bunelul shaved only for important days. He shaved with the razor he had from the army, from the time of the Tsar. I, who was almost eleven, winced around him:

"*Tătuca*, please, take me with you, *tătuca!*"[97]

I was waiting with my heart in my throat; if *bunelul* said "no," then it was "no" and that was the end of it. Finally, he just said:

"Come!"

Bunelul took a jug with wine, baked bread, and a stripped serviette made of thin linen, and we left.

We, the children, when we saw that the Russians were coming toward the village with the tank, went up on the walls, and our mouths dropped.

"Look how they are coming! Look at those carriages with no horses!"

One said:

"No, these come with the devil, because if they go without a horse, they are with the devil, for sure…"

The dark-green car stopped next to us, leaving behind a trail of heavy exhaust. Three soldiers came out of it and turned

---

[95] A way of addressing an older man or someone who has authority in the community. Younger brothers could also address the elder brother with the same appellative.

[96] This was the traditional way of receiving a guest of high honor.

[97] "*Tătuca*" is an appellative used for father ("tata"). In this case, the grandfather played the role of a father for the boy.

toward the multitude, which had gathered all together:

"Zdravstvuite, mujiki![98] We have come to liberate you!"

People looked around amazed:

"From whom do you want to liberate us?"

"What do you mean from whom? From the Romanians!"

"But what are we?..."

That was it: the seed they threw did not want to sprout on that land.

Bunelul came forward to give them bread, but the Russian refused:

"No need, old man, we have bread!"

"But this is how it is from God with us: when we have guests, we receive them with bread and salt!"

"What God? Man makes bread, not God!"

Well, my *bunelul* seemed as if he were becoming a little smaller. He understood that there was something shady going on, and there was a murmur among the people. Someone said aloud:

"These people have no God!"

Then, they began talking to the people. The Russians told them that in Russia the whole village works together, and everything they gather, they divide equally in the fall, that rich people are not honored, and that the poor must lead the world.

Hearing this, the people began leaving toward their homes, and only the curious children and the village's vagabonds remained near the tank. *Bunelul* continued to translate to them what the Russians were saying.

When the "official meeting" ended, they said to *bunelul*:

"Do you live far, old man?"

"No."

"Let us see how you live!"

An officer and a soldier came to our home, and the others remained there, with the crowd of children and some of the vagabonds. I would have wanted to go on the tank as well, and I was very sorry that I had to leave, but I had no choice, since I was one of the "Bessarabian delegations" for the meeting with

---

[98] "Good day, peasants!" (*Footnote in the Romanian edition*)

the Russians. Our house was well put together back then. When the Russians came in and saw such a beautiful orchard, a vineyard, and an apiary with 150 hives, they began shouting:

"Ah, kulak, kulak..."

When we were in the house, *bunelul* shouted to *bunica*:

"Alixandra, bring some cheese with sour cream and a piece of pastrami!"

In the meantime, he rushed to get a tub of wine and put it on the table. The Russians began to taste the wine, and they complained that it was sour, but the old man brought them honey to mend it.

During all this time, the tsar's portrait was on the chimney, with the bag of money there, so that *bunelul* could brag to the Russians that he kept their money and that now he would be rich.

The Russians ate, and ate, and then the officer said:

"Well, old man, you live well! You will be soon taken to Siberia!"

Bunelul became darker:

"How?!... But everything that you see here I made with these hands! I did not hire anyone to do it!"

He stretched his large hands towards them, ridged everywhere, as the bread made on the fireplace. Then he said again:

"My children and I did all these things!"

He motioned toward us, to where we were sitting in the corner, barely daring to take a breath.

The officer looked at us, and his eyes fell on the chimney. He did not think much: he stood up fast, grabbed the Tsar's portrait, and - prrrrr! - broke it in two.

Poor *tătuca* seemed to be even smaller. Aha, he said to himself, these are the vagabonds who took down the Tsar when I was in Tver! At that moment, he was already looking forward to seeing his guests leave the house.

They did not remain much longer and left. When he left, the officer clarified that he was a *politruk*,[99] a word that no one

---

[99] Political commissar responsible for the political education.

understood. *Bunelul* accompanied them, came back in the house, cleaned the table, and looked at his old woman saying:

"Alixandra, these are not Russians! These are with the devil!"

This was the saying in our parts: they are "with the devil," that is, without God.

From that day on, *tătuca* became very quiet, and he tried to meet people as rarely as possible. The *politruk* had stolen from him the jokes and the cheerfulness he used to have, and he sighed deeply wherever he was. His silence and grief were excruciatingly heavy on me as well, for *tătuca* was right next to mom in the altar of my heart, and their spiritual state was the daily bread for my soul.

If up to that moment *bunelul* had prayed for years in Russian, after his meeting with the *politruk* I heard him saying "Our Father" for the first time in Romanian. I did not understand what that meant. Now, after many years, I realize what a radical change his soul had gone through. The *politruk* had cured him definitively of his love for strangers. I then understood how prophetic Eminescu[100] was when he wrote the last stanza of his *Doina*: "*Whoever loved the strangers/May the dogs eat his heart,/May wilderness eat his house/And nothingness his people!*"

After not even a month, my poor *tătuca* no longer slept in the house, because there were rumors in the village that the Russians would take the best people to Siberia. No one knew how far away that part of the world was. Some were saying that you must go there by train for a month; others thought that it was still wilderness there, with a terrible frost, and that only white bears live there... When he heard this, *bunelul* did not wait much longer. He made a bed in the stable with the horses, and he slept there for a while, always listening carefully. Then, he started to hide in the orchards, in the thicket, or in the forest, until the deportations from 1941 passed.

This is how he was cured of his Russophilia...

---

[100] Mihai Eminescu (1850-1889) is one of the most important Romanian poets.

The devil is afraid of the light...

The autumn came, and the children had to go to school. The Bolsheviks thought that the Romanian school was not strong, so they made all of us repeat one year. So I went again to fourth grade, now in Russian, with reading in Russian, telling stories in Russian, making summaries in Russian, and studying the history of the Soviet Union. They tormented us an entire week with the Russian alphabet, with drawing the hammer and the sickle, and with the memorization of the four words, the Union of the Soviet Socialist Republics, the name of the new rule which we were under. Then, it was mandatory to learn poems about Stalin, about all their satanic leadership. We were very confused, because we heard one thing at school, and we were told something completely different at home...

Things would have worked the way they would have worked, but it was really incredible when they forbade us to wear a cross around our necks, and this really worried *bunica*. She took the small cross from the thread and sewed it behind a pocket from my vest. They also took out the icons from our classroom, and you could not even think of going to confession and communion. In a short amount of time, faith was categorically forbidden.

The priest from Mândâc, Ion Goreaev, was called in to be investigated, and they told him to no longer go around in the village dressed as a priest. Some were saying that the activists tormented him night after night, so that he would give up the cross and his faith.

One thing was not clear to people: why the committee of the party worked over night and not during the day. They tried hard to find an answer for a long time, until father Ion Cojocaru told them the mystery he discovered reading the holy books. It seemed that this new Russian Empire that took over the world was not from God, but from the evil one, the devil. And the devil is afraid of light, for light comes from God, and darkness from the evil one. This incredible news spread everywhere fast, and people began to be afraid of and lack trust in this new order.

In fact, the rumors were getting worse every day. The Bolsheviks said that everything would be collectivized, everything would be taken, and everyone would receive back according to the labor he puts in. There were not very rich people in our village, but each one had a horse, a cow, a chicken, a pig that you would cut for Christmas, and no one wanted to have his household wasted. Thus, people could not stand the Bolsheviks, and there was no longer any person who waited for the Russians to come.

Only the activists were happy, the good-for-nothing who came together from all the corners of the village. They knew what took place in every neighborhood, who lived well, who had a difficult life, so they worked easily on the field. Someone from the district had the leadership of the committee.

This is how things went until next year, when the Romanian Army crossed the Prut.

1941 - the emancipation of Bessarabia

The proof that the "Bolshevik happiness" did not work there was that in 1941, when the Romanian regiments entered the villages, the people received the soldiers with bread and salt.

In Mândâc, the village cooperative that the Bolsheviks established was dismantled within an hour. The sheriff post was installed immediately, people named a mayor from among the leaders, and, contrary to the chaos that was installed when the Russians came in 1940, now, all of a sudden, within 24 hours, order was reestablished in the village.

The new leadership did not take very harsh measures against the Bolsheviks: they gathered the activists at the police station, gave each of them a good beating, and let them go home. They did not have anything else to suffer. They were not judged, they were not put in prison, and they were not deported. In fact, where could you deport them? The Russians had Siberia, but where could the Romanians deport the activists?

In the village, life followed its course. Three or four threshers with good, imported tractors were brought on the field. They established a quota per each person's production, which determined how much you were allowed to sell. The State bought from the peasants at the market place. For each one, everything was counted: this much for forage, this much for seed, and this much for feeding the family. You were obligated to sell the rest of the bread. It was war, and the State needed bread for the army.

In the meantime, many German troops were continually passing on the road at the outskirts of the village, going toward the East. Then, still on this road, the Germans began to take groups of Jews in a convoy to Transnistria. I did not know why they did this. The villagers always behaved well with the Jews. They did not resent them for what happened before, except perhaps in Chişinău, where the so-called revolutionaries like Ana Pauker[101] have made great disarray in the Romanian army and among the Romanian state employees. After many years, when I was in the concentration camp,[102] a wise Jew clarified things for me:

"You should not believe that our nation is made only of prophets and saints. No! We have everything, just like you do..."

In fact, I experienced an event that manifested the Christian behavior of our peasants. Since the bombardments were quite close to the village, I was not going far with the cow, but I held her by the rope, right on the side of the road where the German troops used to pass. One day, I was very close to a well, and I saw a convoy of Jews accompanied by Germans. A young Jewish woman, of a rare beauty, with a long plait on her back that reached her loins, asked a German soldier to allow her to drink water. The German made a sign that she could drink. The girl put her head into the bucket and drank avidly. He looked at her smirking, and all of a sudden - buff! - he shot her right in her neck.

---

[101] Ana Pauker is a very controversial figure of early communism in Romania. Generally, she is perceived as the one responsible for the implementation of Stalinism and for the cruelty of communist persecution in late 1940s and early 1950s. For more info, see Adrian Cioroianu's *Pe umerii lui Marx. O introducere în istoria comunismului românesc* (Bucharest: Curtea Veche, 2005) and Robert Levy's *Ana Pauker: The Rise and Fall of a Jewish Communist* (University of California Press, 2001).

[102] The author talks about the Soviet concentration camps.

Scared, I ran home, leaving the cow there. I rushed to *bunelul*, who worked in the apiary, and I told him everything. He covered the beehive, and we both ran after the cow, because she nourished us. We led her slowly with the rod and brought her home. The convoy went further, and the Jewish woman remained like this, with her head in the bucket, suspended alone between the sky and the earth. Nobody got close to her until evening came, but she was not there in the morning; at the border between Slănina and Drochia appeared a fresh tomb, without a cross, which was a sign that the Christian peasants had buried her.

1944 - Again under the Bolsheviks

I was turning 15 in the spring of 1944. I had not gone to school for four years because of the war and of poverty, even if I had finished fourth grade with a very good average.

It so happened that *bunelul*'s eldest son, uncle Vasile, needed a trustworthy worker at his lumber yard, not far away from the train station. He took me to teach me to cut the wood in cubes, to keep the receipts, and to pay attention to what the vender was doing. The yard was in a long warehouse that had a small room with an iron stove where I was staying with the vender. One day, in the middle of March, as I was staying next to that deposit on a pile of wood, I saw some people with long coats, and I understood they were armed Russian partisans. The train station was filled with people, as it was every day. There were entire echelons of refugees going one after the other to Romania, because the people knew now what the Bolsheviks could do when they would return.

After the sunset, when the day turned to night, the shots began all of a sudden. There were shots everywhere, with no mercy. The bullets flew through the air as the beetles fly in the spring, and the train station was filled with screams.

After the burst of gunfire diminished, I came out. Just before the train station, there were many people who were no longer moving, in puddles of blood, with their eyes toward the sky, as if they were following the souls that had left them. A woman had a dead child in her arms and roared desperately: "May you be cursed, Stalin and Hitler!" A burst of gunfire put her down, and she collapsed with the child's body over her.

By morning, there were twenty-thirty people in the room where the vender and I were. They were covered in blood, dirty, and had small children with them. Slowly, they all left wherever they could, as far away as possible from the accursed place.

The true battle started afterwards, between the Russian partisans and some infantry units from a Romanian battalion that was two kilometers away, in the village of Tsarigrad. The Russians needed to get the train station, so they sent armed units to support the partisans, and they crushed the Romanians. The following day, the train station at Drochia was already controlled by the Bolsheviks. When the dawn came, uncle Vasile came to take us home with the carriage. We took the boxes with documents and whatever else we could, and we left. On the road, we passed by the places where the bloody battle had taken place the night before. There were bodies of soldiers everywhere, shattered and scorched, and a terrible man took their clothes and boots. After a few days, the soldiers were taken and buried, as if nothing happened.

This is how the Russians "liberated" us a second time!

Immediately after they were put in power, the committee of the party from 1940 was reestablished in the village, and the party organization started to form based on it.

1945 - At the school of Soviet "patriotism"...

In 1945, the Middle School was organized in Târnova, 12 kilometers from our village. I registered for fifth grade, together with other children of different ages. We had colleagues who had taken some classes in the Romanian high schools, and I admired them for their elegance and high education. During those times, education was serious. A high school student had to speak fluently in German or French, and the baccalaureate was taken with a committee of instructors who took him through all the subjects. You could not copy, listen to someone else's answers, or have the answer already prepared. All the students in high school knew how to cube a stack of hay, not like today, when if you take that toy[103] from them, they can no longer click all day on it, and they are a *tabula rasa*!

Things started changing in 1945. The old school programs were replaced, and the Bolshevik ideology was massively introduced. It was mandatory for every object of study to have an introduction, one third of the textbook, in which you found out that the science studied - biology, zoology, or mathematics - was well developed due to the wisdom of the "great leader" Stalin. Only due to him! The "great leader" had his picture in every textbook, with some mustaches that looked like they could sting you like needles!

In order to be educated in the spirit of Soviet "patriotism," we would make preparations for the so-called parade. We had a crazy military commandant, a *voenruk*, and he made us run wherever there were more weeds, wherever it was most difficult. He used to say that running strengthens the body. The new leadership needed powerful people who could face any hardships. How could we have known that so many hardships were waiting for us?

The school director was Jewish, Halimski, a communist Jew, of course, because he would not have been charged to lead education otherwise. He had protruding eyes, and he spit all over when he talked.

After a while, the caps of the older boys bothered that director. The caps had on them the name of the Romanian high school where the boys had studied before. He gave the order to replace all of them with some Soviet military caps, the so-called *budionovka*, with a horn in the middle. Everyone had to start wearing them.

One of the older students Victor Guțu, asked him:

"Why does this cap have only one horn in the middle?"

To make fun of us, the director said:

"You, Bessarabians, must accumulate all wisdom in this horn!"

And he added imperiously:

"From tomorrow, you must all come with these caps!"

---

[103] The computer (*Footnote in the Romanian edition*).

The next day, all the boys came to school with lamb hats, and Victor came with this usual cap, with the high school emblem.

The students from the upper years rejected the entire Soviet system wittingly and did not accept anything that was imposed as "education." On the contrary, when they sensed that the so-called "educational moment" was coming, they made jokes about it, saying:

"Wait a moment, the lesson is finished and education begins!..."

One day, we saw a large drawing on the school's wall, in the hallway. It was done with coal by a very talented hand. There were two known figures in the foreground: the "great" Stalin, drawn with horns and listening devices in his ears, and Professor Rosenberg who whispered something at the "great father's" ear. The message of the drawing was very explicit. This case was staggering, and it raised the attention of the entire leadership of the district. The chiefs of the NKVD[104] came to the school immediately, the first secretary from the party, military persons, and all of them were running in the hallways, worried.

Every classroom was taken out, led by the class chief. The first secretary spoke first, and he solemnly told us that the Red Army is close to Berlin and that the "fascist beast" will be crushed in its lair. Then he added:

"Now, when our entire country fights fiercely to destroy fascism, some students from your school act in a manner hostile to Soviet power!"[105]

He asked us to confess willingly who scrawled the wall of the hallway. There was a silence like in a grave, even if all of us knew that only one boy in the entire school, Victor Guțu, could do such an accomplished drawing. Seeing that no one had the courage to admit any guilt, a commission passed through all the

---

[104] The Soviet secret police.
[105] The Soviet power often justified its atrocities by presenting itself as fighting fascism. In fact, fascism and communism are two faces of the same coin.

rooms and carefully checked our notebooks. When the crowd of students came back to the schoolyard, we saw how two armed soldiers were taking Victor Guțu toward the NKVD.

For several weeks, they took us one by one, students and teachers, in a room at the end of the hallway, and they intimidated us in the same manner: "If you love your Country and its great Leader, you must observe what your colleagues do and give us a written report about it." What motivated people varied: if they were weak students, they were promised help with their exams. If they were from a well-to-do family, they were promised protection for their parents.[106] However, to the surprise of the "workers" from the "back room," the students did not keep their mouths shut.[107] During one of the breaks, Gavroş Ciubotaru told everyone how he promised that he would be an informant but only about Halimski. The director heard about it, and he decided to suspend Gavroş for a month. The student protested, and a compromise was reached: Gavroş had to apologize to the director in front of everyone, in the courtyard. But he refused:

"How can I apologize to some bastards who sell our people and our faith? It will be better if am expelled, so that I can return home and breathe fresh air in my parents' orchard; it needs to be prepared for spring, anyway!"

And Gavroş did not come to school for a month and a half.

Their attempt to introduce, among the students, the practice of being an informant failed because of this attitude.

There were some teachers who were not Bolshevized. We had good teachers, who were against the Sovietization of education. Our math teacher Mr. Belinski was one of them; he was a tall, thin man, with blue eyes like a chicory. He had extraordinary finesse, and he was so eloquent that it seemed as if he were giving birth to each word in the very moment he would speak it. He had finished the Conservatory, but there was

---

[106] These families were usually deported or arrested, so the "protection" was against such events.

[107] Here, the Romanian expression for "keep the mouth shut" is "keep the tongue behind the teeth."

no need for music in school, so he taught mathematics. He really cared a lot about us, and when he saw us struggling to breathe after each run, he asked the *voenruk*[108]: "Take it easier on them, don't you see that they are burning out? Don't you have any human mercy?"

The most beautiful memory I have of Mr. Belinski is from around the New Year. It had snowed white and clean on the promenade with chestnuts from the schoolyard. He had found a sleigh somewhere, he put bells on the horses, and he took all the students, big and small, for a ride with the sleigh across the promenade. He had also baked some beautiful loafs of bread and gave a piece to each one of us; then, we began caroling. When our celebration reached its height, the directors of the school dispersed us, but we continued to sing for a long time through the streets of the village, in small groups. That evening of singing, organized by Mr. Belinski, remained in my soul for my entire life. We both remembered it with emotion over the years, most of all, when I saw him again in a symphonic orchestra in a concentration camp in Siberia!

The girl with a fragrance like basil...

My story with Lealea Cojocaru began around that time as well. I had met Lealea a few years back, on a Sunday, when I went to play on the village's pasture. I saw a group of girls playing and reciting riddles. Among them, there was a girl around seven-eight years old, with brown, wavy hair, and with blue eyes of such brilliant radiance; I looked into them as into a mirror. She had just finished chanting a rhyme, and the girls were asking her:

"Come, Lealea, say it again..."

They were calling her Lealea, out of love; her true name was Lidia.

She did not give up:

"I am tired; I want to go home..."

I went to talk to them, and I told her to tell me the rhyme

---

[108] A military instructor.

with Father Abraham. She held me with her small hands from the neck and began to pronounce the words as in an incantation; I held her by her fingers, following the rules of the game. Then she asked me to help her cross the bridge, because her mother had forgotten to come after her. The bridge was narrow, made out of two boards put together. I told her to hold tight on my neck, and I held her tight to my chest. She had a frail body and she smelled beautifully, like basil. Something passed through me that day; I don't know what, like a thrill, something inexplicable that I cannot explain even today. I did not even realize when we were on the other shore. I put her down, she thanked me, and then she left and was gone for four years. All this time, I have not seen her, even once. Her family moved to Mândâc, and I lost track of her. Slowly, she faded from me, and only her eyes remained in my soul, those beautiful and deep eyes in which I had seen myself as in a mirror and for which I wrote some lines:

I had never seen
The sea with its billows,
But I beheld the blue
In a girl's eyes: my mirrors...

In 1945, when the Soviet people came and organized the school in Târnova with students from all the surrounding villages, I met Lealea again in room 5A, where she studied together with a boy from my village, Coliuşa. I went to Coliuşa's room often, because we would talk about homework and about things at home, this and that. Lealea was in the first row, always silent, with her head bowed. She recognized me, but I did not. She had grown by now; she was 13 years old. Coliuşa asked me:

"Do you know her?"

When I looked closer, she had the same eyes. She was no longer that little child I had helped cross over the bridge; she was differently built, and only those eyes had remained from that butterfly of a girl. But the thrill came back to me immediately. I looked at her, she bowed her head, and I do not know how, but I asked her whether she still wanted me to help her cross over the bridge.

"Now I can cross the bridge by myself!"

From that moment on, I never left her alone, always keeping my eyes on her! One day, it had snowed a lot, and two boys her age threw her in the snow, piling all the snow on her. I rushed at them like an eagle, and I suddenly began throwing them around. She ran to class, but her little hat knitted from Angora and sheep wool remained at my feet. I picked it up, shook it, and gave it to her saying:

"Here is the trophy from the battle!"

She said:

"Thank you, *bade*[109]!"

"I have a name; if you call me 'bade' again, I won't come to your class any longer!"

I don't remember what she answered, but then she told me:

"I pray you, do not beat those two..."

"Why not?"

"Because I do not want you to be a bad one..."

That's what she told me. On that day, I did not understand. She said it because she said it! I only now realize the kind of soul she had within her...

After this, it happened that I got sick with typhus. I was sick for a month, and after I got better, I went to her classroom to ask her to help me, especially in mathematics, because I was not too good at it. I was a little thick-headed, because I did not understand how two pears[110] and three apples were five fruit. How can you add pears to apples, because the result is not apples, nor pears? Anyway... She was my tutor for a month. She prepared me for the exams. You can imagine: sitting next to her on the bench while she tutors you... I felt how her heart was beating. She was not next to me, but within me...

Next autumn, a new middle school was founded in Mândâc, and they put all of us, the older ones, in a class. Lealea sat on a bench next to me. She did so to her mom's sorrow, because her mother did not really like me. One day, Lealea's

---

[109] An appellative used for older brothers.

[110] "Prasade," a regionalism, in original.

father, *nenea* Venea, called me over to their house and asked me to bring them Negulescu's *Destinul omenirii*.[111] I had barely walked in, when *tanti* Aniuța grabbed my ears and said:

"Say honestly, rascal, how did you charm my daughter to sit with you on the bench?"

"It is no charm, but a child's game that I learned from her when she was little!"

"Come over here, Cosânzeano!"[112]

Lealea came closer, with her head bowed.

"Is it true what he says?... Say something; have you swallowed your tongue?"

I thought that she would immediately beat both of us.

"Mom, don't insult him!" Lealea said. "I was little, we played in the pasture, and I played with him, playing the riddle with Father Abraham. I then asked him nicely to help me cross over the bridge, because you hadn't come after me..."

"Well, this is a long story, husband!" her mother said looking to *nenea* Vanea. "It seems she has been a big girl for some time now!"

"Aniuța, leave the children alone! You are not from the *Siguranța*!"[113]

Tanti Aniuța had menaced me only so that I would not harm her daughter, and I left home happy that I escaped only with that. Not long after that, I found a card in my notebook for my birthday. Lealea had knitted the date of my birth with her hair.

Next year, the classes were separated, and we had to separate, since I was older. Our friendship though grew stronger, because the thrill that passed through us when we were children grew continually, like a snowball.

When I finished seventh grade, there was a graduation ball at school. The director spoke and told us solemnly that we were a historic generation, the first one in the village of Mândâc that finished seven years of Soviet education toward the benefit of

---

[111] *The Destiny of Humanity.*
[112] Cosânzeana is the name of the female character in many Romanian fairytales.
[113] *Siguranța* was the secret police.

the "great leader" and the "cherished communist party."

When the party really got going, I decided I had had enough so I took Lealea, and we both went out. We walked holding hands, recollecting memories from school... From time to time, we stopped to look into each other's eyes. When we arrived at her door, I was faced with the moment I had waited for, for so long. Just when I gathered all my courage and got closer to Lealea, a voice tore apart the spell:

"Come, it's over! You, go into the house, and you, go home and take care to be a good boy from now on!"

"*Siguranţa*" had spied on us in darkness...

Lealea asked her mom to allow us to go to the pasture the next day, so she could see her grandparents' house again, where she had grown up until she was seven.

"Okay, however you wish!"

I don't remember sleeping that night. In the morning, I took Lealea, and we both went ahead, walking along the houses. The war and the famine had darkened the places of our childhood. The mill was sitting lonely on a slope, with no water to make the turbines work and, as such, no bread either. Once green and filled with children playing, the pasture was now scorched and empty. The boards from the bridge had been stolen, and Cubolta had become a small creek that you traversed by foot. With great emotion, we searched the place where we first met. We stopped on a little hill, Lealea looked long at me, and the next moment the whole valley of Cubolta was filled with a fragrance of basil...

And that was it... On July 6th, deportations began, and someone whispered to me that they took Lealea as well. Her father had died in the spring, and she and her mother had moved to Târnova. I ran all the way to the train station in Târnova, I ran from one end of the train to the other, but I did not see her anywhere. I found out later that her mom held her tight, not allowing her to come out, because she knew what I was capable of. If I had seen her, I would have jumped on the train for sure, to go with her to Siberia. Not only then, but even now, if I were to relive my life, I would do the same!

The first investigation

During the summer of 1947, the chief of the NKVD section in Târnova, Kashirin, would often raid the village, targeting the wealthy people. The son of *bunelul*, uncle Vasile, was always in his sight. One evening, my uncle managed to escape from him and run, but, in the morning, my cousin Boris was terrified and he told me how Kashirin had terrorized everyone in the house. I did not spend much time thinking, and I said: we are going to Chişinău to lodge a complaint!

We managed to go up to the first secretary of the Central Committee, Kovali, and the Prime Minister Rudi, and we told them everything with many details, thinking that they would bring about justice. We thought that the leadership in Chişinău finally found out what kind of evil people were in our village! They listened to us, talked to us gently, and told us to be sure that no one else would touch us from then on. We were so impatient to go home to tell them the great joy that we were promised in the Capital!

After not even two days, I was arrested and taken to Târnova, to NKVD. After I was taken in, an officer gave the order to send me to the cellar, so that my mind would settle a bit. A soldier took me to the door of the cellar, pushed me with his gun down the stair, and locked the door behind me. I rolled on the stairs, I busted my lips, hurt my bones, and I remained there on the floor, in darkness, waiting to see what would come next. All of a sudden, I heard a voice next to me:

"Are you Christian?"

"Yes."

"Come up here, on the stairs, because it is cleaner!"

I only then realized that the cellar was filled with dirt, because all the inmates had relieved themselves on the ground, having no other option. I went up the stairs, and two human, gentle hands felt my face: "But you are young, boy!"

As he was sitting next to me, I felt his beard, and when I touched his chest I felt a cross, and I understood that he was a priest.

We talked the whole night. I told him how I went to Rudi to seek justice, and he said to me:

"You, my boy, have a soul that is too open to people. During dark times, man's greatest enemy is his tongue, when he talks much and has his heart open. With strangers, the Christian must be gentle as the dove and wise as the snake. If you understand this well, it may be easier to carry your cross!"

I did not pay attention to his words then. Later, when I went through all the stages of life in the concentration camp, I realized how great his advice was.

They took me for investigations in the morning. They kicked and punched me, beating me in any way possible, just so that I would say where I was and what I did. I thought that they did not know anything, but they knew everything. Those in Chișinău had informed them. Kashirin wanted to find out now where uncle Vasile was hiding.

He grabbed me abruptly during the investigation, to scare me:

"What are your connections with Pentelei and Vasile Oloinicu?"

"Pintilie[114] Oloinicu is my grandfather, and Vasile is my uncle."

"I know this. You are all a band of thieves! What are your connections?"

"My grandfather is not a thief; he is a hardworking man, who has love for people!"

At that moment, I felt something hit my face and my stomach. My whole body was full of excruciating pain, and I collapsed on the chair, with blood in my mouth. Kashirin remained next to me, with his pistol toward me. I began shivering, and I would have liked to die. All of a sudden, my eyes stopped on the floor, on the pinhead of a nail that shone strongly. The crucified Savior came to my mind, and one thought flashed into my mind: "They crucified Him with such nails on the cross"... I felt another hit in my side, and I heard Kashirin ordering the soldier to take me to the cellar.

The silence of the earth took me in again. I wanted to find the priest, to tell him what happened to me, but he was no

---

[114] The NKVD investigator had mispronounced the name.

longer there. I wondered whether they were torturing him some place as well. Fidgeting like this, I fell asleep. I woke up being shoved by a boot and taken again to be interrogated. This time, Kashirin was leaning on one corner of a table, smoking.

"Well, Vanea, did you become wiser in the cellar or are you still stupid?"

"Of course I became wiser! I think that if I make it out of here, I'll go to Chişinău, or even Moscow, to tell the leaders what you do here!"

"And do you think that anyone manages to escape alive from our hands? If you do not want to rot in the cellar, tell us who sent you to Chişinău!"

"Who could have sent me? I went alone, to defend my people!"

"Sit down here and write in detail with whom, where, and to whom you have complained."

I wrote everything as it happened. Kashirin read it and made me sign it. Then he told me that regardless of where I would complain, it would get back to him, and he would make it so that I would be shot like a dog. I told him:

"In 1941, I saw the Germans shooting a Jewish woman who had no fault, from the convoy,."

"True," he replied, "they shot innocent people, but we strive to find guilt in people and we shot them afterwards… Now go home and be careful to not fall back into my hands!"

I ran rather than walked home. Tărcuş welcomed me in the yard, wailing with joy, and *bunelul* waited for me on the threshold, with tears in his eyes…

1946-1947: The famine

The worst plague that came over Bessarabia during those years was the famine. Now, looking back, I think that it was created artificially, to break people's resistance. It is true that the draught was terrible, and it did not rain the entire summer. However, regardless of how bad the weather was, our people always had some food supply in the attic, saved for the next year. With this supply they would not have died of hunger if the activists had not forced them to give a portion to the state, the *postavka*, day and night, cleaning their attics of the last grain of wheat.

Scared, poor people began to invent all kinds of hideouts: some made double walls for their storages; others hid the bread on the bottom of wine barrels. In almost all the households, people began using wheat grinders because if you wanted to grind wheat at the mill, you had to pay with wheat as well. Peasants considered bread to be the image of Christ. In other words, it was the image of Christ which the Bolsheviks continually watched and arrested.

The wheat they took from people was taken to the train station in carts. There, the activists dumped it out in the open, because there were no warehouses, and sometimes it stayed out in the rain until it molded. They were not interested in the bread; they just wanted to take it from the peasants, so that the peasant would remain poor and be controlled completely by the communists.

Toward winter, things were even worse. When the pond by the mill and the brook froze, people began to gather the reed to cover their houses and to make fire. When the whole valley of Cubolta was cleared of reed, those who still had strength cut the osiers and the poplars from the banks of the stream. Then they began burning the fences and even secretly taking the wooden crosses from the cemetery during night. Wilderness had begun to enter not only the earth, but also in the souls of people...

People were saying that some, madden by hunger, slaughtered dogs and cats to eat them and that others caught sparrows and crows. The only measure that the activists took was to bring, in the middle of the village, a bucket full of fish oil that smelled horribly. They gave us this obligatorily, as a measure against rachitis.

Toward the end of winter, people began to die of hunger, one after the other. The gates from the cemetery were no longer closed. The dead were brought there and thrown into a grave because there were no more people to seal the tombs, to follow the Christian tradition.

Father Parfene, who lived at the outskirts of the village, no longer had strength to take his wife to the grave when she died.

He put her on a carpet and dragged her to the cemetery. There, he found a few people and asked them:

"Help me put her in the grave! Then I'll pray an 'Our Father,' and join her, and then you can throw dirt on us both!"

People got scared; they thought the old man lost his mind, and they ran away leaving him with the dead.

The feast of the "bright future"

As the drought had begun in the south, from the steppe of Bălţi, there still was some fruit in the north, and the peasants began going there in search of a piece of bread, a crumb of polenta, or something to eat. They sold the icons they had in the house, carpets, golden things… they sold anything, even for the small amount of food they could get.

We were lucky that *bunelul* was wise; he made a big hole which he filled with beets for forage, he knew how to hide some bread, and we had our cow and a few sheep. However, when we reached spring, famine invaded our house as well. Then, *bunelul* prepared around twenty lambskins and sent me with them to Bucovina, after food. I was already 18 years old, I was resourceful, and *bunelul* trusted me.

I went into a freight train together with some lads my age, and we arrived in Cernăuţi after midnight. You could not get lost there, because there were two great currents of people: a part of them were going to the town of Sneatin, with bags and pouches filled with things that they wanted to exchange for food; the others, the majority of them, were getting ready to go to the factory "Jucika," to the *jom*[115] hole.

Being with my head in the clouds, I did not arrive at central market of the town of Sneatin, but taken by the larger current of people, I found myself next to the hole with *jom*. The hole must have been 10 per 20 meters, and it was filled with a yellowish paste of beet noodles from the sugar factory nearby. The moment I arrived there, a tall, huge man warned me that I have to pay five rubbles if I want a place on the edge of the hole.

---

[115] As explained in the following paragraph, this was "a yellowish paste of beet noodles from the sugar factory."

After I gave him the five rubbles, he gave me a board and advised me to bring some brushwood, to take out *jam* and make some tarts to eat.

I will never forget the scene that I saw then. The stones themselves were crying, pitying the poor people who were fidgeting in the *jom* like worms in a wound! Undressed in the lower part, women and men altogether stirred in that stinky stuff, trying to get something from the deeper parts, where the *jom* was more yellow. They took it, mixed it with a drop of oats,[116] made some tarts, and ate them. After they swallowed them rapaciously, many became yellow, began to tremble, and vomited. Some died there, on the side, with a piece of *jom* in their hand - instead of making a cross, they kept that *jom* in their hand... The bodies were covered by a swarm of flies and remained there, but the crowd didn't seem to notice them, having only one purpose: to get as much *jom* as possible from the hole.

It was there that I saw for the first time how people who were devoid of faith and conscience were brought to the point of losing even the simple human instincts. Swarming around that hole for weeks, sleeping under the clean sky, without washing and without praying to the Savior, some got to the point of relieving themselves in their pants, and still others were relieving themselves in front of everyone, on the bank. That damned hole seemed to be the last stage of torments, the last toll that the Bessarabians had to go through. I had the impression that all of Bessarabia gathered there, to taste from the feast of the "bright future" which "the great father"[117] prepared for the people. When I saw all these things, I took the lambskins under my arms, held them tightly, and I started toward the train station

---

116 The Romanian here says, "o boghiță de hurluială." The translation above does not truly do justice, so let me explain here the words, as they were explained to me by Mrs. Svetlana Brîncă. "O boghiță" is the diminutive of "o boaghe," which designates a very small quantity, as much as you would take with three fingers. Today, "hurluiala" is a mixture of cereals, such as wheat bran, corn, millet, flex seeds, or hemp seeds. In 1947, during the famine, "hurluiala" was rather made of wheat bran mixed with chaff.
117 Stalin.

in Cernăuţi, from where I took a freight train toward Sneatin.[118]

I crossed the river Prut together with several other strong lads - the Prut is a rushing river, and if you try to cross it alone, you'll get under osiers - but I made it, I had arrived at the market. There, people of all ages - children, women, and old men - had things to sell: skins, furs, but especially carpets. Also, it was a covered market.

I stayed there almost the whole day, and no one asked me anything. When I had lost all hope and was starving - I had eaten the two tarts that *bunica* had put in my bag when I left - a short old man, with a sheep hat, came toward me and asked me how much I wanted for the lambskins. I told him that I wanted food, and the old man told me to follow him, and that he would buy them from me. I pondered it a bit and told myself: "come what may, I'll go and that's it!" I was afraid that he could kill me and take my merchandise, because I heard that things like that had happened before, but I had no choice.

The old man took me a bit further from the market, to a wooden cart with a horse:

"Look, my dear, this is the horse that feeds me... Let's see now what I can give you for your lambskins..."

He looked at them and verified them in all possible ways, because there were certain requirements for them and people would not buy them in any condition. He counted out twelve of them, and he gave me back eight of them saying:

"With these, you will take care of your hunger for some time, until you find bread in your parts also."

For the twelve skins, he gave me a bucket of barley, two buckets of potatoes, and two bowls of beans. This was a tremendous joy for me. I put all of them in a sack, and the old man told me:

"I take you to the train station, because it is on my way. Go straight there, without looking for anything else! If you manage things well, it will be enough!"

I listened to the old man, climbed into the first freight train, and went straight home.

---

[118] Sneatin is currently a town in Ukraine.

Then some rain made it to our parts as well, and in the autumn of 1947 we had a good yield of corn, and the village began to regain some vigor. However, the convoy to the cemetery did not stop. Up until 1948-1949, people were still dying because of the famine, because they had eaten not only *jom*, but also earth and mud, and their bodies ceased to function. People no longer had the strength to even wail for their dead. They went quietly to the cemetery, with their eyes buried deep in their sockets, each of them wondering whether there would be anyone remaining to accompany them on their last road...

"The Sword of Justice"

The story of the "Sword of Justice," for which I was arrested and sent to the concentration camp, began around the time when I was in 7th grade. One day, after hours, the *voenruk*[119] came and commanded us:

"6th years and 7th years, come after me!"

He took us to the attic and made us bring down bound volumes of books, registers, catalogs, giving some to each one of us. Then, we formed a column, and he took us to the *sel'sovet*,[120] in the building of the former town hall. There was already a pyre where they burned the religious books. The *voenruk* ordered us to throw everything into the fire. At the beginning, we did not understand that in those bound volumes there was a small library of Romanian books that had been kept in the school's attic: story books, history books in Romanian, and religion books. Then, we began seeing how the heroes of our stories were consumed into the fire one after the other: "The Goat and the Three Yeanlings,"[121] "Făt-Frumos born of a tear,"[122] Ileana Cosânzeana... After them, the history and religion textbooks... Everything that was written with Latin

---

[119] As mentioned above, the Russian word designates a military instructor/commandant.

[120] The soviet rural organization.

[121] A children's story written by Ion Creangă, previously mentioned in Margareta Cemârtan-Spânu's story.

[122] A children's story written by Mihai Eminescu, the Romanian national poet, a good friend of Ion Creangă.

alphabet had to be destroyed.

Vasile Țurcanu, my colleague from Drochia, had a larger coat on him, from his father, and he hid a few books under it: Petru Negulescu's *Destinul omenirii*, [123] two history books written by Iorga, [124] and a Gospel.

When the fire grew stronger, God brought through a strong wind that raised the papers and took them far away. Some people said that a piece of paper with the image of Christ crucified landed on the cross of the church steeple, because this is what is given to Him from the Scripture, to be nailed on the cross.

Seeing that he could not oppose the wind, the *voenruk* ordered everyone to stop. Being happy that he freed us, we ran home! Vasile and I went on a roundabout street, so the others would not see that we hid the books. When we arrived at the creek, we sat on the bank and began perusing them. All of a sudden, as if coming out of the ground, a young man appeared next to us and asked us:

"What are you doing here?"

We closed the books immediately, but the stranger reprimanded us:

"Boys, national culture is not to be hidden as something that is stolen. It must be assumed and worn in the world with pride, as the clothing for a feast."

Then he asked us:

"Are you *komsomolists*?"[125]

"Not yet, but we will be, because we have no choice!"

"Why do you have no choice?"

"Because they took us by force in order to make us *komsomolists*."

"Well, before you become *komsomolists*, you should know that there is an organization in Bessarabia that defends Christianity. Are you Christian?"

"Yes."

---

[123] *The Destiny of Humankind.*
[124] Nicolae Iorga was one of the greatest Romanian historians.
[125] The komsomolists were members of a soviet youth organization.

"Well, this movement is called 'The Archers of Stephen the Great.'"[126]

The stranger sat next to us and began to tell us how the Bolsheviks unjustly occupied our land, how they closed and defiled our churches, how they persecuted people for their faith, how they destroyed Romanian homes, deporting them from Bessarabia. Then, he added that we had to resist them, to keep the faith of our people and our ancestral customs sacred, and, if need be, to defend ourselves against the foreigners, even with guns.

He then told us the "Creed" of the Romanian archers, which went like this: "I believe in the Good God and the eternity of the Romanian people, I hate the Bolshevik regime to death, and I will fight against the Bolshevik-Stalinist lie to my last breath."

The stranger asked us where we lived, and after I showed him my house through the trees, he disappeared as he came, suddenly. He left without telling us who he was, saying only that he would contact us at the right time. The right time never came; the "archers of Stephen the Great" were uncovered. Someone committed treason, and they were all arrested, 140 people, since the organization was already large.

I met this young man, Pimen Damascan, later, in the concentration camp, where we became friends for life. He was liberated before me and returned home, to Soroca, where he taught in a technical high school. After one year, I was liberated as well, and I continued my schooling also in Soroca, where the Pedagogical High School from Bălţi had been moved. We happened to meet on the street. We held each other with great joy, and I went to his house: the state had given him a dilapidated hut where he lived with his wife. After a few years, he became very sick because of the silicon he inhaled in Djezgazgan,[127] and he died of cancer. He played a very big role

---

[126] Stephen the Great, who ruled Moldova between 1457 and 1504, is one of the greatest figures of Romanian history, mainly because of his valiant resistance against the Ottoman armies. He was also recently made a saint in the Romanian Orthodox Church.

[127] Or Jezkazgan, a city in Kazakhstan, where there was a labor camp.

in my life. I became an "archer" and later established the organization "The Sword of Justice" due to him.

I could not say exactly what urged me more to establish this organization. Perhaps what led me to take that path was my first arrest and interrogation in Târnova. The whole situation in those times made me feel a sense of revolt boiling within me as magma boils within the earth. We endured so many hardships - *bunelul* was forced to sleep in the stable out of fear of deportation, Kashirin chased my uncle with a gun, and activists beat my cousins during the night.

I was not the only one boiling inside, but there were many like me in Bessarabia. Our families were deported, our religion forbidden, the plundering from *postavka* took bread from our mouths, and the famine and contempt against us did not cease… All these things weighted upon us as unmerciful wounds, and they made us burst. Even more: I had grown up with the goat and the three yeanlings, and they burned it; I had grown up with "Făt Frumos born of a tear," and they burned it; they categorically forbade me to touch any book on which the names of Eminescu or Goga were written, saying that they were writers who praised the bourgeois order, and the bourgeoisie was the enemy of the working people. Then what was I supposed to do…?!

I also was of a more impulsive, direct nature. I could not stand injustice, Lord forbid! I would have stopped you in the middle of a sentence, cut you with the sword, and nothing less! This is why I named the organization "The Sword of Justice."

The first founding members were my friend, Vasile Țurcanu from Drochia, who was one year younger, and I. The two of us made the decision to become brothers. How? We took a nib, trying to find our veins, to unite our blood. We did not find the veins, but we scratched our skin, and some thin blood like wine came out, and we became brothers.

Then, one of us, I don't remember who, said:

"Do you remember what the archer said? We must also become archers!"

We took the archers' "Creed" and founded the organization. Then, after the "Creed," we also established the last stanza of Eminescu's poem, "Doina", as a sort of password: *"Whoever loved the strangers/May the dogs eat his heart,/May wilderness eat his house/And nothingness his people!"* If you did not know the verses, you were not an archer!

In time, we attracted others to the organization, so that our nest had grown to twelve people. Among them, Petru Lungu from Cotiujeni, today's district of Briceni - may God rest his soul, for he died of cancer. His brother was in the army with the Soviets, and he promised he would procure us some weapons. Due to the romanticism of our youth, we did not realize that we could not overturn a soviet tank only with guns. No... We wanted weapons immediately!

Before receiving the weapons - which we did not receive, after all - we could not sit and do nothing. We wrote a letter to Stalin in which we named him the "leader of demons" and we detailed all the horrors and trespasses done against us. We also wrote to the Union of Writers in Chişinău, the "union of bootlickers" of the regime, from where the majority of lies had originated, and we also tore them apart with our strong words.

From my childhood, God gave me this gift to express myself, and I expressed myself quite courageously, as best as I could back then. We wrote these letters, signed them "The Sword of Justice," and sent them.

On July 4th, we found out from a trustworthy man that they would begin to deport people on July 6th. We went around for two nights to all the people in the village, and we let them know, urging them to run.

Then, you can't imagine what thought struck us. We found a dead chicken, we tied it from one leg, and we hung it on the sign on which the name of the village, Mândâc, was written. Underneath, we wrote: "I made egg after egg, but Stalin did not have enough!"

We did things of this kind, whatever came to our minds back then, because we could not go and fight Stalin!

As any organization, we also had, of course, meetings. We met either at my place, or at father Pavel Istrate's place, and we made a plan of activities for one or two weeks. Like everyone else, we were hoping back then that the Americans would come and would save us from the Russians. Yah! Even their president who had walking problems, Roosevelt, had sold us out for good at Yalta, especially us, the Romanians between the rivers Prut and Nistru. Bessarabia was Romanian land. What would it have cost him to support us, to at least remain united with Romania, be it under communism, be it however, but at least united with Romania? Because of this, we cannot find our path even today; because of this even today people here cannot make a decision about who they are: Moldavians, Romanians, or who...?!

The Treason

There were also two Romanians[128] whom we tried to coopt into our organization, Guţanu Grigore and Serioja Ţăpuşă. I do not exactly know why these two betrayed us. Perhaps they wanted to bring others into the organization, and thus they revealed that there was a secret organization, "The Sword of Justice," against the Bolsheviks. The NKVD found out, took them into interrogations, and scared them:

"Confess everything; we found out that you want to bring this one and that one into 'The Sword of Justice!'"

If they hesitated, of course they were menaced:

"If you don't tell us, you'll go where they go!"

The weak man's nature bows, and they told them everything, out of fear. They narrated how we tried to bring them into the organization, how we listened to "The Voice of America" in secret, at *bunelu*'s radio with batteries, how we planned to make connections with the *banderovists* in Ukraine to get some weapons - all of them sufficient reasons for the NKVD to begin the arrests.

In the spring of 1950, the first one to be arrested was Bobeică, a photographer who was in the Romanian army and was older than us. This photographer violated one of the golden rules of our organization. We had decided in a meeting that absolutely none of us should carry any piece of paper about the organization, about its name, or about its members. When they picked him up, they found the list with all the members, and

---

[128] The author probably means two citizens of Romania.

they only had to find each one of us. The most dramatic arrest was that of Vasile Țurcanu.

He was taking courses at the Pedagogical School in Bălți, and he had an exam in Moldavian language.[129] An entire platoon of soldiers surrounded the school just for him. They did not know exactly who we were; they had no idea that we were some poor young lads that you could just blow away like we were nothing. They thought that they would encounter violent resistance from us and that there might even be human victims. They surrounded the school, placed guards at all entries, and asked the director to take them to the classroom where the student Țurcanu was. The school's director, Filip Feodorovici, had been a lieutenant colonel in the Soviet army, but he was a Moldavian from the West of the Nistru and a good patriot.

His daughter, Katiusha, a young woman of rare beauty, both spiritual and physical, was teaching Moldavian language at the Pedagogical School. She was a model of Romanian dignity. Vasile was in love with her, and she was in love with him. When Filip Feodorovici came in the classroom together with the soldiers to arrest Vasile, Katiusha stood up from the desk, yellow as wax, sighed deeply, and said no word, because she knew what the Bolshevik police meant.

The director was shaking, and one could see that he feared the lieutenant, even if he was a lieutenant colonel. Nobody dared make any movement. In that complete silence, one could hear only the gnashing of handcuffs. Vasile was taken out of the classroom, and the only one who dared to accompany him was Katiusha. After this, Vasile was taken under arrest, and the interrogations began.

On the same night they arrested me as well. I had just returned from a dance, where I was with my sister, in Drochia. These dances were beautiful parties for the youth, with dancing, tombola, and other reasonably fun things. On that evening, I was even chosen the king of the ball. In the morning, at 4:00 am, we went back home. *Mama*, who worried about me, had not

---

[129] The Bolsheviks changed the name of the language from Romanian to Moldavian.

been sleeping the entire night.

The moment I entered into the house, I heard people running in the courtyard. I wanted to go out to see what happened. The door opened abruptly, and I heard a terrible yell in Russian: "Hands up!" Before I could realize what was happening, they turned me with my face to the wall, raised my hands, and hit me in the neck so badly that I had blood coming from my nose. Then they put me on the floor, commanding me to not move and not yell. *Mama* began shouting:

"Thieves! Thieves!"

I shouted back to her:

"*Mama*, these are not thieves; they arrest people!"

They shoved mom immediately and began to search the house.

They took every little piece of paper with writing on it, books in Romanian, pictures, everything that they thought would serve them. But they looked especially for weapons. When they saw that they could not find anything, they brought the hammer from the car and broke the oven, the hob, and a part of the stove to see whether there was any weapon hidden there. They created a real hell: they were covered with ash and soot, and we were covered as well... When they finished their search, the sun was already up. They took me in the truck, in handcuffs, and they tied me to a chain in the car.

In the meantime, the village heard that Vanea the son of Zenovia, the grandson of father Pintilie Oloinicu, was arrested. In the middle of the crowd that came there, I saw *bunelul*, and I thought then that he looked so much like the priest in the cellar. When the car's engine began to rumble, *mama* rushed toward the gate, raised her hands to the sky, and fell on her knees. I barely had the time to shout:

"*Mama*!... *Tătuca*!..."

Someone covered my mouth immediately, and we left. Flanked by two soldiers with automatic riffles, I went like this, with the truck open, to Chişinău. With the car speeding by, I said my goodbyes to every village, and each time I felt as if something broke in my heart. Surrounded in a dusty haze, my mom, sister, grandparents, and the entire village had come to accompany me. I kept them in my heart as an icon, as some saints, everywhere I was taken by the waves of life.

"The gate of hell" - 104 Livezilor[130]

In Chişinău, they took me out and pushed me into the KGB building, at 104 Livezilor. The first preparation of my file as a detainee began in a cold room, with thick iron bars at the window. I was naked like Adam, and they took all the markings on my body, checked my mouth and my behind, to make sure I would not have any explosive, they took pictures of me, from the front and profile, and they gave me clothes to put on. When all this ritual of taking me in had ended, the one who brought me there received a receipt that I was delivered to the investigators.

I was taken into a cell - better said, I was thrown into a cell - and the door was slammed behind me. It was a wooden door with metal on it, with a peephole for surveillance and a small window through which you could get a tin or a can. I studied in detail every corner of the room. It was two by three meters. At its end, there was a small, latticed window and a lightbulb well protected by bars. During the day, a little light could get through there. The walls were grey, and there were holes in them, a sign that someone was executed there. Next to the door, in the corner, there was a big wooden bucket, with a cover on top and some chlorine for disinfection. There was no bed; they gave me one only on the second day. I sat on that bucket for a while, but then I was taken by sleep, so I fell asleep on the cement. I slept on the floor the entire night, turning from one side to the other. Whenever I got stiff on one side, I stood up, rubbing that side, and went back to sleep on the other side. I actually had no real sleep!

For three-four days, or even for a week, they did not call me in for interrogation. By then, I was peaceful. I was afraid when they came to arrest me, but after the arrest I became peaceful, because I understood that this was my cross and that I had to bear it. It was supposed to be this way and not another

---

[130] This was the address of the KGB building in Chişinău.

way. I waited for the death sentence. So they left me alone for three-four days, while I started to become acquainted with the first tortures of prison: hunger and lack of sleep.

The feeding regime of prisoners was a can of warm water, nine grams of sugar with three little fish, plus 450 grams of rye bread, that you needed to administer for the entire day. I was healthy and vigorous, so I ate the bread in one-two minutes. Then, the rest of the day, I licked my elbows,[131] as we say, if I could reach them. Sometimes, I also received some pigwash, and that was it. As for sleep, after they gave me a bed - that is, a wood board with an unctuous mattress filled with straws - they told me that I was not allowed to sleep before bedtime. At the age I had, the desire to sleep was terrible, so a great period of torment followed. There were moments when I slept standing, and after each moment of sleep I felt that it was easier on my soul. The desire to sleep and the permanent hunger began to grind at my being…

After they kept me this way for a few days, I was taken into to be interrogated, in a small office, with thick iron bars at the window. I was ordered to sit on the chair, and the investigator began to ask me questions in Russian. He asked me if I needed a translator, and I told him that I did not, that I understood everything he was asking me. He asked me in Russian, and I, being obstinate, replied in Romanian.

The investigator got angry:

"You said you did not need a translator!"

I told him:

"Just consider it: who needs a translator between the two of us? I understand what you ask me, but apparently you do not understand what I reply!"

I was very stubborn, as I have already said!

"Why don't you answer in Russian?" he asked me again.

"Because it is easier for me to talk in the language of my ancestors. I am ready to endure even the pain of death in our language!"

---

[131] The Romanian expression "a linge coatele" implies that one has nothing to eat.

Eventually he had no choice and he called the translator. He asked me in Russian, I answered in Romanian, and the translator translated my answer. This is how we struggled during the entire interrogation. I did the same thing at the trial: I did not want to speak in Russian.

The interrogations at Livezilor Street took place only during night. First, the lights went out and you had to go to sleep according to the rules, with your head toward the small window and facing the door, so that they could more easily watch you. When they thought that you fell asleep, they opened the door of the cell, shook you, and yelled: "To the interrogation!" The most common interrogations began with an electrical bulb. They fixed a powerful lightbulb on your face, half a meter away from your face, they asked you the question, and you had to give the answer. The interrogator repeated always, rhythmically, in Russian:

"Speak! Speak! Speak!"

It may have been that this method had a psychological influence on the one interrogated, breaking his will.

You had to be watchful like a beast, careful with everything you said. It was best to endure it and be quiet, because silence is always golden.

This torture with the bulb was excruciating; it burned your head and your entire face, and your eyes would redden terribly. Two butchers held you on the chair, with your face toward the bulb, until you lost conscience and fell down. When you fell, they threw water on you, and when they saw that they could not get anything else from you, you were dragged back to the cell.

I did not say anything at the beginning. I was silent, and I pondered what answer to give so that they would not catch me with something. I was worried that I would destroy our movement because I did not know that the entire organization had been arrested. I thought that I was the only one arrested, and I was very afraid that I might betray someone. I was wondering whether that young man who had given us the archers' "Creed" might have been an instigator. I found out only later that they had arrested him as well and had condemned him to 25 years.

So I was silent, and when I could no longer take it, I turned my head. At times, such an interrogation took hours, as long as my body could resist. Then, I fell down, they threw water on me, but I was no longer good for anything. I could not speak, and I could not even walk. Then they dragged me as if I was a rag, and they hit me there on the cement, in the cell.

After the interrogations with the bulb, the beatings followed: beatings with kicks and punches, hitting me wherever they could. The most terrible interrogation took place when I cracked my skull. I still have that scar. There was a special team from NKVD, the so-called team of Silayev. There were four-five total, and they broke the prisoners who would not give in during the interrogations by torturing them, as a last resort, with the door. They put their fingers in the door's hinge, and they tightened it until they crushed their fingers.

First, they took me to interrogations like usual. The main thing they wanted to find out was what connections I had with the people across the border. They thought that I was too young to organize an anti-Bolshevik movement and that someone older, from outside the country, must have organized it.

When they saw that they could not obtain the desired answer, they put my hand in the door and tightened it. When they loosened it a bit, only to tighten it again stronger, I pulled away with the rage of a wild beast, I tripped because I stumbled over the leg of an interrogator, and I hit my head on the table's corner. The blood gushed out, darkness overtook me, and I no longer felt anything.

I woke up the second day in the cell, with my head bandaged and the fingers from my left hand purple and swollen badly. My covers, shirt, and coat were covered with blood. I tried to get up, but the entire cell began to spin. Slowly, my mind seemed to clear. I began to think of the people at home, my poor mother, my *bunelul*, my *bunica* Alexandra... I soon realized that it was only a beautiful dream, and I was beaten badly and locked in the cell, just to be taken out to the interrogations again. I then understood that only the Almighty God could save me from the claws of Satan. I prayed an "Our Father" prayer in my mind, and I asked Him to protect me from the butchers' hands. A guard and a woman in a white robe came to the cell. She washed my wound with some liquid that burned terribly. After they left, I tried to eat, but my jaws did not obey me. I crouched again and I covered myself with a blanket. I was thinking that they would torture me again until I would give them the answer they wanted, and if not, they would kill me.

The worst thing was that doubt began to sneak into my mind, the thought that I might have made a mistake when I organized the "Sword of Justice." I began to remember all the events that aroused in me the rebellion against the regime: *mama* was menaced by the activists with a trial because she had hidden the last small barrel with wheat; my cousins were beaten in the night by Kashirin; *bunicul* Pintilie was a fugitive from the home he built himself... I remembered the train with deported people in the train station in Târnova, full of the most industrious people from the village and with Lealea, the first girl with whom I fell in love... I then heard a voice inside of me that told me outright: Never doubt yourself again! After I made this confession by myself, in that cell, my soul was a bit relieved. For a whole week, they no longer took me to the interrogations, they gave me a better portion of food because I was sick, and they allowed me to sleep.

They seemed to have put all the other members of the organization through the same torture, through Silayev's "factory." After they got what they could from each one of us, they decided to confront us. They brought us together two by two, confronted us, and began the classical interrogation: "Do you know him? Have you worked together? Where did you organize your meetings?..." The order of the interrogation was repeated with each one of us. They first confronted me with Vasile Țurcanu. He was limping from one leg, and he had a bruise on his left eye that covered half of his cheek. The moment he saw me, he started shouting:

"Treason, Ioane, they betrayed us!"

They hit him immediately in his back, and he fell. They threw water on him and put him on the chair. When he regained consciousness, he whispered again, as to himself, "Treason, treason..."

They asked him first:

"Do you know him?"

"I do."

"What role did he have?"

"He was the captain of the organization."

Then they asked me:

"Do you know him?"

"I do."

"What role did he have?"

"Deputy-captain."

The interrogations continued in this way, according to the same structure, with all the members of the organization face to face, from the first to the last. They had the list by now and knew everything, for those two, Guțanu and Țăpușă had betrayed us.

I met Guțanu again after many years, after I was liberated. He taught music in the same school with me. I did not tell him anything; I only looked at him with disdain, from head to toe. He never asked for forgiveness. He was terribly afraid of me, like someone running from fire, and he always avoided me. He had a tragic death. He had a stroke, remained paralyzed for three years, and then he died. His judge was the Almighty One, not me. The other one, Țăpușă, died before I returned from the concentration camp. The interrogations at Livezilor Street took half a year, from May to November 1950. Then, they handcuffed us, threw us in a black car, and took us to trial, the Supreme Court of the Moldavian Socialist Republic. They put us before three judges who had our files from the investigations, files that have been studied and annotated. The first thing they asked us was to accept the lawyer they assigned to us. The eldest in the group accepted, but we, the three younger ones in the group, Vasile, Petrică, and I categorically refused.

"Why do you refuse a lawyer, young man?" the judge asked.

I answered:

"Give me, please, one lawyer from the Soviet Union, from all of the Soviet Union who could defend an 'enemy of the people'! This is how you try me, as an 'enemy of the people.'

Which soviet lawyer with a sound mind would defend an 'enemy of the people'?"

He said to me:

"Well, you are feisty, aren't you? They did not arrest you for nothing!"

The trial began behind closed doors. There were only two witnesses and nobody else. When they saw us in the box for the accused, they did not dare look at us; they only looked down. They sensed the terrible drama in which they put us. It could have been a tragedy, but our luck was that the Soviet Union had to enter the International Organization of the Red Cross that year, and the United Nations imposed, as a condition, the abolition of the death penalty. They had repealed it right before our trial. Then, in 1953, they reintroduced it. So, luckily, none of us received a sentencing to capital punishment. We received, however, very long sentences.

When we heard that we escaped alive and that we would not be condemned to death, we, the young ones, jumped for joy, this is how happy we were! After they took us back to Livezilor, a medical committee came to check the three of us within half an hour, to see whether we lost our minds since we had jumped for joy when we received such terrible sentences! I was condemned to 25 years total: 10 years of hard labor in the concentration camps, 10 years of exile in the far north, and 5 years without civil rights. The punishment of exile to the far north was a hidden form of condemnation to death. If they took you in the tundra region and dropped you there on the snow, without an axe, without a knife, and without anything, how could you survive? You had to manage with your bare hands, to dig, to make yourself a burrow, if you could! There, in the tundra, the villages were not like in our parts, one after the other, but there were hundreds of kilometers between them. They would take prisoners to the fields, in between villages, and leave them there. Those who had this mission knew the exact coordinates and transmitted them to the centers of surveillance in the villages: "within that perimeter, at that latitude and that longitude, we dumped that prisoner, a very dangerous criminal." The centers would take over the surveillance, monitoring where each prisoner would move, how they survived, if they were alive or dead.... If a prisoner had endurance, will, strength, and help from God, the center took him in because they were interested in such people. However, 99% of the exiled no longer saw the light of day; they were consumed by beasts, the frost, and the general unfavorable conditions for life.

I found out about all this later, from the prisoners who had tried to escape. They went through the tundra for weeks and were caught and taken back to the concentration camps. There was even "folklore" about the concentration camps, which included these stories about the exiled, about the most spectacular escapes, and also poems or songs of all kinds. From this "folklore" I remember Goga's poem that we, the Romanians, often sang in the concentration camp:

Why did you take me from your side,
Why did you take me far from home?
Had I remained home with a plow,
Had I remained... but now I roam...

I think the exile in the tundra would have taken me too. Beyond the status of a political prisoner, I was also registered under article 33 as a "very dangerous criminal." However, I was lucky because of the so-called "melting of glaciers" during Khrushchev, when many files were retried. After retrial, they kept the 10 years of hard labor and canceled the 10 years of exile and the 5 years of civic degradation.

The Russian prisons

A few days after the trial, they began taking us to prisons.

The first destination was the central prison in Chișinău. We arrived there at sunset, it was drizzling. When we entered into the yard and they began to count us, there was a blackout in the entire area. Since they could not do the necessary formalities without electricity, the process of taking in the slaves was interrupted.

Soldiers with dogs seemed to emerge from the earth and surrounded us. For three or four hours, they kept us in the rain, with the weapons pointed at our faces, and we waited quietly, soaking wet, because we knew what awaited us if we tried to run. After the electricity came back, they took us in. It was the same ritual as on Livezilor Street: they undressed us completely and checked any markings on our bodies. They had to correspond to the ones from the investigation file. It was sufficient to have only one new sign, and you were immediately isolated and taken for interrogations: when did it appear, how, and why? The personal markings were very important, and they accompanied us during our entire detention, until they freed us.

We only remained in the Chişinău prison for twenty-four hours. They took us to the train station the second day and loaded us into the famous wagon *Stolâpin*, built specifically for prisoners. It had bunks on three levels, separated from the hallway with mobile iron bars. One bunk held ten prisoners; they were tightly glued to one another. In the hallway, the sentinels were patrolling, and there was a soldier with a dog at every end of the train car.

This is how we went to Odessa. At the Odessa prison, as in all Russian prisons, the *zeki* - the short name for prisoners - were put into two large categories: the common law criminals, and the political prisoners. In the first category were the thieves, people without any morals and without mercy, who made life in prison even more unbearable. The political detainees were those condemned on the basis of article 58, the so-called "enemies of the people." At the beginning, the political prisoners were differentiated according to their cultural level, studies, nationality, but over time, they were all homogenized, made to wear a uniform and became a hungry crowd. You could rarely see one who succeeded in bearing the dignity of a human being.

In the Odessa prison, the political detainees were mixed with the common criminals, and the latter made the rules according to an unwritten law they had. At the meal hour, *urka*, one from the thieves' nest took a portion from each prisoner for his band. Those who were faster and ate the meal before the *urka* came to them were beaten without mercy. One evening, the door of my cell opened, and six political prisoners came in. They were brought from Siberia to be interrogated. *Urka* came to them and asked them where they came from. One of them answered:

"It's none of your business, urchin? Get the hell out of here, you devil! I don't want to get my hands dirty with such dung!"

When he heard these words, another thief got up from the bunk and shouted:

"Why do you offend the boy, mutt? Filka, twist his neck!"

Filka raised his hand to hit him, but one of the six grabbed his hand suddenly, twisted it behind him, and threw him down. Then, all the new comers jumped on the thieves.

One of the thieves began shouting, knocking on the door by kicking it:

"Boss, open, the fascists[132] are murdering us!"

The door opened, and the guards rushed in:

"What's with this disorder?"

The people began shouting:

"These thieves terrorize us, they take our food!"

The guards ordered all the thieves to take their things and go out to the hallway. After their departure, we were all relieved.

This is how I saw the first brawl between prisoners.

Then, one evening, they told us that we would be leaving "in stages." You were never told where you were taken. They just loaded you in the train car. The conductor knew where the train was going - why did you need to know?

It was December, and everything was already frozen. We had to go from the prison to the train station in a column, two by two in handcuffs, on an icy, slippery road. The column moved slowly through the darkness, and our feet were slipping all over the place. The soldiers shouted furiously at us to move faster. At one point, a poor old man slipped and rolled a few times, taking with him the one to which he was tied. They were shot on the spot, and two dogs jumped on them and mangled them. They told all of us to lie down and counted us ten times with strong flashlights, while their dogs waited to jump on us. After they were convinced that only those two were missing,

---

[132] The Bolsheviks' propaganda was that all who opposed them were fascists.

they wrote a report stating that those two wanted to escape and were punished by death on the spot. This is how it was done: they wrote that capital punishment was applied, without a trial, because it was an attempt to escape, and the problem was solved.

Two soldiers remained with the two shot bodies, and they pushed us toward the train station, as if we were cattle. It was clearly only one stage, for the station was full of prisoners. They loaded us into the *Stolâpin* and, after an infernal voyage of two and a half days, with terrible frost, we arrived at the new destination: Moscow.

In Moscow, they separated us from the common criminals and took us to the prison named Krasnaia Presnea. This is where I met the Banderovists from Ukraine, with whom we had planned to get in contact with, to get weapons and ammunition when we started the "Sword of Justice." The Banderovists were Ukrainian nationalists who fought for the independence of their country. They took their name from Ostap Bandera, a history professor at the Lvov University, who defended the theory of Ukraine's independence and did not recognize the sale of 1654, when Bogdan Hmelnitzki sold it to the nobles in Russia. Later, Bandera ran from the Soviet Union and died, apparently in America.[133] The Banderovist movement began during the war, first against the Germans and then against the Bolsheviks. They were more instructed and more prepared than us. They also had great reserves of weapons, grenades...the only thing they didn't have were canons. They had very organized units. During the night, they would attack villages and robbed food stores or would come to the house of a rich kolkhoz president, fight with him, take all his food, and leave. They only took food, nothing else, and this is how they survived. In prison, they were very united and merciless with all Bolshevik elements. For example, in Krasnaia Presnea, in one of the rooms, they recognized one of their Ukrainian traitors, Nemii Noga, who whipped the children who gathered the grain ears left on the field during the

---

[133] Bandera died in Germany. Many thanks to David Dulceany for pointing it out.

famine. The moment they recognized him, they decided to punish him. The room was large, with 50 people, and the bucket used for relieving themselves was also large. They dragged him to it and told him:

"Kneel, you serpent, and confess! Speak, who ordered you to whip children for some grain that was rotting anyway? Those ears were mixed with the sweat and blood of mother Ukraine! This is how you built communism, villain?"

They grabbed him by his feet, put his head into the bucket, and threw him out. Then they hit him a few times and dunked him back into the bucket. The guards outside saved him. They saw what was happening and took him out of the cell.

After this, the Banderovists took care of another Bolshevik in the room, Zveriev, who had been the deputy of the Minister of Food. He regularly received from home packages with white bread, sausages, salamis, Dutch cheese, and luxury cigarettes, and he had a feast by himself, not giving a crumb to anyone. The Banderovists thought they should educate him. When the guards gave us the morning portion, they gathered from all of us some of those small fish, rusty from the metal buckets where they were kept. We were angry with them: we were hungry, and they took that little piece from us too! But we had no choice, power is power, and if you do not submit to it, it crushes you. Zveriev had just received the package from home and enjoyed a fine cigarette, taking the smoke deep into the chest. One of the Banderovists came to him and asked him:

"Give me one smoke too!"

As he was arrogantly smoking on the bunk on top, he answered:

"You'll smoke when your wife brings you a smoke!"

But the other one did not back down:

"I'll smoke right now!"

Immediately, the Banderovists came next to him, having the twenty rusty small fish on an aluminum plate:

"Come, get down here!"

They got him down by force and put the fish in front of him:

"Come, take them one by one and eat all of it, with the head, the guts, the tail, just like we eat!"

"Me?!"

He did not eat things like that…

"Eat if you want to live! If not, you will be executed on the spot, in the bucket!"

He ate all twenty fish.

"Now do what a Christian must do!"

He did not understand what a Christian must do because he was a Bolshevik.

"Give nicely to everyone from your food! Make as many portions as there are mouths in the room and share them with your own hand!"

This is how the Banderovists reeducated Zveriev!

We stayed in Moscow for two weeks, and then we left again in the next "stage." The new destination was the most terrible prison in the former Soviet Union: the Ruzaevka Prison on the Volga. The prisoners would run from it like from fire. The environment was terrible, draconic; you had the right to speak only in whispers or through making signs. When you made signs, your hands had to be in front, as close to your body as possible. Any deviation was punished with solitary confinement in a black and wet cell, where you only received a can of water and 300 grams of bread per day. This is where I had the occasion to eat camel meat for the first time, some kind of sinew with long threads, wrapped as if around a match.

It was said that many of the notable people of Russia were murdered there, in Ruzaevka. Even in our neighboring cell, at number 17, it was known that Vavilov, the greatest geneticist of the 20th century, had died tormented terribly.

We did not stay long at Ruzaevka either. After two weeks, we were loaded again in the train and taken in the "stage." This time, it was a cattle train arranged especially for prisoners. However, regardless of how arranged it was, it was not as secured as the *Stolâpin* wagon.

It was January 1951, on a terrible frost. I got to be on a bunk close to the toilet, in an infernal stench and a horrible cold. Next to me, there was a history professor from Ukraine. We were sleeping glued to each other, like canned mackerel. During the night, he woke up to go to the toilet, and he did not return for a long time. After a while, I felt that I was cold and the whole train car began to get colder. What had happened? The professor broke two-three wooden boards from behind the toilet, took out the bars from the window, and, taking advantage of the slowing down of the train, he escaped. Only the good God knows what his fate was, whether he stayed alive or they caught him!

We continued our voyage to the Chelyabinsk prison in the Ural Mountains, and from there, after a tiring trip of almost two weeks, we arrived in the steppe of Kazakhstan.

Karlag

There were hundreds of concentration camps for detainees in the steppe of Kazakhstan, grouped into a few bases: *Karlag, Steplag, Minlag*. They were to become later the great industrial centers of the Soviet Union: Karaganda, Ekibastuz, Djezkazgan. Each basis was some sort of a town endowed with the minimum necessary for the prisoners. There was also a military unity that was sufficiently armed for suppressing any revolt. All these military units communicated among them and were centralized in a general headquarters that was in direct connection with the Supreme Security Council in Moscow.

Seen from above, these towns with their thousands of lights probably seemed like a huge necklace of beads placed on the chest of the great soviet monster.

Our contingent of prisoners stopped in Karaganda, the main coalfield in Kazakhstan, where many coal mines were built. There, the mines came one after the other, uniform and gray, forming the so-called *Karlag*, the camp with a severe internal regime. A camp could have up to five thousand prisoners of all nationalities, the general language for communication being Russian. All around, there was only the steppe. You had nowhere to run, nowhere to hide. Then, they promised large sums of money to the natives for catching "the enemies of the people," so any escape was practically impossible. I was assigned to the Dubovka camp, first to the quarry, then to the coal mine's construction. We lived in some wooden long barracks, fifty over thirty meters, on bunks built on three levels.

It was terribly cold during winter. The temperature would reach as low as negative 45 degrees Celsius. When we worked for the mine's construction, our happiness was that we often fell upon coal, so that we could fully supply the two big iron stoves in our barrack. We put in them five, six, even ten shovels of coal, and we made an infernal heat inside. The stench was also stronger - a terrible stench, of the unwashed, of body odor.

The most difficult time was when the Buran blizzard started. This wind took the snow mixed with sand far away. This happened every two-three months. In those moments, a thick rope was extended from the barrack where we lived to the barrack where we received food, and we went in a line to get the meal, holding the rope under our arms and the hands tightly together; if the wind blew you, it would have taken you someplace and covered you with sand. When the Buran stopped, we were all taken out for cleaning, because it created great havoc all around.

Our work consisted in the construction of the coal mines, from the buildings on top, where the work in the ground was managed, to the tunnels, made for serving up the coal. This is how the mine was built: the geologist engineers indicated the depth of the coal layers, which could be two, three, or even four in number. The tunnels were built mandatorily beneath these layers, so that the coal could free fall into the trolleys that circulated in the tunnels. A mini electrical engine pulled these trolleys, and they took the coal to the pit for construction materials, from where trucks would take it. At the beginning, we dislocated more barren rock than coal, and the rock piled up on the surface in a huge mound that became, over time, like a true Egyptian pyramid. Since that stone was contaminated with much marsh gas and mixed with enough coal, this pyramid would burn day and night, like an oddity.

It was fine as long as we worked on soft rock, but it was much harder when we hit hard rock, and our strength weakened because of the small portions of food we received. We had a daily norm: a certain number of cubic meters of rock had to be drilled, loaded, and taken up to the surface. If you wanted to eat, to survive, you worked frantically to accomplish it. If you were indifferent to life, then you would be content with the simple portion from the camp, 450 grams of bread, and you would then later become dystrophic and shortly die.

People worked in three eight-hour shifts. The rest of the time, when you were not working, you would have to manage your things: you washed laundry, you sewed... Whoever had a needle for sewing was considered a rich man. Whoever did not have one, managed however he could. Also, all the camps were endowed with rich libraries. You could find all of classical literature there. You could also find scientific literature, which went through the soviet purgatory, of course, so that it could correspond to atheist education. Whoever could memorize things was lucky in that camp! I learned Pushkin and Lermontov by heart, but especially Esenin, with whom I was in love. I did not have any Romanian writers and poets, absolutely no one. I only had what I wrote in a notebook, some of our poems that I still remembered.

They made this literature available for us because they wanted to reeducate us. However, this helped me in a different sense. First of all, it helped me to train my memory all those years. Second, I accumulated so much knowledge: about what had been written, how it had been written, and many other things.

I had the great joy of procuring Shakespeare while I was in the camp. I gave away the costume I had had from before, when I was still free, for a half liter of *țuica*,[134] and then I got for that *țuica* a volume of Shakespeare with six comedies and six tragedies. It was worth ten costumes, not one! I slept with it under my head and learned by heart all the words of the characters.

When I received it, the prisoner who brought it to me said:

"May God protect you and the book, and may it be that you both get back to your Moldova!"

That was exactly what happened. After liberation, I returned to Bessarabia with the book in my bag.

---

[134] *Țuica* is a traditional alcoholic beverage in Romania usually made from plums, something similar to brandy.

My dear măicuță[135]

During that time, we were allowed to write two letters per year, and even those on only one page of a notebook. The text had to be stereotypical: I am healthy, I am well, I have everything I need... Those letters went first through the censorship of the administration, and from there, the majority went to the trash, from the trash to the chimney, and from the chimney up into the atmosphere...

Luckily, we did not work in isolation, but we had connections with free people through the drivers who transported the construction materials in the camp. If you knew how to manage it, you could befriend one of the drivers, put something in his hand, and if he had a good heart, he would send your clandestine letter, which did arrive home.

This is how I was able to write to my mother, to whom I thought I was most guilty. She did not even know why they arrested me. She only knew that I could not make peace with the wrongdoings the foreigners had brought upon us. I remembered how those beasts beat her when they took me from home and how she remained in the middle of the road, on her knees, yelling behind the car that was taking me. I don't know how, but I felt like writing to her in lyric form, about that tragic moment of our separation:

I left you, dear mother... You, grieving by the window,
You watched alone, in pain, the dirty, weedy road.
So often did I walk on it from school - your eyes would follow-
When I was small and joyful, quite ready to explode.
Your mind now wonders; it asks me where I am; straying thoughts
Bring back my childhood's image and take me home, my place...
A scalding, heavy tear connects so many dots
And from your eyelash washes your humble, painful face.

---

[135] This is the diminutive of *mama*.

Your years flow without a question,
Snow slowly covers all your hair.
Your waiting at the door is my only beacon.
For you, to see me once again - your only prayer.

At the end, I added a few phrases that made it seem like I were on the verge of bursting out crying:

My mama, my dear holy măicuță, forgive me for all the pain that I brought upon you, but especially forgive me because I was not able to defend you from the rooks that rushed on us! I do not want to lie to you that I am well and healthy. I can tell you that I am alive and that I fight for reaching the day when I can come to fall on my knees and ask you for forgiveness for all the pain that I caused you. Do not be sad, mama; there are millions like me in this devilish and crazy country, and someone must raise the Sword of Justice sometime and tell them that they are not all powerful in this world, with all the cannons and tanks that they have. Almighty is only the One in the heavens...

I wrote then some lines for *bunelul* and *bunica*, and I folded the letter praying that it would escape the vigilant eye of the party and that it would reach the loved ones at home. Then I also wrote a "standard" letter, through the administration, so that I would be covered if I received an answer.

Weeks had passed. It was toward the end of January, and one evening the entire brigade, weary and weak, waited breathlessly to hear the announcement whether we would have a day of rest on Sunday or not. When we came out of the shift, the brigadier, Ghünter Antonovich, looked at all of us with sadness in his eyes and, after a short break, said as if for himself something in German: *Arbaiten und arbaiten!* Understanding that we would not be able to use the seventh day of the week the way God left it for our parents and grandparents, each one of us retired to his lair, covered in sweat and dust after six days of tiring work...

On Sunday morning, a terrible frost came over the camp. It stung our noses and our ears, and it reached our bones through our rags. I took all the clothes I had, hoping that I could bear it.

The roundup was difficult. Everything seemed as if it were against the order left by the One above. The column and the dogs were more agitated than ever. The beasts barked without ceasing the entire trip to the quarry, as if someone sicced them on us.

The quarry was quite deep. During the summer, it was warm and stuffy on the bottom, and the air was not sufficient; during winter, it was unbelievably cold. The icy cold stones became hostile, and there was no way to sit on one of them; thus, you were forced to move almost the entire time, so you would not freeze. Time would flow so slowly that I had the impression that the sand in the hourglass stood still. The cold was taking hold of us more and more. We felt a drowsiness that pulled us to sleep.

The silence was sliced by the howl of a beast, which made the others bark again and be agitated. We looked around confused, not understanding what was happening. The soldiers on the sides of the quarry became more watchful and took their weapons from their shoulders.

The wind above the quarry began to move, and we heard whistling coming from far away. It began to snow, and the wind was stronger every minute. We did not even realize when the *Buran* began to unleash its fury. It was a continual roaring, as if all the beasts of the entire Gulag of the "Red Monster" were howling. The snowflakes began to mix with the sand, and they hit our faces mercilessly and entered through all the openings on our clothes, at the collar or through the sleeves. If you did not move, you were surrounded immediately by a small hill that grew fast around you. The plague was unleashed with an anger I had never seen before. I had the impression that the entire satanic cohort was dancing in the air and rushed down on us.

Visibility was becoming more and more reduced. We finished the work, but we remained stunned for some time, not knowing what to do. Any wrong move could make you fall down, and you would immediately become prey to the satanic plague. Staying in one spot was not helpful either. Slowly, we began getting closer to one another and embracing each other as in a fellowship. Finally, the gray mass made out of *zeki* stuck together became a unit, in which hope for life still palpitated. The *semantron* sounded without stopping, commanding us to leave the quarry and to go toward the exit, but no one could hear it. The violation of the rule could also bring upon us another plague: the bullets of the brave lads of the "Red Monster" could rush down on us without any mercy. In that state of stiffness, some of the guards came toward us without weapons and began calling us to move toward the exit, holding unto one another. It was for the first time that I heard them having a human voice, speaking with some compassion...

With huge difficulty, rather crawling than walking, we arrived at the exit, where they began counting us in an unusual way, taking us one by one in a hurry. When the last one crossed the door, they were relieved because none of us had escaped. They commanded us to start going to the camp without menacing us with their guns.

Nature seemed to calm down for a few moments, only to rush down on us again. However, we felt as if we were safer, and our poor hope grew in us, after we only had just a bit of hope, like a grain of mustard, when we were on the bottom of the quarry. The dogs were all around us, our daily convoy. How much happiness it is to know that you are valued once again, carefully protected!

The column moved slowly, as a funeral convoy. The shouting of "*shag v pravo, shag v levo!*"[136] were no longer heard. The convoy, the dogs, and the *zeki* crawled with difficulty, and people continually wiped the sand out of their eyes.

Once we were out of the quarry, we were all taken into the arms of the empty and hostile steppe. There is a huge difference between facing the *Buran* with sheepskin and felts and doing so dressed with our rags! The sand mixed with snow entered through all possible and impossible places, lashing us with cruelty. At one moment, the storm became even stronger and

---

[136] "A step to the left, a step to the right," in Russian in original. The expression is used for marching, as when all the people in a convoy have to have the same rhythm: left, right, left, right.

blew all of us together in a pile, one next to the other. We woke up next to the convoy and the dogs, all mixed together. No one realized this was happening; the dogs no longer showed their teeth, but only yelped, their tails between their legs. We stayed one next to the other, trying to protect ourselves, however we could, from the merciless bursts of the *Buran*…

We were one and the same![137] It is hard to say how long this miraculous state lasted, but one thing is certain: after any Apocalypse, "the lion eats hay with the lamb from the same place."[138]

After a difficult road that squeezed from us any bit of energy that could still be squeezed, we could glimpse the silhouette of the camp, as if through haze. Vasilie, next to whom I stayed the entire time, was ironic:

"Vania, we can glimpse our 'parents' home'!"

(After a while, for us everything had become *"rodnoi,"* parental: dog, convoy, camp, Gulag, SSSR…)

Indeed, we sensed immediately that we were close to the camp. The convoy leader yelled with a severe voice:

"Convoy! Observe the distance!"

The dogs immediately sensed the *zek* odor and began barking and baring their teeth; the camp opened the gates after a thorough counting and took in its "offspring," *vraghi naroda*![139]

The trip to the quarry and back took us almost half of the day, so we did not get to our lair, but we were aligned and taken to lunch. There was no sense in using my spoon for the soup, because there was nothing to fish in it. It was hot, so I took the tin and drank out of it; it seemed like it did not even stop in my stomach. A mush made out of some sort of mixture followed. It was something more consistent, and it was good enough to stay in my stomach. Since thoughts start from the belly many times, I thought: it would be so good if I could jump into a heated oven, to burn there alive, but to have some heat at least for a

---

[137] In Romanian, "o apa si-un pamânt," an expression showing the lack of difference. Word by word, it is translated with "one water and one land."

[138] See Isaiah 11:6.

[139] "The enemies of the people," in Russian in original.

second! I cleaned the tin with a piece of bread and, warmed by the parental mercy of the "dear party," I ran all the way to my lair in the barrack.

In the place where I usually put my head while sleeping (I did not have a pillow), I saw a letter that Jozeh, the barrack leader, left there. In the blink of an eye, jumping like a feline, I was at the third level of the bunk. My joy was beyond me: it was a letter from *mama*. It seemed that there was more light in the entire barrack, because it felt as if *mama* together with my entire village, Slănina, were there with me. When I was a student in the second grade and the teacher asked me where the capital of Romania was, I replied without doubting that it was the village of Slănina. Thus, when I was up in my lair, *Mama* and my Country waited for me to help me in bearing my punishment.

Silent and patient as always, *mama* had dropped a few tears on the notebook paper where she had spread her lament:

Dear Vania,

Mama's naughty and unruly boy, you must be a lad as strong as a pine tree. We have received your letter, and it was a great joy to find out that you are alive. Poor dad cannot find his place since they took you, and he mentions you at every step...

From the other few lines that followed, I found out that she had decided to bear anything, and that she would not enter into the kolkhoz. Her decision was final and irrevocable to her last breath, so the brave "dear party" had taken care to make a furrow with the plow so that they could not touch the osiers from the valley. Only a mother like this could have brought on earth an enemy of the Party! Thus, the *Sovrom* had swallowed also our poverty from the osiers, and *Mama*, the Capital, and the Country suffered the breath of the Red Monster together with me!

Under what *mama* wrote, Andruska had added a few lines:

We received a letter from the lads in Altai. They told me many things about their lives. You cringe! They wrote me that the girl you had loved became a wife out of need. You should be at peace with this. From what I understood, life there is the same as where you are. Then, you know that Lealea is not someone to be left at the margins of the road! But God is great!

Andrushka.

After I read these final lines, a terrible despair took me. Everything I held dear on this earth was now subjected to ridicule, and I could do nothing about it. Right at that moment, Leandr Aleksandrovich came toward me. He was a Polish Jew, doctor of science, and he was like a father to me during all the years in the concentration camp. He saw the letter and understood that the news from home was not too good. He caressed me paternally and told me:

"Vanea, you must learn to have patience! The path of the cross for us is still long, and no one knows where its end will be. I am certain of one thing only: no one is eternal on this earth..."

I dragged myself toward my barrack, feeling my legs heavy as led. On that evening, I read and reread the letter many times. I turned from one side to the other a thousand times, without falling asleep. Eventually, my thought dwelled on *bunelul*, and I finally fell asleep. In a dream, or I do not know how, one letter came to me, and I wrote it on paper the following day, so that I would not forget it:

Letter to bunicul

What can I write you, dear grandpa,
With your beard greyed by time,
What can I write you, dear old man,
When the world is filled with crime...
Thousands of people just like me have
Written of the good, of the bad
But like in a dream, they left, passed on,
Their egos buried in the sand.
Should I write how in these parts
The wilderness is spread?
Or should I tell of how man sells man,
How many hearts have bled?

Why should you know the pain we have
When in a column taken,
Why would you know the dust from roads
Or work that is forsaken?
I left you at the brook, by poplars,
When the weather sewed its shiny clothes,
And when the silver drops of dew
Awoke the petals for the shows.
I left to wander in the world
To look for justice and for law,
But slow, I drown in foamy waves,
Drinking this world's poisoned flaw.
You're very old by now and wish
To see me on your threshold,
How I would bring a cart with hay,
To feed the calf in winter's cold.
You thought that in your old age
We would all be around you,
But the times have separated us
And gave us rivers of tears, too.
When the archangels sing to you
To go to them, in painless worlds,
I pray to all with a great zeal
To let you live and still have strength.
I would not want you to bring news
From our cursed earth,
To break their eternal peace
By telling them of our dirt!

"The wake"

In Dubovka, our work in the mine was extremely dangerous. We worked at 280 meters beneath the ground, dislodging the rock in order to build the galleries for extraction. We broke the layer of rock with drills and jackhammers, loaded everything in trolleys to be taken to the surface, and dug trenches for the water drainage. Then, another team came after ~d placed props and formwork boards, poured concrete, and the gallery was ready for extraction.

After two or three weeks, we had reached a layer of soft rock and we were advancing fast with the dislodging. The concrete finishers who consolidated the galleries had not finished their work, so they remained far behind.

The day of the accident, our team descended to work in the first shift, as usual. We checked the wooden poles for consolidation, to see whether they were cracked, and we began working. There were nine of us total: three with drills, three with jackhammers, I loaded the rock in the trolley with a mechanic scoop, and two others gathered the rock together, so that it would be easier to pick it up. It was like being in hell; it was a place full of an infernal noise, dust, and sweat.

At one moment, the poles could no longer withstand the pressure, the rock crashed, and the reinforcement collapsed. Our luck was that we were working on a layer of hard rock, on which we had pained for some days. The ceiling above us did not collapse, but we were trapped. We all gathered around Lukshtash, the team chief, who was a prisoner from Lithuania. We all thought how excruciating our end would be, and we did not utter one word. After a while, we heard Lukshtash's trembling voice:

"Brothers, even if we are swallowed by the earth, our hope is still with our Good God. If you want to resist, do what I tell you. Each one of you must bring your battery and your *tormozok* here!"

The battery was a kind of lantern fixed on your working helmet. It worked for eight hours, the length of a shift in the mine. The collapse interrupted the natural flow of time and we could no longer calculate it. Lukshtash thought that we should keep track of the passing of the hours with these lanterns that could function by turn. As for the *tormozok*, this was a supplementary portion, with two small cubes of sugar and a piece of bread or, sometimes, a few dry small fish that we received when we descended into the mine, to have extra strength for work. The *tormozok* translates to "taking a break," which means that we would stop a little from work to eat. But we did not stop from work because we had to complete the plan! We ate with one hand, we worked with another, and we swallowed everything like this, without chewing it.

Lukshtash took the *tormozok*, divided it in portions, and after every eight hours, when a battery ran out, he gave each of us a small portion, so that we would prolong our lives.

"The tomb" in which we were buried alive was ten meters long, eight meters wide, and around three meters high. If air wouldn't have been coming in through the cracks in the walls, we would have suffocated immediately, but even so the quantity of oxygen was limited. The weight of the landslide had pressed on the cracks in the floor, and the water that had seeped through the walls had no place to go. We got up on some big rocks and waited for the water to take our souls. We no longer had any hope for survival; we had finished our food, we had finished everything, our strength was completely exhausted, and we began to dehydrate. The youngest one of us, Andreiko, began to be delirious, whispering, "Oledia, I love you!"

I looked at that lantern that was still lit, and I thought it was a candle that burned for our memory. All nine of us were witnesses to our own wake for our burial, and we waited to see what the end was like.

I realized at that moment that my thoughts were the only things that I still had; since thoughts are in spirit, any prison in the world could not handcuff them. I became somewhat peaceful, and I did not fear death. As any man who lives his last moments, I only felt the need to ask all my dear ones to forgive me, especially *mama*, to whom I had caused the greatest pain. I could hear how she reproached me: "You see, mama's dear, look what happened to you because you were restless?"... Then I heard *bunelul* reprimanding her: "Daughter, pray to God, because if he had more days to live, then he would escape all torments!"... I also felt the strong need to ask my country for forgiveness because I had succeeded only to do so little for it.

Then I remembered the most beautiful moment of my life: Lealea giving me a card on my birthday, where she had weaved my birth date with her hair. It seemed I could hear her telling me with her warm voice: "Let me stay next to you for at least a few moments..."

I then began yelling with all my might:

"Nooo! Nooo! I do not want you to die here too!"

The others were scared, thinking that I also began to be delirious. Someone began reciting a poem from Shevchenko, in tears, and no one dared to interrupt him. Then, silence fell upon us again.

The weather was becoming warmer and warmer. The level of water increased, and the volume of air was diminishing. Then, without even realizing, I began praying, saying, "Lord, have mercy! You cannot be so cruel to let us drown in our own tears! Lord, Master of heaven and earth, forgive us, sinners, our trespasses, cleanse our minds and souls, and give light to the path that leads to You!"

In the meantime, the fifth lantern was changed. Life melted in us slowly, imperceptibly. Petrică, a Moldavian from Transnistria, who had not ceased telling us during all this time that we would escape, said again:

"We'll escape! We'll escape for sure! The entire *Karlag* is now searching for us!"

"Are these measured words, or are you just throwing them out like this, into the wind?" Misha Diakon asked him. "Be careful, because there is no wind here to take them away!"

"No, I pondered well! Think about it! We will escape for sure! It's not only the whole camp that is looking for us, but rather the entire Soviet Union. Not because they need us - they don't need us because they will bring hundreds in our place. They need this central artery, so that the mine can advance. This mine is strategic for them because it creates the energetic basis of the Soviet Union. This thought is my safety belt, and my soul clings unto it!"

The lad thought well. When we no longer had any hope to be saved and were already waiting to die, we heard some hammers knocking in the wall. We immediately put our ears to the rock! There were again some knocks. It was a great joy, and we seemed to regain some life. We lit the sixth lantern and waited. It took eight more hours until they reached us. They made a big breach, and the first one in was the brigadier Kostas, asking:

"Is there anyone alive?"

He saw Lukshtash first and took him in his arms, since they were both Lithuanians, and they began crying. We also began crying and shouting at that moment, urging one another with our last forces toward the saving breach.

When we came out, platform-trolleys with sheets waited for us. They loaded us and took us to the section with compressors, where it was warm. They took off our clothes and rubbed us all over with alcohol mixed with cider. Then they checked again any distinct markings on our bodies matching them to the record, to be sure that, even there under the earth, we did not make an exchange of prisoners with the Americans. Then, they gave us some dry rags to get dressed in and two small cubes of sugar to manage until morning. Then they sent us to the camp, where we were hospitalized at the infirmary.

They kept us there for a week so we could regain some strength, and we were called in to be interrogated with the hope that we would "confess" which one of us organized the "sabotage" against the "great soviet construction"! We answered that none of the nine souls buried alive could have thought to sabotage "the great construction" risking his own life! Further, Misha Diakon and Andreiko dared to show the investigators the true cause of the collapse. They told them how the administrators chose the best pillars and took them out for their personal use, and sent down only the rotten pillars, which could not hold the earth. Seeing that they could not obtain anything from us, they tried to convince us to go back into the mine because preparing another team took time, and time was money. However, we refused categorically, especially when we found out that five concrete finishers who followed us with the consolidations had been crushed on the spot by the earth falling on them at that moment. We had seen death with our eyes once, we felt like we had participated in our own wake, and we had had enough! Because we refused to work where the camp administration sent us, we were punished with one month at the BUR (*barak usilennogo rejima*), a sort of prison-barrack with very strict and harsh regulations. Then they dispersed us to various other concentration camps.

Ekibastuz

I was sent to Ekibastuz, to an open area for coal extraction. I was assigned to the second brigade of constructions. The chief was a man of a rare goodness, Avdeev, the son of a White general. [140] After the Bolshevik revolution, the general had emigrated with his entire family to China, but his son, loving his country, decided to return. The Bolsheviks arrested him on the spot and gave him ten years of hard work for spying. This Avdeev was a man of great character, and one could see he had good knowledge of construction.

It was in the Ekibastuz camp that I met Pimen Damaşcan, the young man who had told us about the Archers of Stephen the Great when we were still high school students. The moment he saw me, he embraced me and said:

"You became a real man, Ionele! I am sorry you ended up here too, and I feel guilty about it..."

I appeased him telling him that I would have ended up in the camp even if we did not meet because I would have followed the same path. Then I asked him to tell me how he had ended up in Ekibastuz.

He told me that he had worked for one year at the copper mine in Djezkazgan, where they forged on dry land. People died there like flies. Every month, a new group of fresh forces came in, and small groups of sick people, the majority of them crippled, left. After one year, he could no longer manage it. The dust made him cough for ten-fifteen minutes without stopping. They diagnosed him with silicosis and sent him to the hospital-camp in Spask. The doctor there, a German prisoner, treated him well, and after a while they sent him to the quarry. Because of the dust, the disease returned, and he was sent to work as a locksmith, his specialty, after the German doctor insisted on it. As he knew German very well, Pimen managed superbly because the majority of the machines were German. He even repaired the personal cars of the camp administrators. One day, the chief of the camp came to him together with two civilians,

---

[140] The Whites were the forces that opposed the Red Bolsheviks during the revolution of 1917.

gave him a drawing in German, and asked him to explain it. There, in the camps, the Russians had a lot of German technology, which they captured during the war, but this technology had to be put together, directed, repaired, and maintained, and their civilians did not know German. Pimen could read those drawings very well. This is how they took him in as a mechanical specialist on the Ekibastuz site.

The death of the "Father"

During the first days of March 1953, the conditions in the camps suddenly got worse. Every barrack was controlled in the morning and in the evening, there were guns on the watchtowers, and guards patrolled the area with dogs all the time.

At the beginning, I thought that they had discovered an escape plan and that was the reason they had increased the security. Then, I saw that the portrait of the great "Father of all peoples,"[141] which was usually hung on the garrison's building, had a black ribbon on top. The reactions were varied. Some could not believe it because they thought he was immortal; others naively rejoiced, thinking that they would be liberated. The most explosive were the Banderovists, who immediately got together in groups, shouting and singing. On that evening, bedtime was set early, so that they could disperse us and lock us in barracks. In the morning, all the three thousand prisoners were taken outside and arranged in columns. Surrounded by guards, Tatarin, the chief of the camp, stood before us on an elevated platform. With a solemn voice, he announced to us:

"Citizen prisoners! I am authorized to tell you some news that saddened profoundly the working class of the entire world! These past days, the heart of the father of all peoples, Joseph Vissarionovich Stalin, ceased pulsing!"

At that moment, something completely unexpected happened. From the weak chests of all the humbled and hungered prisoners, cheers of joy broke out. People threw their hats in the air and shouted as strongly as they could. The

---

[141] The author refers to Stalin.

soldiers standing on watching towers awaited the commands of their superiors with their fingers on the triggers. Only God protected us from the bloodshed that could have happened. After the roar diminished a little, Tatarin warned us, gnashing his teeth:

"I am telling you that we will punish cruelly any deviation from the rule during these days of great pain for the proletariat!"

With this, our convocation finished. The prisoners went back to their usual program, but the rumors, discussions, and presuppositions began to stir everyone's mind. Each one of us expressed his opinion about the possible changes; we dreamt, whether we confessed it or not, of emancipation.

Aleksandr Isayevich Solzhenitsyn

One of the days that followed, the electricity was shut off on the yard where we worked. The blackouts were our joy! We ran immediately to the foundry, where people worked with metals at high temperature, and we could warm our frozen bodies a little. At the foundry there was someone who had come recently, transferred from a brigade in construction.

He was a tall, thin man with a long face, a pointy beard, and a pair of piercing, black eyes. He seemed to be around forty years old. He was a history teacher, had been in the military service and became a captain in the army, and then ended up in the soviet camps as an "enemy of the people." He did not talk much; when he spoke, he pondered his words before pronouncing them.

The moment we came in, revived by heat, we began speaking, saying that now, that "the father" had died, we would be liberated and would go home. He stayed at his place and listened to us carefully. Then, he said calmly:

"We will not get out from here so fast! For the Bolsheviks, we are a great problem. The world's public opinion is agitated as far as we are concerned, it supports us, and it protests against the regime. As it stands, they are forced to liberate us, but they do not know how. Once liberated, we would speak at home and describe what we did, how they treated us, or what we ate, and our relatives will tells others about it. We are a thinking biological bomb that they fear more than the atomic bomb. Why? Because the erosion that we will produce in society speaking the truth about the "red happiness" will be the decisive erosion that will lead to the collapse of the regime!"

We did not really try to see what he wanted to say. Why would we bother with so much philosophy? They will liberate us and that's it! But he was right.

He was an extraordinary man, exceedingly warm and kind. I liked him from the first moment and I felt close to him. However, to be fully honest, I was almost on the point of grabbing a brick - I did not have much intelligence then - to prove to him that I was Romanian. He told me:

"You are no longer Romanian, you are Moldavian!"

He had been a history professor in the Soviet Union, and he was a slavophile at his core, believing that the Slavs would be the race that would dominate the entire earth. He told me that I was not a Romanian, and that Bessarabia was something different than Romania. I could not make peace with this...

I valued him much even then in the camp, but only after the soviets fell, when he sent each one of the survivors his book, *The Gulag Archipelago*, I realized who he was. I knew from the camp how he wrote the book. The people from his brigade told us that after the guards took the pages he had written several times and then punished him with solitary confinement, he had stored the entire work in his memory, dividing it and organizing it on the beads of a prayer rope that he always kept in his hand. Then, he repeated the book daily until the day of liberation, just like a prayer, like praise dedicated to the millions of martyrs from the Gulag.

He had within him the soul of a writer. This is a gift from above; it does not happen by chance. You must know the language very well, you must know how to write, how to use words and form them with complete ideas into sentences. This gift is a talent offered from above, only from God. Solzhenitsyn had this gift.

Only the owl can still be heard in my country...[142]

All the soviet camps had to have a "cultural" building called KVC (*kul'turno-vospitatelinaia ceasti*), a kind of "reeducational club" where the prisoners were fed with Bolshevik ideology and where many informants of the administration swarmed about.

These informants were an interesting species. They could sell out anyone, either out of fear or for various small advantages. There were many of them - you can find weak people everywhere. The prisoners hated them and punished them mercilessly. If someone was discovered to be an informant, he was stabbed during the night, and some people put in his mouth a note on which they wrote "Judas." That was it. The Banderovists especially were very ruthless with the informants.

One of those days, I also went to the KVC for "culturalization." On a long table, you could see the collections of the party's newspapers from all the Soviet republics. They all had the same themes: the contribution of the great Stalin to the development of all fields; the success of the plan in all branches of production; the momentum of citizens in the great construction of communism; and the impending victory of the proletariat in the class struggle taking place in capitalist countries.

Stunned from reading this, I wanted to leave, but right at that moment a short and thin old man came to me and asked me with a squeaky voice:

"Are you from Moldova?"

"No!"

"But where are you from?"

"From Bessarabia."

"Isn't that the same thing?!... Look, I would suggest that you read an article by your great poet, Emilian Bucov."

I immediately understood that he was an instigator and, measuring him up with my eyes, I replied:

---

[142] People used to say that the song of the little owl announced the death of someone in the village.

"Yes, indeed, he is a huge guy, three times your size. But for me the two of you are one and the same!"

This Bucov, a poet from after the war, went to high school in Cetatea Albă and spoke a pure Romanian language, but you could see from a distance that he was a Russian and an ardent communist, behaving like a great Romanian writer from Chişinău. Like all the writers in the soviet Moldova, he also was a party journalist. I found there, at KVC, in *Izvestia*, an article in which the "great poet" Bucov stigmatized the rebirth of West Germany, which was reunited then in the so-called Trizonia and "menaced" Europe again, he said, with the "Teutonic invasion."

When I finished reading the article, the old man approached me, as if rising up from the earth, and asked me:

"Doesn't he hit the Fascists well?"

I answered peevishly:

"What do you want, old man, that Germany would again be separated into Federal Länder, and that the united Russian kniezates would annex all of Europe?"

"I'm not saying this, but they should no longer invade us!"

"Why? So that we, with the sweat off our brow, obtain our *grobushka*[143] peacefully, here in the camp?!..." Knowing that he would go to write his report, I added:

"Old man, even if the earth were to swallow me, I wouldn't change. This is what you should say to your master!"

I turned to leave and behind me the old man shouted with hatred:

"Screw-ball, you'll regret it!"

Angry, I went toward the barrack, and on the road I wrote in my mind a letter to Bucov, planning to send it to him at his address with the Union of Writers, for me, the "union of the regime's bootlickers." The moment I got to my bunk, I took my pencil, my notebook, and I wrote:

---

[143] Crust of bread, in Russian in original.

Letter to Em. Bucov

In Chișinău you write your poems,
On alleys carelessly you walk,
And freely smell your linden flowers,
Your place protecting with your talk.

You are afraid and yell at Teutons
To stay away from our field.
Bucov, I also do not want your owners,
Nor see my people to them yield!

Today I see crucified peoples
On iron, heavy crosses hang,
You always sing that they are happy
Under the boots of the new gang.

Close your factory of verses,
In Chișinău no longer write,
If you don't see how times are going,
If you can't tell the dark from light!

I sent this letter to the Union's address, he received it, and I received as my "honorarium" ten days in solitary confinement. I was accused because I dared to send a letter avoiding the censorship. Why so much hatred and venom that I attacked such a "wonderful soviet poet"?

Of course, I had a "special treatment" in confinement. In the morning they only gave me 300 grams of bread, and then I had to stand or sit until evening. If they caught me lying down, they took my bed and I had to sleep for one to two weeks on cement, catching pneumonia and rheumatism. There was nothing for me to do other than sitting and waiting for the moment when they would take me out. If, God forbid, I did anything stupid, if I yelled or anything like that, they would extend the punishment for one or two days more.

After I finished my "honorarium" of ten days, you know what came to my mind? I should not have written to Bucov, but instead I should have stigmatized all writers. After two months, I wrote to the entire Union of Writers a poem called *The Torches*:

> *Looking at you back through centuries,*
> *You, torches that took light,*
> *The light that for us and those tomorrow,*
> *Cannot be turned out,*
> *My soul burns like a volcano, boiling,*
> *When I see that new torches do not ignite today.*
> *The doinas[144] that you sang a long time ago*
> *I heard with my ears,*
> *And these songs are so marvelous*
> *That they move both the old and the young.*
> *With your weak plume creaking,*
> *You took from the soul as if from an ocean*
> *The pearls eternally shining,*
> *Enriching the treasure year after year.*
> *With your charm you overpassed*
> *The nightingales from other countries,*
> *But now, linger without songs,*
> *We admire in secret our past instead of admiring the future.*
> *Today, nightingales no longer sing for dawn,*
> *But one can hear only the noise of crows,*
> *And instead of the blackbird that sang beautifully,*
> *Only the little owl can still be heard in my country!*

After I wrote this, I felt so relieved; I appeased my soul. I could no longer bear so many lies, but how could I have shot them? I was not in the army, and I had never held a weapon... I shot them with this letter. Of course, I received ten more days of solitary confinement.

The Spask Camp - "the house of wisdom"
In the middle of spring, three brigades from Ekibastuz were

---

144 The *doinas* are folk songs that express a mixture of feelings—desire, love, revolt. They usually take the form of a lament.

assigned to the construction of a railroad segment eight kilometers away from the camp. Every day, we carried the gravel in wheelbarrows for the leveling of the roadbed, and then we carried the tarred rails on our shoulders.

We were all only skin and bones, and the clothes were getting gnawed from the rails, so we shortly got bloody shoulders and were covered by wounds. They greased us with a swab soaked in iodine, but the wounds cracked again, stuck to our rags, and hurt even more. As if this was not enough, I began having stomach pain from dragging the rails by chains.

One day, a small group of sick people came from the Spask sanatorium. They had been sent back to work. One of them came toward me, asked me my name and where I was from, and gave me a note. The note was from Petrică Lungu, with whom I had formed together with Vasile the "triumvirate" of our organization. After my meeting with Pimen Damaşcan, this was the second miracle that happened to me in the camp.

Petrică Lungu was a good boy, shy like a girl, delicate like a lady, silent and still, but wise, very wise. He had studied for two years at the Sanitary School in Bălţi before being arrested, and now he used his knowledge at the hospital in Spask. On the note, he wrote me: "Ioane, the glaciers are moving; they will try us again. You must come so we can discuss what to say at the trial, so that they don't give us more years, but rather free us before the term is over." After Stalin's death and Beria's arrest, many files were reexamined and many had their sentences reduced. Some had been even liberated.

Petrică also wrote me: "I work as an assistant for the main surgeon in the Spask camp. To arrive here, you must simulate some disease. 90% of the prisoners have stomach problems, one way or another, so fake a stomach disease."

As I really had those pains from carrying the rails, after three months they sent me to Spask, together with twenty other sick people. The trip was difficult, with a temperature of 35 degrees Celsius, in a closed van where not even the dog could put up with it. Angry beyond measure because of the heat, the dog grabbed the soldier that was guarding us and almost tore his throat. He did not succeed, but he tore at the soldier's right hand, the one the soldier used to defend himself. The soldier signaled to the driver, the van stopped, an officer opened the door, and the dog jumped out and ran out into the steppe, mad from the heat. It was one of the few successful escapes…

We arrived in Spask very late, completely numbed from the heat. Spask was some kind of sanitary center where they brought the sick prisoners from all the camps in Kazakhstan, men and women alike. There was no longer a separation there, because these poor people were no longer good for anything. Some had a leg or a hand missing, others had no nose because of frost, or still others had tuberculosis. All the diseases in the world were treated there, but in the most primitive fashion. Nevertheless, the chief-surgeon was a former military doctor from the German army named Rosenberg, who had miracle hands. He worked so well that he was often taken out to see the communist "nobility."

The camp had the dimensions of a town with twenty thousand people, but all sick or invalid. The barracks were still rectangular, but lower than the previous ones, and the small windows had thick iron bars. When I entered there, I was assigned directly to the section of those who were supposed to have surgery. Petrică had arranged everything, but very discreetly, without revealing that we knew each other or that we had a common file. Only the doctor, Mr. Rosenberg, knew who I was. Petrică had told him about our organization, how we established it, how they caught us, and the doctor had praised him:

"You are courageous lads, bravo! Get Vanea over to me, and we will do something to help him!"

They began to prepare me for surgery. They examined me, checked my belly, and listened to my heart. When I understood that this was no joke, I asked Petrică:

"Man, the two of you are crazy, do you really want to cut me? My stomach is fine, glory be to God… I eat iron and I make nails!"[145]

He told me to stay still because the doctor knew what he

---

[145] The narrator means that his stomach functions like a well-oiled machine.

was doing. After he examined me thoroughly, the doctor told me:

"We will operate on you tomorrow!"

I froze:

"What do you mean?"

"We will operate on you tomorrow! We will take out the appendix!"

To encourage me, the German added:

"Don't worry! In our country, we take out the appendix for all children when they are four months old, and then they have no problems their whole lives. For you, we will take it out now. Whether it is bad or not, we must take it out, since you came here. Why did you come, for cuckoo flowers...?"

I had no choice, and the second day I went to the surgery. There was no table for such things there. They laid me down on a bench, and four strong guys rushed toward me, as if they wanted to beat me. Each one of them grabbed me by one hand or one foot. They held me down, like they would the cattle, because they had no other choice. There was only a little narcotic on hand, so they stingily anesthetized me.

Then I heard the command:

"The knife!"

I felt how my flesh cracked on the right side, just like the cloth does when the tailor cuts it. Then, the doctor started to work with my intestines. What he did inside of me, only the German knows! I only know that it hurt so much that I thought I was going mad. But I clenched my teeth and told myself: "I am the leader, so I must endure it! What would Petrică say if he saw me crying or roaring?" And I did not cry. At one moment, when I thought that he took out all of my innards and put them into a vat to disinfect them, I groaned once terribly, like a calf.

When the surgery was finished, I thanked the doctor and asked him if I could leave. He laughed so hard that the whole room resounded, and he signaled the four men to put me on a stretcher. They took me on a bunk, put a sachet with warm sand on the cut, and told me:

"The pain, lad, will begin only in a couple of hours. So far, it was nothing!"

And they were right.

The second day I could move a little and they took out my stiches on the third day. I could already speak with Petrică at ease, without being suspected: I was a patient, and he was the doctor's assistant. We planned together how we should behave at the trial, what we should say, and what we should do to get the sentence reduced.

I remained in Spask for ten days, and during this time Petrică took me with him several times to show me the sections with sick people.

He took me to the barracks with dystrophic people, who were lying on the bunks, waiting to swell up and die. He told me how sixty to seventy corpses left the camp daily and were dumped in the common grave. There, before they could cover them, they began to decay, leaving an infernal stench. When the grave was filled, they brought big bulldozers and threw dirt over them.

I also went to the barrack where the women stayed. There was one woman with her hand cut off. She only had a stump instead of a hand. She had a burning desire to become a mother, and God knows how she became pregnant and gave birth to a child beautiful like an angel. I have no words to describe the love and the maternal passion she had while caressing the child with that stump of a hand...

Petrică told me that the mothers were allowed to give birth and then wean the children; after that, the children were snatched from them and taken to the soviet orphanages. These mothers did not know whether they would find their children again or whether they could be mothers again, and their pain was so great that it made them lose their minds at times.

One day, I went to the barrack of the mentally ill people, or the "house of wisdom," where there were all kinds of people: scientists, doctors of sciences, Bolsheviks, leftists, rightists, but all having lost their minds. I received a spectacular welcome there. When I went in, someone whispered respectfully: "Foreign guest!" One of them, a short old man who believed he was the grandson of Mahendra Bir Bikram-Shah Dev, the emperor of Nepal at that time, sat on a bucket and with a blessing gesture invited his subjects to sit on golden chairs. Then he declared solemnly that he, together with his good friend, Koba the seminarian (Koba was Stalin's nickname), made the laws according to which the entire universe is moving, and they were very tired.

After this, taking a bow toward us, he said:

"Your excellences, we will put an end to all the ugly attempts coming from our happy Albion. We will cut off the legs of all those who dare try to escape. Whoever will raise his hand against the kingdom will lose a hand. Whoever tries to listen to the crazy whispers from abroad will lose their ears. No one should dare to put his nose into what is not his business, because he would lose his nose!"

"Your Highness, but this is already a dictatorship!" someone protested.

"Correct. But the bright future of humanity cannot be built without dictatorship. I am tired now, so His Luminescence pastor Danilevsky will talk to you about this mystery."

The "pastor" pointed toward a yoga patient who had been standing on his head since we came into the barrack, with his hands and legs wide apart:

"Behold, your excellences, this perfection of world order. We lived half an eternity with our legs down, keeping our head at the place of honor. But our head could not lead us further. The Great Explosion of human wisdom then took place, so everything was turned upside down, and thus the second half of eternity began, when another organ leads, but not the head. This is the final explanation of things!"

After this "explanation," the old man on the bucket proposed to begin the ceremony of our acceptance among the lords of Albion. Petrică bowed very properly, pushing my head with his hand as well, and explained that we did not prepare well enough and that we did not bring the gifts with us. Then, walking carefully back, we went toward the door.

When we got out, I breathed deeply and looked behind me to see whether anyone was following us. I was shocked, and I wondered what was the terrible sin these people committed. Petrică told me that they probably pay for the sins of an empire that sowed only pain and terror in the world. How many innocent people from so many countries lost their minds because of the sufferings brought upon them by the "loving father of all peoples"?[146]

Petrică also told me how these people were used as guinea pigs for psychological experiments. Two or three times per month, the civilian doctors administered secret substances to them, and then they checked the effects. Sometimes, after these experiments the patients remained unmoved for days.

I think that the scene that I saw in the barrack of the mentally ill deserved to be made into a movie. It's worth it. It is an impression that shows what the Bolshevik regime could do to the population from the former Soviet Union. It is the tragedy of a people that was brought to dementia...

One evening, still in Spask, I saw another dramatic scene: the "way of the cross" taken by the invalids to the quarry where they were forced to work for a piece of bread. Going to work and returning from work were more excruciating for them than the work itself because the majority of them moved with great difficulty. Some did not have a leg; others did not have a hand, an eye or a nose... They went two by two, holding each other, and some were supporting themselves with sticks. It took them two hours to go for one kilometer and a half, and this time was counted as outside their working schedule.

When they could no longer drag themselves, some just rolled down on the ground, and others put stones under their heads and slept there, on the side of the road, until next morning.

Their work at the quarry did not contribute much. Those who had two hands broke the rock with the sledge-hammer, and those with one hand rolled the rock with a crowbar. But how much could some such as them truly bare? The true purpose was to torture them. When the colonel Chechev, the chief of the Camps Direction, came in inspection once a month, he reminded them mockingly that "movement is life," as the Marxist-Leninist doctrine teaches.

---

[146] Stalin.

All these things stirred up a boundless interior revolt, and I swore that I would never forget them, until the Final Judgment!

"The Lark"

After I left Spask, the final camp where they took me was Aktas. The winds of change were already blowing, and we were beginning to hope. We heard of the first revisited files and the first prisoners liberated before the term.

I had not written any request to have my file reexamined, but I was called one day to the camp office, where I was told officially that the Supreme Court of the USSR reviewed the file of the members of the organization "The Sword of Justice" and decided to maintain the sentence for the accused Lungu, Bobeică, Țurcanu, and Moraru, but it annulled the 10 year term of exile to the far north.

I had done four years of punishment, so I had six more. I was thinking of the scene with the crippled people coming from the quarry and the tragedy in the "house of wisdom." What if I end up like them? And if not, will my poor grandparents still live long enough to see me again, to wait for me? What about mom, with her crushed spirit? Despair began to take a hold of me, and I thought more and more often about breaking out of prison.

Around that time, the administration of the camp had softened the work regime. They knew that the terms were being diminished, and they tried to give us reasons to remain there after liberation because they needed a workforce. The KVC was more active than ever. The prisoners were allowed to organize a theater and even a true orchestra.

This is how I met again, to my great joy, my former math teacher from Târnova, Mr. Belinski. He played the violin. When I saw him, I thought that it was him, but it seemed just like in a dream. I went on the stage, I approached him, and then I asked him:

"You are a professor of mathematics; how did you get here?"

When he heard me speaking Romanian, he lost it and could barely ask me who I was.

"I am one of your students from Târnova. Do you remember the feast of St. Basil, on that alley with chestnuts at the mansion?"

Then he ran up to me, embraced me, and started to cry. Then he turned toward the public, holding the violin with one hand and the bow with the other, and said:

"If there is even only one Romanian in the audience, the concert will be Romanian!"

He turned toward the orchestra, touched the strings of the violin, and magic sounds began pouring on that stage. When he played the *Ciocârlia* (the Lark),[147] we were all mesmerized. We followed his bow as it traveled across the strings, how he brought up the lark in the heights of heaven, and how he brought it down to the meadow, where the others birds were accompanying it. Lord, such beauty!

The audience remained speechless, and Boris, a Tatar friend, the painter of the camp, asked me if my violinist is from earth. Then I remembered the words Pimen had told me a long time ago, on the shore of the brook in Slănina: "One must wear one's culture in the world as the clothing for a feast."

After less than two weeks, professor Belinski was sent away to a new "stage," in an unknown place, and we no longer heard of him.

Lidia Monastâriova

During all this time, the thought to escape had not left me at all, and I thought that the theater that started in the camp could help me because they left periodically to travel to concerts in other camps. It helped that Mr. Beresnevich, a Russian director who was the leader of the group, noticed me and insisted that I join them. He saw in me some feminine aspect and gave me the role of Manea from V. Shcvarkin's[148] play *Foreign Child*. Manea was supposed to be a beautiful little Russian, slender, and I did my best to play my role as best as I

---

[147] *Ciocârlia* is a very famous and beautiful traditional tune.
[148] I am not certain of the transliteration of the name. In Romanian, it appears as Scvarkin. It may also be Chichvarkin.

could. We played the piece in our camp, and now we had to go to the women's camp for a performance there as well.

The women's zone was 100 meters away, separated from us with barbed wire. Between the two camps there was a neutral strip, and anyone stepping on it was shot without warning by sentinels. Now, with Khrushchev's relaxing of the regulations they allowed us at times in the women's zone because they thought we might get attached to one another and thus remain there even after liberation.

We left the camps in two cars: one was loaded with the props and everything that we needed, and the other full of actors. Beyond the barbed wire, the women waited for us all crowded in the club. They had yellow-earthly faces and faded overalls. We followed the director like a flock would follow its master, and we then started to look around.

Backstage, Mr. Beresnevich took me straight to Lidia Monastâriova, the leader of the women's theater. She had been an actress in Ukraine. During the Fascist occupation, she had worked as a translator for an administrative institution, and the Bolsheviks accused her of espionage for the Germans and so sentenced her to forced labor in the camp.

Mr. Beresnevich knew her well, and he left me in her care: "Lidia, take care of him and make a woman out of him!"

Monastâriova was seven-eight years my senior and was of a rare beauty, spiritual and physical. She was very refined, and she spoke well and properly. She had black, bright eyes, and her whole being was surrounded by a mystery that one cannot describe.

She stayed with me to help me get ready. She took my shirt off and gave me a spotted long dress that went down to my knees. She gave me a pair of sandals, arranged my wig, my wrap, and perfumed me slightly behind the ears. During all this time, I had the sensation that I was next to a mysterious pyre. At one moment, we no longer found anything else to say to each other, and we remained like this, looking at one another. She was the first to shake off the spell. She turned to one side, and then to the other, looked at me, content with her work, and there was nothing else between us. The show ended, we received applauses, congratulations, and a small bouquet of artificial flowers made by the prisoners. Monastâriova came to accompany us to the gate of the camp. On the way to the gate, as I was slowly walking next to her, my sinful heart could no longer bear it, I took her next to me and kissed her, in a passionate and masculine way.

This gesture was very bewildering for her, but I found this out only later. For the moment, after we separated, we continued to exchange letters. I told her a few things about me, about Bessarabia, and, with Mr. Beresnievich's help, I sent her a small album that I made with pictures of my loved ones from back home. She was very joyful and moved by this. Then, I found out that she was liberated, and I lost track of her.

After a while, it happened that I was called to the parlor by a woman. It was Sunday, the day of rest, and I had just returned from my shift. I had not shaved yet and I was dirty because I had not managed to wash the coal off me yet.

They took me to the meeting room, and I saw a distinguished woman, dressed with a long overcoat, with a small hat and a shawl over her shoulders. I thought that it was a mistake or that she may have been one of the researchers that sometimes were conducting studies about the prisoners.

She looked at me for a long while, and then she told me:

"Vaniusha, don't you recognize me?"

At that moment, I saw her black, bright eyes, and I realized that she was the actress Monastâriova. She opened her arms and embraced me. I was very uncomfortable: I was so dirty, and she was so clean and frail...

I asked her how she reached me, and she told me that she was helped by Mr. Leandr, who was respected by the administration and who had recommended her, saying she was a relative of mine.

Then she told me:

"Vanea, I am older than you are, and I have my world, from which I come. You are young, you must do your studies and move on with your life. There is no chasm between us, but there is a distance... I came only to tell you that when you kissed me, you brought me back my feminine dignity, my human dignity. You did not kiss me, but you kissed my cross that I have carried up to here with so much pain. You kissed the lips that the executioners burned with cigarettes, that they hit so many times, the lips that were nourished with all the rubbish and rottenness just so that I would remain alive…"

She then told me about the most horrible tortures to which she was subjected. They tied her hair to the doorknob, stabbing her with a needle all over and mocking her body. She also told me how she was thrown naked in a cold dungeon, then taken out to interrogation, kicked and cursed…

Two tears trickled from her great, round eyes, and it seemed that her entire suffering was contained in them.

Then she told me again with sadness:

"There was no stone in the camp that I have not wet with my tears; there was no corner in the barrack where I have not cried for all things that I suffered… I do not know whether you will be able to understand now the entire tragedy that I have experienced. Years will pass, and if God gives you to be a wise man, you will realize what I have suffered… Vanea, I chose you as my confessor, but I am asking you to break the law and to not keep my confession secret, but tell the entire world what you have heard from me…"

She then stood up, ready to go. She took two pictures from her purse, one of hers and one of Leandr Aleksandrovich, and she gave them to me as souvenirs. At the door, she turned around once more and whispered:

"Farewell, Vaniusha!"

After her departure, I did not manage to hide the two pictures, and the guards asked to see them.

"Who's this old man with his pipe between his teeth?"

Knowing their cultural level, I answered:

'What do you mean who's he? He is the grandson of Mahendra Bir Bikram Shah Deva from Nepal!"

"And who's the woman?"

"She is his granddaughter, the goddess of patience and suffering!" I said.

The guard gave me the pictures back with disdain:

"You, the sectarians, are a bit lost! Come, get lost!"

I have not heard anything from Monastâriova since then, and I have never seen her, but I cherish her memory as one of the most beautiful in my life. I also keep the last letter I received from her in the camps, as one would keep a gem. She wrote me these verses in Russian:

Walk on the path without falling with your soul,
And give a hand to the fallen, so that you would save them.
In the name of science and of light, raise your candle,
So that you may give light to the darkness that surrounds us…

The release from the camp

The story of my liberation is connected with a woman as well.

My sister had told one of her friends who was a student in Tiraspol that I am in the camp. The girl, being curious, asked her for my address, so that she could write me.

This is how, one day, I received a letter in the camp. It was exceptionally and beautifully written. The girl was telling me that she was a student in Biology in her fourth year and that she would have liked to correspond. I was very happy: if a student wants to talk to me, it is wonderful!

Letter after letter followed, but none of them ended with the classical formulas, "Missing you so much" or something like this. There were no such things between us. However, one could see that our mutual connection was increasing, becoming like a great mountain of something dear and holy. Finally, she decided to raise money, quit college, and come to me, in the camp. The moment her father found out about this, being a hunter, he took his gun in his hand and told her:

"If you try to do such a thing, I'll empty my gun in you. I will hunt you down, wherever you go!"

He silenced her, gave her into marriage, and that was that…

After liberation, I even went to her place and met her family. Later, I went to see her again. Her husband had died, and her son had died as well. I took the album with family pictures from home, because I had children and grandchildren by then. We looked at it together, we talked, and we cried… We both cried, for what else could we do?... But this was much later. Back then, when I was in the camp, I did not exactly know what was happening. The only indication I had was that in her last letter she told me that her father had had a meeting with a "guardian angel," after which he had decided to marry her off by any means. She said she did not have the power to oppose destiny. Reading and rereading the letter, I was overtaken with fear. What if she entered under the sight of the authorities? What if she was suspected for connections with a political prisoner? What if she had to go through the investigations of the "red angels"? After I heard what Monastâriova had told me, this last thought tormented me the most. I burned all of her letters and thought about what I could say during investigations to show that she was innocent.

I was tormented like this until June 20, 1956, when I was called to the office. An older man in civilian dress was waiting there for me. This is it, I thought, the investigation begins! Was she brought here as well? Does she have long hair? Did she bring warm clothes or did she wear thin ones?

I almost blacked out when the civilian told me that he had to communicate something very important to me. I stood up, and he read to me the decree of the Supreme Presidium of the Court of the Soviet Union by which I was liberated, my punishment was suspended, but I was not rehabilitated.

I could not believe my ears. I had done six years and forty days, and I still had almost four more years before the end.

The civilian did not give up and gave me a short "instructive" speech:

"Listen, boy! You were young and full of romanticism, so you could not understand the meaning of the new times. All of you have committed an error; you did not understand our politics, and you rebelled when we came to liberate you. Now, you must cool down and realize that our country has an invincible army and you cannot do anything with your fantasies. You will have to learn the communist way of life and adapt to society!"

His sermon cut me like a knife, but I kept my mouth shut tight and did not fight back at all because I wanted to see my mother and my grandparents. The civilian added that I had to be very careful with my actions because the KGB would follow me closely. Then, he ordered someone to take pictures of me and to complete my release certificate. He made a document for my trip home, and with that document I could get my passport in the district of Târnova.

On the land of my Bessarabia...

On June 22, I left by train toward Moscow, and from there, still by train, toward home. When I crossed the river Nistru at Movilău, coming unto the land of my Bessarabia, I remembered the verses of Lermontov, written when he was exiled to the Caucasus. This is how they would sound in Romanian:

> *Farewell, unclean Russia,*
> *And you, people in blue uniforms,*
> *And you, great lords,*
> *And you, enslaved and brutalized people!*

I looked immediately around, to see whether there was any "mind reader." Then I realized that I was not correct. I remembered all my Russian comrades with whom I shared my years in the camp. I remembered Dima and Nikolai, who accompanied me to the gate at my release, Boris, Sergey, and the actress Monastâriova. I seemed to hear Mr. Leandr, with his pipe eternally between his teeth, whispering reproachfully: "Vaniusha, it's not all of Russia in the way the poet described it!"...

My mind turned again to the house that I was approaching. If I had wings, I would have flown to get there faster. I could not say who I wanted to see more: *mama, bunelul, bunica,* my cousins, or Tărcuş? I don't know how to say it, but Tărcuş was for me a symbol of our existence, a symbol of friendship and faithfulness, much more than a dog, he was like a fellow man to me.

All the persecutions that I had suffered in prison - the beatings, the cold, the hunger, and the humiliation - were difficult to endure, but being away from my parents' home, from my parents, from my *bunei*, to whom I was very connected spiritually, was the greatest burden for me. Being separated from them was the greatest torture that I endured there.

Now, as I was getting closer to home, my heart was beating faster. I finally arrived in the villages and began going toward the house of *bunelul*. When I came by the gate, only Tărcuș was in the yard. He sat on the porch, on an old mantle. He was really old. He made two attempts to bark, and then he jumped up on his legs, abruptly. I thought: now he will knock me down! Indeed, he rushed at me, but yelping for joy, like in the past. He embraced me with his paws, and he seemed to say that he was with me in Siberia, that we was with all our people in kolkhoz, that he also tasted from the bread of the kolkhoz...

In the meantime, *bunelul* had come outside to see why the dog was barking. When he saw me, he shouted:

"Hey, Lisandra, Zenovie!"

Zenovia was *mama*. They came out, on either side of *bunelul*, and I fell on my knees and I embraced him like this, as you would embrace an oak, and said:

"Please forgive me for everything I have done!"

I felt so guilty for the pain I brought upon them, and they did not even know why everything happened. After our arrest, there were many rumors in the Valea Cuboltei: that we falsified papers, that we stole money... Nobody said the truth. The KGB covered it up well, so that young people would not find out and raise up again "The Sword of Justice."

The old man bent, took me in his arms, shed a tear, and said:

"Get up, my dear boy. Glory be to God for seeing you home!"

In the world...

After I retuned in the village, I registered again at the Pedagogical School in Soroca in the third year.

The first thing I tried to do was to find Lealea. I went to the Police, I gave them the most important info I had about her, and I told them I was ready to pay for the search expenses. After three days, they called me again. Captain Carasi, from the KGB, who was closely following me, was waiting for me in the office.

He told me that the Pedagogical School is full of girls, that I should no longer look for what I shouldn't be looking for, and that I should not forget that I had to serve four more years of concentration camp. When I heard this, I lost all hope.

The Pedagogical School was indeed full of girls, but the age difference between us was ten years, and the spiritual difference was even greater. They already had the stamp of soviet education. Regardless of how great the passions of youth may have been, I could not find a common ground with them.

I often came home from Soroca to see my sick mother and my old grandparents. I had nothing to do in the evening, so I was going to the village's club, to the movies. I met Profira there. When I saw her, my heart leapt within me. I knew her because she had studied in my school and she was three years my junior. One night, we even came home from the train station together, walking for ten kilometers, but back then I was cherishing a holy friendship for Lealea and I could not think of anyone else.

It is true, my mind was still caught up on Lealea, but when I saw that all my attempts to find her hit the wall of the KGB, I understood that I had no longer time to form another friendship. Then, I clenched my fists, and I decided to get married.

After the movie, I asked Profira to allow me to take her home. I went to her house and, whether I needed it or not, I asked her to give me a glass of water. She brought me water in a crystal clean glass. I drank all of it. This must have been a prophecy, a symbol.

I then looked at her and said:

"Profirica,[149] you know me..."

She told me:

"I know you. I know where you came from, I know with whom you were friends, I know everything. What do you want now?"

"You have no idea!... Would you marry me?"

She was silent, silent, silent... I told her:

"Profirica, I see you don't say anything... You are not sure

---

[149] The diminutive from Profira.

because you do not know what happened to me in the camp, what I did, why I was sent there, and why I came back from there... Look, I will give you a whole month. You think about it, and I'll come back in October to get an answer. Is that fine?"

"Fine."

I returned after a month, as we had established. She waited for me with so much love, with so much care, and she told me she would accept to be my wife! There was a party that evening at school, in the village. She was a teacher there, and I was in the last year of Pedagogical School. I went with her to the party, we stayed there a while, we then came home, we sat next to each other, dressed as for a feast and I kissed her, and that was it.

When morning came, I looked for the secretary of the County Soviet, I brought her to our place, we registered, and we became husband and wife from that day forward. I was 28 years old, and she was three years my junior. She was so small and thin, but with a soul as great as a mountain. I went home to *mama*, to my *bunei*, and I introduced her to them:

"She is the one, be good and love her. There is no other one and there will be no other!"

I cannot say that my marriage with Madame Profira was out of a great love, as in Romeo and Juliette. It was a marriage coming from the need of two young people, a man and a woman, to establish a family and to make a life for themselves. Slowly and shyly, love came with time.

We could not have our religious wedding back then because we were supervised closely, especially me. We only had it much later, when the Soviet giant collapsed. That "rascal" of a priest wrote in her papers that "Mrs. Profira Parpalac, God's servant, was married," but in my papers he did not write "*fecior*,"[150] even if I went a virgin to the camp and I returned a virgin!

It was not even one year after we got married, and *mama* died, at 42 years old. *Bunica* died three days later, and *bunelul* after three more months. He had gone to the cemetery, to take

---

[150] The Romanian word "fecior" signifies a man who is still a virgin.

care of their graves, and he died there, over them. For us it was a tragedy, but we endured this as well.

We then began to build our house and to get settled. Adeluța[151] came to the world, and after seven years Inuța,[152] my younger daughter who is now in Kiev, also arrived. The two of us were teachers at the school in the village, and life flowed slowly.

Farewell, Vaniusha!

It was the autumn of 1966. I had finished classes, and I was getting ready to go home. In the office, there was much agitation: the director had received a "goal," a ball that some boys had kicked through the window shattering it, and now he was moving around furiously. The team's captain, Pavlushka, was from my class, so I tried to calm them down. In the middle of the turmoil, someone knocked timidly at the door. It was Adeluța, who called me to tell me something:

"*Mama* asked you to come home fast because there is a lady who wants to see you!" I went home holding her hand, and we arrived immediately, since we lived not far away from school. I came in, and I froze: on the couch, Lealea and Profira, the two most precious women not in the village of Mândâc, not in the district of Târnova, but rather in all of Bessarabia or even the whole world, were sitting next to each other! When I saw them this way, I froze. I halted, and then took a step toward Lealea; she took a step toward me, and then we no longer paid attention to propriety and embraced each other strongly, and the tears began to flow.

Adeluța, poor child, did not understand what was happening, why that woman embraced her father. Profirica endured as long as she endured, but she was supposed to go to school, because we were working in shifts: I worked in the morning and she worked in the afternoon, so that we could take care of Inuța, who was only one year old. She thus began to give me the report:

---

[151] The diminutive from Adela.
[152] The diminutive from Ina.

"Inuţa ate well and slept a bit; I am going with Adeluţa, so we'll leave you in charge of the house."

She then turned toward Lealea. They knew each other since we all had studied at the same school, and Profira had even discovered that they were relatives. She told Lealea:

"You and I are blood relatives, and you and he are spiritual relatives. You believed that your love was a great secret. It was so only for you because we knew everything. Love is the only secret that man cannot hide… Your drama is so tangled that only God could untangle it. Come, remain here in the house and take care so that Inuţa doesn't cry when she wakes up!"

This is how Profirica was: she always knew how to maintain equilibrium in all situations. She took Adeluţa and went fast to school. For four hours, she did not follow me at all to see what I was doing with Lealea…

We remained stunned for a while. Slowly, we began to confess to one another. I told her how it had been for me, and she told me how it had been for her.

It was then when she told me that in Târnova, at the train station, her mother had kept her at her breast by force, so that she would not come out to see me. Later, Lealea found out that her mother had formed a relationship with my uncle Vasile in her youth, but *bunica* Alexandra was against it and wanted a daughter in law from her village. Lealea's mother could not forget that, and this is why she was against our relationship.

Then, Lealea told me of the horrors that took place on the way to Siberia. One night, in that boxcar for cattle in which they were, a child was born in darkness; he was sentenced from the beginning. The women did everything they could for the baby. They tore the umbilical cord with their teeth and tied it with a thread taken from a cross someone had around their neck. They also tore some worn shirts to make him a diaper. The chief of the convoy was infuriated and wanted to take the child from his mother and leave him at the first hospital. But the entire train car revolted and all said as one:

"You either shoot all of us, or you leave the child alone!"

They were forced to leave the mother with the child at the hospital. Then, Lealea told me the most terrible trial she went through. Since they were all crowded, unwashed, after a month or so the entire car was full of lice. They took them out of the train car, somewhere on a dead end track, and forced them to get completely undressed, men and women together, to disinfest them.

"Vanea, when I was home, I did not wash before my mother, so how could I have undressed with so many people present! It was then when I thought for the first time that I would like to die. But I thought that my poor mother, left without me, would be mad from pain, and all of heaven fell upon my head. After all, with a crushed spirit, I had to do what I was commanded to do. Vaniusha, your soul is taken from my soul, and only you and *mama* are able to understand my shame and pain at that moment..."

She began to cry again, but then she calmed down and continued her story.

After a long time, their convoy stopped at Kemerovo, and Lealea with her mother were appointed to a cattle farm, to clean the dung. They worked for half a year there. They lived in a hut next to the farm. In the night, when it was still night outside, they left to do their work, so that the milkmaids would find it clean when they came in the morning. One night, the snow was waist high and there was a strong blizzard. Her mother was going ahead, to make way, and Lealea stumbled and fell in the snow. She sank down in the snow and felt it on her skin, down to the bone, and it began to hit her like thousands of needles. Her mom called her desperately, but she could not answer. She finally found her, shook her as much as she could, and dragged her to the farm. The moment they came in, the women hurled insults at them, accusing them of partying all night long and for being late. A kind hearted Russian took Lealea and put her hands on the warm haunch of a nearby docile cow.

Lealea told me crying:

"You cannot imagine, Vanea, how dear to me was this Joiana.[153] She saved my life when people were crueler than animals!"

---

[153] Proper name used at times for cows.

Their luck was that Lealea's mother was a good seamstress, and she had managed to take her sewing machine with her. It happened that she sewed an overcoat for the chief's wife at the farm, and when that woman saw how well she worked, she took her on as a seamstress downtown. They moved into a more humane small room, and they were allowed to send Lealea to school. Lealea was wise, so she finished school and then went to the Electro-Magnetic Department at the University in Kemerovo. After this, thinking that her mother's heart had softened, she wrote me a letter with the hope of sending it to me. Her mother found it, and she made her burn it and promise that she would never look for me again.

Lealea stopped here and did not want to tell me anything else: how she had to marry, what happened... We both cried, having much bitterness in our souls; after we realized the tragedy in which we found ourselves, she asked me:

"Vanea, do you remember the riddle I did for you the first time when you helped me cross the bridge?"

"How could I not, Lealea! Without that wonderful moment, that is given only once in a lifetime, our meeting now would have had no sense, knowing well that I have two children, and knowing that you also married before me... It is perhaps that riddle that brought you here now..."

"Would you like me to do it again, for the last time?"

She grabbed my neck with her hand, just like in our childhood, she said half of the riddle, and then a chill shot through her whole body and she set her head on my elbow. I have no words to describe what happened then... Then, she took two steps back and told me:

"This is it, we stop here! You have two small children to raise; two little girls who are beautiful like two angels. I owe the man who saved my life..."

She had come to the village to get some papers that she needed in order to move for good to the Soviet Union with her husband, who was German.

She looked at me one more time and said:

"I must go. I don't want to take advantage of Profirica's goodness any longer. Any other woman in her place would have sent me away from the door. She invited me in peacefully and she called you immediately. Vaniusha, perhaps you do not realize the treasure God gave you! When she comes back, tell her that I only came to say goodbye to the most beautiful part of my life. She will understand. From now on, only God can protect us and judge all three of us!"

Lealea turned to leave. I remembered that Profirica had left us some pies. I packed two in a hurry and gave them to her. As she was heading out the door, I saw that Cercel, our dog, came towards us barking.

I said:

"This rascal may do something!"

Lealea bent down, took a piece from the pie, and called him. Cercel came toward her, took the piece, licked his mouth, and allowed her to pet him.

"Well, you see" she told me. "If I tamed you, how could I not tame him?... Now, please go back in the house, do not torment me... Farewell, Vaniusha!"

She turned and left without looking back. Cercel accompanied her to the curb. Profirica was coming home at that time too, with one girl in her arms and the other one holding her hand...

Bless you, prison!

Looking back to my life, I thank God for giving me what he gave me!

I did not regret back then, and I do not regret today either that I was in prison. Many times I want to say what Solzhenitsyn said: Bless you, prison! The prison helped me to know myself, to find my dignity, to know who I am, and to become a real man.

If I lived here, in freedom, I could not have known the people I met in prison, people of such high culture and spirituality. I learned literature, science, art, and even atomic physics from them. After my release, I studied at the university as well, in Tiraspol, but the professors there were not at the level of Mr. Leandr Aleksandrovic, doctor in technical sciences in Warsaw and Sankt Petersburg, or at the level of Mr. General

Dragomir, the professor of political economy in Bucharest, or at the level of the director Bresnevic, or at the level of Solzhenitsyn. And there were many others, not necessarily scholars, but people of great spiritual beauty.

I carry all of them in my heart as my holiest memory. They entered in the patrimony of my soul, and I love them with the same love with which I loved Lealea, my mother and grandparents, and my wife and children.

During all these years of suffering, I often felt God's hand protecting me! When I was saved by a miracle from Melikian's claws, when I remained alive at the mine, when I survived in Spask, where I could have died under the knife, it only could have been God's hand. God kept me alive until now so that I could witness to what happened there, in the inferno.

Thinking about everything that I have suffered, everything that happened with Bessarabia and with this Orthodox corner of the world, I think that God allowed the devil to put our faith to the test. With regret I must say that very little faith remained. However, I think that people begin to return to God again.

The Satanic dragon with two heads, communism and liberalism, that has become the master of the world since the French Revolution, is about to be suffocated, and people will return again to their natural way of being. This is a work that we cannot explain fully. Only the One Above can fully explain what happened, for he is the only one who knows what meaning each thing had.

After a life of bitter experiences, my word to all, but especially to young people, is this: do not get away from the Orthodox Church and study the real history of your people. If the young do not return to faith, the experience of my generation will not be of any help. If, however, they have real faith in their souls, they will be troubled and they will learn something and tell this story further to their children and grandchildren. Then they will perhaps understand that life is not about making money in the West or living off the fat of the land for some time. Their duty is higher: to remain in our country with their sleeves rolled up and their head on their shoulders.

By now, I have lived my life, and I thank God for everything that He has given me. My soul has only one more desire. I rose to fight for Romania, and the beatings that I have received everywhere were because I said that I was Romanian. It is true that, back then, when I established this organization, I did not have in mind to do something for history. I had my head in the clouds. Back then it was the romanticism of the age! I established "The Sword of Justice" as the burning bush of Romanianism, just as the Burning Bush movement[154] in the Sovietized Romania. This is why I desire to receive back, before I die, my documents that attest my Romanian ethnic origin. I want to deposit my bones at the foundation of the country of Romania, and I would like to go to the Judgment of the nations with my papers in order, stating that I am Romanian!

Mândâc, Bessarabia, July 9, 2011

---

[154] The Burning Bush in Romania was a movement of spiritual revival that began before WWII ended. Among its members, there were Fr. Roman Braga and Fr. André Scrima.

In the Darkness of Foreign Lands

Galina Baranovski Shapovalova

I am from a family with four children

I am from Bessarabia, the district of Rezina, the county of Echimăuţi. I am from a family with four children, two boys and two girls. Dad was a medical assistant, and mom taught the practical hour at school. The eldest brother was born in 1939, I in 1940, another brother, Constantin, in 1946, and the youngest sister, Silvica, in 1950. We lived in Rezina until the war; we were just two children then. When the war began, dad was mustered in and taken as medical assistant in the Romanian army.

This is how we all moved to Romania. According to my memory and to the pictures we still have from that time, we were in several places, depending on where dad was moved with his work: Roşiorii de Vede, Drăgăşani, but also in Transylvania, around Făgăraş. The last place before we left for Bessarabia was Alexandria. I do not have many memories from Romania. I only remember a festival where I recited poems. I remember it was a peaceful, beautiful atmosphere. I also remember that there were people lining up to get consultations with dad. There were sick people coming on carts, and I remember how they would wait to be checked by dad.

After the war, dad was forced to return home. Here, in Bessarabia, we returned to our old house, where *bunicu'* lived. My dad's mother had died when he was a child, and this is how only my *bunicu'* remained. *Bunicu'* made sure dad would learn a craft, and he sent him to the School of Arts and Crafts. Dad was very handy, but he was also passionate about medicine.

Later, after he married *mămica*,[155] he studied medicine and worked as a medical assistant. *Mama* told me that when dad was arrested, he had already been working as a medical assistant for ten years. He was known throughout the district of Orhei because his profession was the passion of his life; he put

---

[155] The diminutive from *mama*.

a lot of soul into it, and many people came to him for help.

In 1945, after we returned to Bessarabia, the country was under Soviet occupation, and dad was not very valued because he had been employed by the Romanian army. Shortly after our return, in 1946, the terrible famine broke out. I remember how people would come and die in the yard of the medical assistant. Mom and dad managed to hide some food, so we were all saved. We also had a cow, and we managed to get through the famine of '46-'47 with its milk. However, I went through a terrible hunger later.

In 1949, with the deportations, I was at my aunt's house. I remember how some soldiers came during the night and began knocking at the gate. I was arrested with my aunt. She began crying and telling the neighbors who were gathered there:

"She is not my child! She is my sister's child from Echimăuți!"

They called *bunelul*, who was 80 years old and was not deported because he was too old. He came and took me away. This is how I escaped, but I went through a shock, and I got terribly scared. Roars, shouts, soldiers holding the gun, so menacing… All these things scared me terribly.

The night when they arrested dad

Mom and dad were afraid that they would also be deported, but they escaped that wave of deportations in 1949. My aunt was taken and deported to Kurgan. She was considered a Kulak, which means rich. God only knows how my aunt arrived in Kurgan. Dad was arrested toward the end of July, the beginning of August in 1951. Before then, various committees came to us periodically to check on us. They were from the *Securitate*. They went to the attic, went to the cellar, to the cattle, everywhere… I did not know what they were looking for. Well, they said that they wanted to make sure that we were protected against fire. When I was going to school, the children would ask me:

"Did they come to your place to see whether you have guns?"

The night when dad was arrested, I was home. I heard a

strong bang in the window. I was already scared from when my aunt was deported. Someone asked me:

"Is your *tăticu'*[156] home? I am sick. I need him to do a gastric irrigation."

I told him:

"*Tăticu'* is not here, he is out on the field, where they thresh."

This was around one, two in the night. I told them where he was, and they left. In the meantime, dad came back from the field, and I told him what happened. They came back after one hour or so. It was already getting light outside, and they came and picked him up:

"You come with us. Get into the cart!"

Mămica said:

"Why? Where are you taking him?"

There were several people arrested in the village and taken at the kolkhoz. We found out that dad was arrested at the village's soviet office.

I went there, in the neighboring village, and I saw *tăticu*, and he saw me. But just then they were moving him into another cart, and he began to cry. He did not get to take me in his arms, and I did not get to kiss him. I could not bid him farewell… I was the last one who saw *tăticu*. After that, I did not hear anything from him and did not know anything of him until 1992. I wrote requests to the DA office, at the Securitate in Moscow, at the Minister for Foreign Affairs in Moscow, and I finally received a letter from there in which they told us that dad was shot on March 25th, on the day of the Annunciation.[157] He was tried in Odessa by a special *dvoica*.[158] But I think he was shot in Chişinău.

After dad was arrested, we left to live with *bunelu'*. *Mama* had cancer; it was the last stage. It was said that dad was a

---

[156] The diminutive from *tata*, dad or father.

[157] The Annunciation is a great feast for the Orthodox Church, celebrating the moment when the angel Gabriel told Mary she would have a child.

[158] (*Footnote in the Romanian edition*) A commission formed by two members that was established with the purpose of quickly trying the "enemies of the people" in the Soviet Union during the Stalinist purges.

militant for Romanians, that he was against the Soviet power, and that meant that he was a fierce enemy of the Soviet Union. *Mama* did not know anything about this. What can I tell you? After 1940, when the Russians came the first time, *tăticu* was at his godparents' house, in Echimăuţi. The Russians came there and they shot our godfather before dad's eyes, in his own yard. For dad, this was a shock. Of course, he could no longer stand the Russians, he could no longer stand the communists, and he saw all the misery and poorness they brought. Perhaps he was connected with others… *Mama* used to say:

"I'm dying, and I do not know why they arrested *tăticu!*"

Where are you taking us? Where are you taking us?

After they took *tăticu*, we were dying of hunger. We did not have anything to eat, and *mama* came to Chişinău, trying to get a job here, as a nurse at a hospital. But she had no papers because all our papers had remained in Romania. One morning, when she was getting ready to go to work, two men came to her, where we lived on rent, and they arrested her. They took her to a dungeon and left her there until 2:00 am in the night, without telling her anything. Before this, they also came to us, to *bunelu'*, where I was with my little sister. Several people came, both women and men, and asked *bunelu'*:

"Where is your daughter?"

And they asked me:

"Where is your mother, girl?"

"*Mama* is not here; she is away, to work in Chişinău."

"But why in Chişinău? Who took her there?"

I did not know. They finally found out where she was. I realized that they were looking for *mama* to arrest her, and I thought that they wanted to shoot her and then take us as well. A few days passed and, even if we did not know that *mama* was arrested in Chişinău, having passed through the shock with my aunt's arrest, I was crying day and night with heart pain, and I was saying:

"A misfortune happened with *mama*, and it will happen with us as well!"…

It really was a misfortune.

Every time I tell this story, I feel again all the emotions, I relive that trauma, and my soul bleeds. It is difficult when you go through memories because you go through that suffering that you had again…

It was night, around ten or eleven o'clock. The village did not have electricity. I saw on the road a light coming into the village. I was with my little sister and with a cousin. I said:

"Do you see that car? It comes after us, to take us and shoot us."

My cousin told me:

"How do you know these things? Why do you think it would be this way?"

We then fell asleep. Around two or three in the night, we heard bangs on the door, just like I had heard when they arrested my aunt. I got up:

"Who's there?"

I heard *bunelul*'s voice:

"Open, it's me."

I asked him:

"Why do you knock that hard? Why do you scare us?"

When I opened the door, *bunelul* had behind him four-five soldiers with guns. They dashed in the house, and I began crying. My little sister woke up, and my cousin ran away fast to tell my aunt, my mother's sister.

During all this time, they told us:

"Gathered what you can and come with us!"

"Where are you taking us? *Mama* is not here, and we are only two children. Where are my other brothers?"

"Take your clothes and let's go!"

"Where are you taking us? To *mama*?"

We were scared, and we made a bag out of a cover and put whatever came to us in there. They took us into a truck, where there were an old man and a woman nursing her child. There was also another family next to them. All the soldiers were guarding them with their guns. I began crying even louder. I took my farewells from my neighbors:

"They take us, arrest us, and shot us! If we harmed you in any way, if we sinned before you, forgive us!"

It was 1952, and I was 11 years old, and my sister 2 years

old. I was a child, and I did not understand why the soldiers followed us everywhere with their guns. We were going to the bathroom, and they followed us with their guns:

"Where are you running, child?"

"To the bathroom!"

They had their guns on us all the time.

In prison

They took us to the Rezina prison, where we did not have anything to eat or drink. We had nothing, and we were children. Toward evening, they loaded us in the truck again and took us to another place. I did not know where. They took us to Chişinău, in a prison on Livezilor Street. This prison still exists, and this is where all the thieves and murderers are kept - it is a prison for common law offenses.

Let me go back to what happened to *mama*. At two o clock in the night, they came to her and told her:

"You are arrested, and there is no way out from here!"

"But I have four children! What do you mean? Where are my children? Will I never see them again?"

"Don't worry, we'll bring your children too!"

As they arrested us, my sister Silvica and me, they also arrested my brothers and took all of us to the prison on Livezilor Street. All of us were gathered there, except my 12 year old older brother, whom they left together with the thieves. They took all of us to the prison hospital, with *mama* and brother Costică, who was sick. We all stayed in a room, but with other women and children. We were children, and so we wanted to run around, to talk, but we were not allowed to go even to the restroom.

We stayed there for two weeks. They were getting ready to take us to another place. We had no idea where. One night, they woke us up and told us:

"You go with us!"

They took us again in fear, having their weapons on us, in the middle of the night. We formed a column, and they took us through town: men, women, and children. We arrived at the train station. They loaded us in a special train for transporting prisoners; it had bars because it was used for thieves and criminals. They took us to the Tighina prison. We stayed there for one-two weeks, and then things were clarified and they took my family and other families back to the Chişinău prison.

They took us to Chişinău in the black car.[159] They did not take us on the main road, so that no one would see us. They cramped twenty-five of us in the car: children, adults, toddlers… Not having enough air to breathe, I fainted. *Mămica* shouted:

"My child is dying! Give her air!"

They stopped the car and carried me out. It was raining heavily. I was sweaty and very hot from the car, so I got pneumonia in both of my lungs. I arrived at the Chişinău prison, where I remained unconscious for three days. Only the good God has allowed me to live long enough so that you can see me today.

After a while, they took us to the train again, and they transported us to the prison in Odessa. In this way, from prison to prison, we arrived at the one in Kazakhstan. They told my mother that she was condemned to five years and that she was sent there to serve her sentence because her husband was a counter-revolutionary who fought against the regime and was part of an organization.

It took several months to reach Kazakhstan. We were together with the convicts in the train. We were ten-fifteen people in a compartment. They gave us some bread to eat. We, the children, got sick with dysentery. There were only Moldavians in the train up to Odessa, but then, in different stages, people of other nations came in: Estonians, Latvians, Germans… They were all political prisoners. I was a child, and I preferred to not think about what was in store for us. I was laughing, crying, singing… *Mama* was amazed: "What joy came over you?"

But I was afraid that they would separate us from *mama* and that other evils would come upon us.

---

[159] The author probably refers to a car that had black windows, so that no one could see in.

In Kazakhstan

When we arrived at the destination, something took place which shocked my mother greatly. The children, even the ones still nursing, were separated from their mothers, and the women from their men. I do not know why they did this; perhaps they did not want the children to create problems with the convoy. *Mama* thought that we were separated so that she could be shot, and she was worried for what would happen to us. Once separated from *mama*, we were very sad, and all of us brothers sat one next to the other forming a small pile. Then they took us and loaded us in a car pulled by small donkeys. They took all of us to prison, and when *mama* saw us again, she said:

"I am happy to see you, to be together!"

We stayed there for a month.

We were in the Republic of Kazakhstan. *Mămica* did not know Russian at all, but I went to Russian school for two years. When she was taken to the interrogations, *mămica* took me with her to be her translator. I knew a few words, and I translated the questions for her, and then I told them her answers. *Mama* said:

"My dear, implore them to not send us in the Cossack deserts because we do not know the language, and you will not be able to go to school!"

I cried and implored the comrade to allow us to stay in town because we wanted to study. They had pity on us and did not send us away. They knew that my mother was very sick and that she could die.

During these interrogations, *mama* was asked about her crimes, our crimes, and dad's crimes. Did she know about *tăticu*'s activity? She did not know anything. They took our fingerprints and our profile pictures... We stayed the whole time in the hospital, and they took us to the interrogations from there.

My brother had tuberculosis, and they kept us there so that we would not die, but we lived like the convicts; we slept on wooden boards. They moved us from the prison to the city only when they saw that we were dying. The whole city was full of deported people, and they had no place to accommodate us. They had deported entire villages there, entire regions with

Georgians or people from the Caucasus. You could not understand what language people were using on the streets.

First, they took us to a barrack with Greeks who had been deported in 1940. But they no longer had rooms there, so they finally took us to an office of the Securitate, where people had to come monthly with an ID to prove that they did not run away. When they saw *mămica* with four children, one smaller than the other, and when they understood that they did not know where to accommodate us, a Cossack and a *securist*[160] took pity on us and gave us one of their offices until they could find a place for us.

We did not have a place to sleep there, so we slept on the floor. We had nothing to cover us. It was January. We were hungry and sick... The Greeks pitied us and brought us a piece of bread, an onion, or something else, and they finally told us:

"If you have nothing to eat, go to the railway, where the train with the recruits passes by. Go there and beg for a piece of bread, and this will save you!"

Mămica cried and said:

"Go, my dears, go!"

She made us some small bags, we learned how to say bread in the Cossack language, and we went there and said:

"Give us a piece of bread!"

Whoever had a heart threw us a piece of bread. We were happy and came back home to *mama* with our little bags filled. *Mămica* made the fire with some pieces of coal - for we had a hob - and dried the bread there. We ate it like this, dry. She used to tell us:

"See, children, how God takes care of us, my dear children! See, we will not die of hunger!"

After a while, these people had even more mercy on our mother and us, and they told her:

"Give us the children, and we will assign them to orphanages. You must go to a hospital to be treated."

They gave the little children, my brother Costică and my sister Silvica, to an orphanage. My brother who had lung

---

[160] An officer from the Securitate, the secret police.

disease was sent to a sanatorium. *Mama* said:

"Leave my daughter with me!"

This is how I remained with *mama*.

She went for months to treatment to stay alive. They sent me to school.

We lived for a whole year with that crust of bread. I went to school and received the highest grades of all. The only class where I took poorer grades was Russian because I did not know it. But I began to understand the language of those Greeks, and when *mama* was at treatment, I was going to them to ask for boiled water that I used to eat the crust of bread. From time to time, they also gave me a good piece of something else. This is how we lived there!

After Stalin died, they called us to the office and told us that we could go home or to my mother's sister in Kurgan. *Mama* had written letters to ask to be moved to Kurgan to serve the sentence there. But *mămica* wanted to return to Bessarabia - she wanted to die home. However, we did not have any money for going back. Since she was a bit better, *mămica* took a job at a shoe factory, and she received some coins. At my age, I thought, "How can I also help *mama*?"…

One time, I went to the market and saw some girls selling *rochiţa-rândunicii*,[161] a plant with which they fed the cows. It could be found somewhere on the field, five kilometers away from the city. I began asking at people's doors:

"Don't you have cows so that I could bring you some grass?"

I found some people who wanted some grass. I walked around fifteen kilometers per day to gather this grass. This is how I helped *mama* to get the money for going back. This way, with the money *mămica* gained and with the money sent by our relatives from Bessarabia, who sent us from time to time some packages with corn meal and other things to eat, we gathered the money and we returned to Bessarabia. My little sister, Silvica, stayed behind because she was severely sick and could not have survived on a seven day long trip. *Mămica* thought that

---

[161] I am not certain what plant this is. The botanical name is Convolvulus.

it would be better for her to stay at the orphanage than to have to throw her from the train if she died. She thought that, when she got better, she would go back to take her. Then, if she, *mama*, died, no one would mock Silvica, and they would raise her there. Home, everyone mocked us. They called us the enemies of the people, counter-revolutionaries... We did not have any right.

We had a very difficult life when we returned

When we returned, we went to *bunelu'* in the village, to *mama*'s village. They did not allow us to return to dad's village, where our house was. My dad's house had been confiscated and became a post office. Then, it was demolished, and nothing remained from that house.

We did not receive back father's land either. We had a very difficult life when we returned here. Nobody helped us. I remember that we woke up in the night, it was cold, and they sent us on the field, where there were some straws, so that we could make it a bit warmer in the house. My youngest brother's finger blistered because of the cold. So we woke up at 2 o'clock in the night, so that the guardian would not see us, and took a few straws from the pile, came back in the cold and the blizzard, and could make it a bit warmer in the house.

It was terrible in Kazakhstan, but it was terrible back home as well. We did not have anything to eat, and *mama* sent me to get some bran to mix with a little flour and salt. We put it on the hob, dried it, and ate it. We had to toil much to survive. We did not have money for textbooks. My youngest brother took people's cows to pasture to get money for textbooks.

Mama was very sick and could no longer work. However, they forced her to work in the kolkhoz because there were shares we had to pay to the state for meat, eggs... *Mămica* wrote to the authorities and complained that she was dying, that she had three children she could not feed, and she asked to be excused from going to work in the field. They never excused her. *Mama* died in 1958. I continued school and finished ten years. I had very good grades; I was among the best students. I applied to the medical school, and I succeeded. My brother

Constantin sang beautifully, and *mama* wanted to make him a priest because my grandfather's brothers on my mother's side were cantors and priests. *Mama* came from a very faithful family, and she was very faithful herself. She used to say:

"Costică will be a priest for sure!"

After she understood that he would not be able to be a priest in that regime, seeing his talent for music, *mama* took him by the hand a few days before her death and went with him to the "Ciprian Porumbescu" school of music in Chişinău. *Mama* told them she could not help him, and he was taken in at the boarding school. I was in medical school, my brother was in music school, and *mama* was content that her children did not have to beg in the village. My older brother could not learn because he had been sick with meningitis from his childhood. However, he was hired as a worker in constructions.

Take care of your brothers!

Before dying, *mama* told me:

"I am dying, and all the parenting will now fall on your shoulders. You must do everything I did not do. You children must be dignified successors of your parents. Do not steal, do not murder; if you have nothing, go and beg from people. If they send you away, go one more time. Try again. Know that it is written: 'Knock, and it will be open, ask, and it will be given.' You only have your dignity of a pure girl. Be careful not to lose your dignity! It will be the same when you are married: do not lose your dignity. If your father is alive and if he comes back, tell him that I loved him until my last breath and I was faithful to him until the last moment of my life!"

For me, *mama*'s words remained as a commandment, as a testament.

"My dear child, you still have a sister in Siberia. If you want, you can look for her. She is there alone, in Siberia, and she does not know her family. Look for her, my dear child!"

My mom is for me my standard and my support. She was a special human, with a great will; she was a great human who lived for a short time but did many things for her children. I believe that, in heaven, she and dad are proud of us, her children. Who could think that we, who started our lives without any help, would manage to make such beautiful lives?

I would like to show you a poem *mămica* wrote in Kazakhstan. She says:

> *By the flowers, leaves, and deer,*
> *Bad you've cursed me, oh, dad dear,*
> *You cursed me on a Monday,*
> *So the world I covered all day.*
> *You cursed me on Tuesday, too,*
> *So I remained alone, and you*
> *Could help me not in wilderness*
> *To feed my children, powerless.*
> *And when we see that night has come,*
> *By cold like death we're overcome,*
> *For our blanket small it is,*
> *And everyone says, "I'm cold, please!"*
> *Galea wants it so she's covered,*
> *I desire it with ardor,*
> *To Vitali, it never gets,*
> *And Silvică cries with regrets.*
> *And Costică, having no fold,*
> *Cries and shouts: Mămica, I'm cold!*
> *Seeing all these things like this,*
> *I wake up, all is amiss!*
> *I begin to cover them,*
> *And to think, why me, why them?*
> *Why am I in so much torment?*
> *What did I do to men so bad*
> *That God sent me this bitterness*
> *And sent me out in wilderness*
> *With many children, fatherless.*
> *Lord, if you ever want to do*
> *A miracle, genuine and true,*
> *So my time here does get shorter*
> *So I can say my luck was better,*
> *So I can go back to my home,*
> *To see my family, my very own,*

To die back home, where I am from,
Regrets, I would have none at all,
For I would die in my own village.
There is no more cherished thing on earth
Than the village where I was born.
But if the Good God wishes not
That I would have what I may not ought,
Then please forgive me all of you,
My word in writing I leave for you,
And I pray you to forget it not,
To know that luck I did not have
And that I carried my life in senseless sands
In the darkness of foreign lands.

When my little brother, Costică, reached a difficult moment one day, a moment of despair, I gave him our mother's letter and told him:

"Costică, may it be that *mama*'s letter gives you courage!"

This letter encouraged my brother very much.

All the Bessarabians from the village thought that *mama* had died in Siberia. They said: "Frosea could not have resisted; she threw herself under the train!" They came to her sister and told her: "Your sister must have committed suicide from all the suffering she endured." This rumor was spread in the entire village, but it was not true. *Mămica* told me:

"Fight, children, until the end, so that you are victors!"

The meeting with my sister was staggering

Mama died, and I began to look around among my acquaintances to see how we could find our sister. When she left from Kazakhstan, *mama* asked some Bessarabians to take care of her. Silvica told us that whenever they visited her, these people were telling her that she had a little brother, Costică. She received news from them for a while, but then they moved out or our sister was moved to some other place. She stayed in one orphanage until she was old enough for school, and then they moved her to another orphanage with children from elementary schools, and then in another one with older children. I eventually found her…

I was already married, and my husband knew that I was looking for my little sister. One day, he came home and told me joyfully that he had found her. An answer came back from where she was. I wrote to the director of the orphanage and asked him whether there was someone willing to accompany our sister home. We were too poor, and we could not go there to bring her. The director sent his wife; he was Korean, and he was deported there. This is how they brought her to Chişinău.

The meeting with my sister was staggering. When we left her there, in Siberia, she was two years old; now she was in second grade. They would keep the orphans at the orphanage until a certain age, and then they sent them wherever they could. She was very happy when we met; she was joyful that she escaped from there, that she found her sister. For a long time, she did not tell me about the pain she had in her soul, but then, one day when I was with her, she told me:

"Why didn't you look for me earlier, so that I could get to know my *mama*, so that I could know what it means to have a mother? You were happy: you said *mama* and *tata*, you had our parents' affection, but I did not have any of this… This pain stays in my soul…"

I married early so that I could keep my brothers around me, both of them. After I finished medical school, they gave me a job in the city, and I worked as a medical assistant. I took care of my brothers and of my children. I helped my brothers in school, and then I helped them to get a living. After this, I had the desire to go to college as well, for I only had gone to medical school. I had two children, but I started to go to the exams for Medical School.[162] I finally passed only the fourth time.

I was decided to go to college. First, I was accepted to the Biology and Chemistry Department, which was affiliated with

---

[162] Faculty of Medicine. In Romania, the Medical School is not done after a BA degree, but you can apply to it directly out of high school. Mrs. Baranovschi Şapovalova went first to a medical school after which one can be a medical assistant (a school of arts and crafts), and then she went to the university for Medical School.

Medicine. But my dream was to become a doctor; I had wanted to do this since I was little. I remember that whenever I was asked, "What do you want to be when you grow up?" I always answered, "A pharmacist." I thought that to be a pharmacist is to be a doctor! I used to take broken vials and needles from *tăticul*, and played doctor. This was my dream, and it seemed that if I did not fulfill this dream, then it meant that I had accomplished nothing.

I was finally accepted to Medical School. I already had two children, both students in school. I was 27 years old when I went in, and I finished it when I was 34. I did Chemistry and Biology first, and then I did Medicine. I taught Chemistry and Biology for the upper levels, and I studied in Medical School at the same time. I finished it with very high marks - I was an exemplary student.

After he graduated from musical school, my brother Constantin[163] went to the Art Conservatory. He then joined a traditional folk music orchestra and, over time, he began arranging and composing different pieces, and so he became well known. This orchestra went to various countries to play, either socialist countries or in the West. The Securitate never allowed him to go. His compositions were played abroad, and some people even asked where the composer was. They answered that he had stayed behind in his country.

I felt God in my sufferings

Mama taught me the Creed and some prayers from an early age, and I had communion only when I was in seventh grade, after we came back from the deportations. The next day, when I went to school, there was a caricature in the classroom: Galina Baranovshi was on her knees before a cross, saying, "Lord, have mercy." All the children laughed at me:

"What, did you go to church? Did you have communion? And did God help you?"

This was a shock for me, and I alienated myself from God. However, He did not leave me, and He has always helped me...

---

[163] Constantin is the name from which the diminutive Costică is taken.

I went through difficult moments; today, I would have been dead or paralyzed after a serious meningitis if He did not help me. On one occasion, when I was very sick, something told me: "You will be paralyzed. Say *Our Father*!" While I was in that terrible state, I said the prayer.

I always felt that God helped me in my sufferings. But, you see, doing two majors in sciences, I was taught there that there is no God. I danced during Great Lent,[164] and I went to weddings during Great Lent... Since I was a doctor, I took ladies to a gynecologist, so they could have abortions. You see? I committed terrible crimes. I did many things, but God sent me priests among my patients, and they helped me to understand what I did... Now, I cry and pray God to forgive me: "Forgive me, Lord, for I am fashioned by Your hands!"...

When I returned to Bessarabia, I also wrote a poem for those who were deported. I wrote it when I was in a tragic moment and felt oppressed. This poem was the cry of my soul:

> Little leaf and forest brother,
> Don't you beat me, dear mother,
> And I beg you, curse me not
> For they'll take me to deport me.
> Take me far away they will,
> Over freshwater, and then, still,
> Over endless sand,
> In a far away country,
> In the Russian land,
> To where none would find me!
> I will live in prison,
> No sun, no water given.
> Light there will not be,
> For people are evil, you see.

---

[164] The Great Lent is the period of fasting before Pascha. (40 days plus the Holy week). It is a period of cleansing and preparation for the renewal brought by the Resurrection. In Orthodox tradition, people abstain from food coming from animals, including dairy products, alcohol, and sexual activity. They are supposed to dedicate more time to prayer and alms giving. Celebrations of any kind are discouraged during this period.

I will be forsaken,
For people are pagan!
I will have no mother,
And I'll only suffer;
Parents I won't have,
And I will taste no fruit!
And what's still worse,
All my brothers are cursed!
And I will cry, and cry, and cry,
Till my eyes are lost and dry,
With bloody, bitter tears,
For unanswered prayers.
Write me something, mother,
Write me any letter,
Write me with hidden words[165]
To know how things are at home,
Write me little verbs,
To make me cry and moan.
God will surely see
How I suffer here,
And for my ordeals,
Hearing my appeals,
He will send a miracle
Clear, loud, and visible,
That I would go back home,
From the bitter, abusing world.
Little leaf and forest brother,
Don't you beat me, dear mother,
And I beg you, curse me not
For they'll take me to deport me...

Chişinău, Bessarabia, the 16th of June, 2011

---

[165] Communication from and to home had to be encrypted, so that they could bypass the censorship.

From Cosăuţi toward the Valley...

Teodosia Cosmin

My parents were simple people

I was born on June 9, 1938, in the village of Bubuleşti, the county of Floreşti, the district of Soroca.

In 1940, when our dear Bessarabia was separated from Romania, I was only a small child, a baby, and I did not know that my country was divided. My parents were simple people, peasants; they worked the land. We were eight brothers. There were six elder brothers and sisters; I was the last but one child. Some of the brothers died while they were children because of diseases, and we were only three sisters and a younger brother, Iacobaş,[166] who died during the famine. He was one year old.

In 1945, dad was arrested and taken to Siberia. He had a very sad destiny. He was taken to a camp, in the region of Kransnoyarsk. He was not allowed to write. *Mămica* received a letter from him by chance. On the road from the camp to the work place, dad found a piece of paper, and he wrote on it a letter to *mama*. He threw it on the road, hoping that a good man would find it and put it in the mail. And so it happened. Dad wrote that they were very strictly watched, that they were not allowed to look to the left or to the right, and that they were suffering from famine. It was already the beginning of 1947, and *tăticu* wrote that it was very difficult, that it was cold, and that they were sent to forced labor. We did not receive any other news from him. While he was still with us, *tăticu* told us what the Soviet Union meant, what communism meant, and so he prepared us. He told us that the world would change, and he told us to not become pioneers,[167] to not enter in the Komsomol:

"These antichrists will force you to step on icons, to deny your faith... Regardless of how difficult it may be, be strong and do not become pioneers and Komsomolists!" I remembered this for my whole life.

---

[166] This is the diminutive of Iacob (Jacob in English).
[167] The pioneers were the members of the youth organization of the Communist Party. It was the first step in becoming a member of the Party.

The times of the famine

Without *tăticu*, it was very difficult for us during the time of the organized famine, in 1946-1947, because the Russians came and swept our attics. They took the last grain. It was very difficult during the famine. Our luck was *mama*, who was a very strong character. One of my sisters, Ilenuţa, died of hunger during that time. I remember how she used to say:

"*Mămica*, if God just brought dad home, so that he would bring us two loaves of bread and two pretzels!"

She did not desire anything else. Just two loaves of bread and two pretzels. It was very difficult. We went through famine, typhus... *Bunica*, dad's mother, died then as well, still because of hunger. Ilenuţa, who wanted two loaves of bread and two pretzels, and Iacobaş, the youngest brother, only one year old, died too. He was just a babe. He died in terrible pains. I wrote about this in a small book. I cried all the time I wrote about it. I had two new handkerchiefs, and while I wrote about this moment, when the little brother Iacobaş died in terrible torment, I filled them with tears. I cried until I was wasted. Then I washed my face with cold water, came back to myself, and wrote again.

This is how it was with our brother: *Mama* was away during the day; she had to take the cow to give it away because they took quotas for meat. There were huge lines, and she had to stay for days. My brother was almost one year old, and when *mama* came home in the evening to feed him, he sucked greedily from her breast. He got sick. He had dysentery. When he was close to his death, *mama* was crying, I was crying, and so too my sisters Eugenia and Pelaghia... He could not die. Our lament could be heard, and he had tears on his cheek. He was close to his death, and his tears flowed. A neighbor came and said:

"Go out, all of you, and I'll hold his candle; he cannot die because he hears your lament."

We all went out, and he died in great torment.

The famine of 1946-1947 passed. In 1948, the famine subsided a little. But let me tell you what we ate out of hunger. We ate weeds, flour from *cioclezi* - you know, that stalk from corn... *Mămica* crushed it well and mixed it with a little wheat of bran, so we had something to eat. When the oil is done, there are some remains from the sunflower - we call them *macuh*.[168] We ate those as well. We thought they were sweet like honey. *Mama* had to gather 20-25 cubits of cloth because back then the cloth was measured in cubits. She used to say that if she survived, she would make us some other dowry. She said:

"Clothes do not feed us. I'll sell everything, so that we may be saved!"

She went and she traded ten cubits of cloth for a *macuh*, a little bread. We had dishes. On Palm Sunday, she sold the dishes - she gave them to people who were better situated and who had some food and lived better than us. It suited them because they bought these things almost for nothing. It was very difficult... It is very difficult to describe those moments.

1949 seemed to be a good year...

Then, 1949 seemed to be a good year. But on July 6 we were deported. The day before deportation we had people over helping us hoe the land. During those times, people helped one another because it was difficult to work the land as we were just a few women.

On July 5, 1949, it was our turn to hoe the land - corn, sunflower... what we had. *Mămica* was of strong character. Regardless of how difficult it was, she knew how to get to the end of things and to resist in difficult times. After they finished hoeing, *mămica* told them:

"Let us have a dance!"

They held each other's hands and sang and danced. In the evening, they came home. On that day, I played like a fool. You could see it was not a good sign. I played with a girl in the neighborhood all day long. We played, wrestled, and laughed the whole time. Especially me; I laughed with tears. She laughed as well. Then she stopped, looked at me, and said:

"Teodosia, what's up with you?"

---

[168] As already explained, *mahuc* (also spelled *macuc*) are the remains of sunflower seeds when oil is made from them.

"I don't know, but I want to laugh, to jump!"

It was not a good sign. In the evening, when *mămica* came home from hoeing the land, she put all of them at the table, to have dinner. By then, I was sad, very sad. It was as if I was taken someplace by my own thoughts. I could hear what they were saying, but I could not be attentive. I had pain in my soul. Someone even noticed this and said:

"Look at this child how sad she is! What may be the problem?"

Mămica said:

"Did you see how many cars were on the road today? Why so many cars?"

Someone said:

"Don't you worry; the cars have their business."

Someone else said:

"I hope there is not another war!"

These cars were going here and there; they were assigned to villages and districts, to pick up the deportees.

These people stayed at our place for a long time. After dinner, they talked. You know how it is in the villages: people say jokes, talk about things... It was getting very late. One of them even said:

"Look how long we are staying at your place today! As if we weren't meeting again tomorrow!"

Mămica said:

"Who knows? It is a long time until tomorrow..."

What else do you want from us?... Our life?...

These people left home around midnight. *Mămica* prepared the beds, and we went to sleep.

We fell asleep. We slept for an hour, perhaps two, and then we heard knocks on the door. *Mămica* got up to open it. I was very sensitive, and I woke up as well. I grabbed my mother's shirt, and I went with her to the door. *Mămica* asked:

"Who's there?"

I recognized his voice. It was the secretary of the village's soviet. He said:

"Open, do not be afraid. It is I!"

"What's the problem? So late! What are you looking for at this hour?"

"Do not be afraid, open!"

Mămica opened, and armed soldiers, armed Russian soldiers, with their berets with the hammer and the sickle and the red star on the foreheads, invaded the room. Once they stepped inside, they shouted:

"Fast, in the car!"

Mămica began shouting and pulling her hair:

"What do you want from us? You arrested my husband, you took him from five children" - we were five children when *tăticu* was arrested. "I gave you grains for quotas! You swept my attic, and there was no grain left! I gave you the cow for meat! What else do you want from us?... Our life? Take it!"

This is what they did during the famine. They swept the attics. They did not leave one little grain. If anyone hid something in the basement, the attic, or in the earth, they still found it and took it. They took even the last bucket of corn. It was so terrible!

When I saw them, I froze out of fear. I could not say a word. I think I was pale. My hand froze on my mother's shirt. The Secretary said:

"You don't have much time, half an hour. Don't waste time! Take whatever you have and throw it in the car!"

Mămica turned to the walls, where we had many pictures with the family and icons. She began kissing the pictures, the icons, and we began to get ready. *Mama* said:

"Clothes will not keep me warm. Where are they taking us? Perhaps to death..."

The secretary put his finger on his lips and said:

"I don't have the right to tell you. Only this: you can take whatever you want."

But how? I was frozen still. My sister began covering the child, my nephew, who was only four months old. The neighbors heard my mother's shout. We lived next to a rocky shore, and my mother's cries echoed out toward the village.

The neighbors came and they began throwing in the car anything they could grab: pillows, some sheets, a bucket, a cauldron, a plate… They gathered everything fast and took it to the car. Our turn came too, and we went in the car. I came a bit to my senses. The Russian soldiers guarded us with their weapons on us. I raised my eyes to them, and I remembered how they forced us at school to learn poems about their heroes, hymns about Stalin. I remembered a poem about Stalin, about their Lenin, and their "heroism," and I looked at them with a painful gaze, the gaze of a child, and I thought: "These are the heroes about whom we learned poems by heart? These heroes come and snatch us from the nest of our parents' house, to take us God knows where?…"

If we die, we'll die together!

From our place, they went on to other houses, including to the house of an old woman, Ileana Vieru. They rushed her to get in the car as well. She took some of her clothes. When she was about to get in the car, the lad across the street wanted to help her, to give her a hand, but they did not allow him. The entire village was already up. My sister Pelaghia was married, but she was on the list with deportees as well. When she heard and saw that we were in the car,[169] she began howling, pulling her hair, and shouting:

"*Mama,* my dears, I am coming with you!"

Mămica shouted:

"No, Pelaghița,[170] run, because we do not know where they will take us! Maybe they will take us to our death!"

But she said:

"If we die, we'll die together! I want to be with you!"

The people who were gathered there, the villagers, formed a wall to defend her because the soldiers jumped to catch her and take her to the car. But someone took Pelaghița on the side and hid her. The truck left, and she escaped. She remained a fugitive for two weeks, so that she would not be caught and deported. We left. Everything that we had in the house and

---

[169] Since she was married, she lived in a different house, so she was not taken at the beginning.

[170] This is the diminutive for Pelaghia.

around the house, remained there. We could take very little.

The trucks left the village toward Floreşti. When we arrived there, at the train station, I, being a child, wanted to count the train cars. But they did not allow you to do even that and pushed us with the guns to get in the train as fast as possible. They loaded us in the cars in which they transported the cattle - they loaded us in the same cars. Our family, *bunicuța* Ileana,[171] and the others who were from our village went in one car, next to the engine.

The road to Siberia took one month

By evening, all cars were filled with people. They gave the order to leave. The car was overcrowded. You had no place to pass. Everyone had his or her own luggage. We stayed on the floor. Since the car was in the sun the whole day - it was July, and it was very hot - we felt like we were in an oven. When the train left for Siberia, the people who remained on the platform began crying. They were lamenting, shouting, trying to hold on to the cars...

"Write to us, tell us what happens to you!"

In that turmoil, *mămica* began singing. She began singing the song with which people used to accompany the lads who were leaving for the army. But *mămica* made up different lyrics on the spot, and everyone began accompanying her and singing. It was then, on the spot, that the words of the song were being born:

> *From Cosăuți toward the valley,*
> *From Cosăuți toward the valley,*
> *There formed a large, long alley.*
> *Of and of again...*[172]

---

[171] *Bunicuța* Ileana is the old woman mentioned above. *Bunicuța* is the diminutive from *bunica*, the word for "grandmother."

[172] I could not find any equivalent for this expression in this context. In Romanian, "of" is an interjection that one uses when one sighs, especially in connection with some pain, physical or psychological. One may say, "Sigh and sigh again," but I thought that leaving it in Romanian would maintain the poem's musicality.

Of and of again...
And the alley's on three pines,
And the alley's on three pines,
For the deportees in lines.
Of and of again...
Of and of again...
Deportees from Bessarabia,
Deportees from Bessarabia,
Filled with wailing, grief, and woe!
Of and of again...
Of and of again!

And the entire car was moaning and crying. The train was already in movement. As I told you, it was very hot. They closed the door and locked us in. There were only two small barred windows. The toddlers fainted because of the heat. There was a terrible stench. In the corner, toward the door, they put a bucket, and this is where we did our necessities. They stopped us and took us down from the train cars two times per week. The armed soldiers stood on both sides so that no one would escape. We had to relieve ourselves there, under the train. Imagine that there were virgins, children, young lads, and older people! We were of all ages. And all of us there, under the car.

The journey to Siberia took a month. The food was dry: black bread, fish, or whatever else they gave us, but it was very bland. We had water from a reservoir from the engine. They gave us a bucket for the little ones, so that we could wash them once a week. We arrived in Krasnoyarsk, in Siberia, right in the region where *tăticu* had been. We knew from the letter that *tăticul* was in Krasnoyarsk, and we thought we might meet him. We did not know that he had died. He died on the 2nd of May, 1949, right in the place where they deported us. But we did not know he was dead, and we were thinking, "Where may *tăticu* be? Perhaps they would allow him to come to meet us..."

Once we arrived there, groups of twenty deportees were organized to be taken to bathe, and they were flanked by armed soldiers. When they took us to bathe, they ordered all of us to get naked: women, men, children, young lads, young girls, all together. They pushed us in those booths to wash: "Faster, faster, wash yourselves!" And again:

"Fast, get dressed, and in the cars!"

It was terrible! *Mămica* told us:

"Do not look around! Put your eyes down! Do not look around!"

I'm telling you, there were young people, girls, and old people, and they pushed us in those booths as if we were cattle. This is how we washed. Then, fast, back to the cars and on the road. We arrived at a station after a month, as I told you. They commanded us to get out.

It was raining; it was drizzling, as if through a sieve. It was toward the end of July. And we... with our luggage... They gave us some money. They allowed the children to go buy something. But what could you buy? Black bread and some salty fish... You could not buy anything. But we bought what we found, for we were hungry. They kept us on that platform for 48 hours.

Four weeks in taiga

Cars came to take us to the taiga. We went to the taiga from that station, around 40 kilometers away. We loaded the luggage, and we went on top of it, in the trucks. This trip in the truck was also very difficult because it was bumpy, and the truck would incline from one side to the other, almost to the point of rolling over. So again there was crying, shouting, and all those things...

We arrived in the taiga. There were some wooden barracks without doors and windows... It was obvious that before us there were other deportees and prisoners. They tucked us in those barracks. There were some wooden bunks, like drawers, two to a bunk. Every family received one of these decrepit beds, made with an axe. They made the men repair the doors and the windows because there were thick forests, with many wild animals, so they had to make the doors and the windows to keep out the beasts, the bears, and the wolves.

We stayed in these barracks in the taiga for a month. There also were a few houses that belonged to the locals. Before we

came, there had been other deportees because we saw their
names written on the wall. They were German, Polish... We
also wrote our names on those walls. After a month, they loaded
us again and separated us with the purpose of taking us to
different regions. In our barrack, there were also four deported
children without parents, from the village of Pragina, next to the
district of Floreşti. Their mother was in prison because she
could not pay for the state quotas, so they tried and arrested her.
Their father had died of hunger. They took them, four children
without parents, and deported them. They were there, with us.

They told our family, *bunicuţa* Ileana, our neighbor, and
others where we had to get off. But God was with us. We fell
asleep, so we did not get out where we had to. We went by train
further than the place where we were assigned. In the morning,
when the chief came, he did not know what to do with us.

"You had to get out at that station!"

We all raised our shoulders... How could we know, in the
wilderness, in foreign places, where we had to get out? After
all, they sent us some other place. He reported that there were
four families that did not get out where they had to be. They
took us to the steppe, to the plain of Amur.

The settlement number four

As far as you could see, there was nothing else but the
steppe. Only deserted fields. Wilderness! From time to time,
there was a small settlement with thirteen-fifteen houses. Very
small. They had no name; they were known only by numbers.
The first settlement, the second... We were in settlement
number four. We were assigned to a *sovkhoz*.[173] When he saw
us, the chief of the *sovkhoz* said:

"What can I do with you? I have no houses, I have
nothing..."

He did not expect to have people assigned there. There was
an empty train car. There were people from the city in the
settlement, who came to mow the hay because there were cattle
farms and they deposited the feed for winter; this grass was very

---

[173] (*Footnote in the Romanian edition*) A kind of collective farm.

good. They also seeded barley and other things. The chief said: "Since there are still workers from the city, you will stay in the train car until fall."

We arranged our modest luggage in that car. It was late, so we went to sleep. We woke up in the middle of the night. We were scratching. We were all itchy, and the children were crying. The bedbugs and all sorts of insects from the car's planks were biting us. We woke up, and *mămica* did not know what to do with us. She found a little bottle with gas that may have been used by others as well. She put gas on us too. We could not fall asleep all night. In the morning, we cleaned up a bit, we washed, we put gas on everything, and we remained there.

We, the children, slept on the hob

Mămica worked with the calves, and my sister milked the cows. She was young, thin, and she had to milk fourteen cows. In the beginning, she barely managed to milk five-six cows. But the other women who milked cows helped her. There were other deportees from the Baltic States. They had been deported earlier, in March. They were learned people, with higher education. Some were physicians, others professors, others engineers, but they all worked there, at the cattle farm. The women helped my sister who, slowly, got used to it and became one of the best.

Mămica worked with the calves, and we, the children, stayed home, looking for something to eat or for firewood during the winter. They gave us straws instead of wood. But what could you do with those straws when the frost would get to -40 degrees Celsius during winter! We had a very difficult time with the cold and the food. During the autumn, we went in the field and took whatever was left there: a potato, a beet… We still found a few pieces. But it was harder with the fire, and it was very cold.

After we made the fire, we the children used to sleep on the hob. As long as it was hot, the hob burned us, but then it was terribly cold. This is why all of us, deportees, are sick. That cold hob would stick to our bodies. Poor *bunicuța* Ileana had a piece of fabric from home, and she made some sort of a sock that she put on over the night. The cold was terrible. In the morning, the adults went to their work, to the farm. If it happened that they were delayed at work in the evening, they could no longer return home that night because there were many wolves. The wolves surrounded the farm. I know because I went with *mămica* sometimes, and you could see their eyes, like the candles, one next to the other, howling. If I was with *mămica* at the farm, we were afraid to come home and we slept at the farm.

The children looked for firewood because it was very difficult to make the fire with straws. The locals, the Russians, threw away not completely burned coals from their stoves. We found a bag, picked them up, and divided them among ourselves: "You take a little pile, and I take a little pile." I was shy and more reserved, and the other children sometimes forgot about me when they divided the coals. But the Russian children also came by and saw how we divided the coals. They saw that the children did not give me my share, and they said:

"Look, it's her turn, you must give coal to this girl too!"

Briefly, it was tragi-comic!

We, the children, learned Russian fast. We sometimes played with the Russian children, even if they called us all possible names. I remembered how *tăticul* used to tell us: "I may not be alive one day. Who knows what fate you will have! Be strong, be dignified, and never give up before the enemy. Do not cry, and always have a smile on your face. Even if it hurts, retain your dignity and keep your head up!" I tried to be this way. Sometimes, we would quarrel with the Russian children because they called us "the enemies of the people," "gypsies," this, and that. All manner of insults. But I did not give up. I answered back:

"You cannot be both Gypsy and Moldavian. Look, the Gypsies are dark - we are not dark! We have blue eyes."

At the end, there were always fights between the Russian children and us. As they were more numerous than us, they managed to overpower us, and we used to run to the barrack. We entered in fast and locked the door, and I still did not give up. We had that small icon from home, and I used to go with it to the window, show it to them and say:

"You see, here is God! He will protect us, but your Stalin is not good!"

It was something serious to say such a thing about Stalin.

God will bless our Pascha

This is how we lived for three years. By that time, a little house was made, and they gave us a part of it, with aunt Ileana[174] and the four orphan children.

Let me tell you how we celebrated the Holy Pascha in Siberia. Over time, *mămica* had gathered some flour, eggs, and all that was needed. She made the fire and baked a Paschal pie, as it is done in our regions. At our place, around Floreşti, the Paschal pie is round with cheese and with the sign of the cross on top of it. Where could we bless it?[175] *Mămica* was a very faithful woman. She was orphan, with no parents, and she got close to faith and the Church since she was very small. She had a very beautiful voice, and she used to sing in the choir of the church. She knew the entire service by heart. Aunt Ileana was also a very faithful Christian.

So, with Pascha... The Russians came and looked at our Paschal pie as to a miracle. We colored eggs with onion peels, with whatever we could, as it is done in our world, according to tradition. At four in the morning, *mămica* and aunt Ileana put that pie on a towel together with the eggs and salt. They sang and prayed to God.

And she said, "God will bless our Pascha!" The Russians did not know about Church and God there. They knew about nothing in that wilderness. Whatever was prepared, we put on the table. We said, "Christ is Risen!" We ate and we did everything according to tradition. We sang liturgical songs...

---

[174] Aunt Ileana is *bunicuţa* Ileana. Both words, "aunt" and "bunicuţa," are not used with their usual meaning, but designate an older person, so close to the family that she receives family names.

[175] In the Orthodox tradition, people take the non-fasting food to church on Easter night. At the end of the Paschal Liturgy, the priest blesses all food, and the people eat it there, after the long Great Lent, or take it home and eat it with their family.

And I am telling you that the Russians began to look at us differently from that moment.

Going to the school from the settlement

We, the children, did not go to school because nobody called us there. Our settlement was small, and the teacher did not call us to go to school. The school was in a small, wooden house. We went there when she was having lessons with the children, and we looked through the window at how the Russian children sat and learned. She made it seem as if she did not see us. She took short glances at us, but she did not say anything.

Nobody had called us to school for two years, and no one had taken care of us. But a woman who was also a teacher returned to that settlement. She was a teacher, and her husband was chief at the milk place. That woman had a good soul. She saw us immediately and realized that we were not going to school. It was already the third year, in November. She told us:

"My dear children, why don't you learn? Why don't you come to school? It will be very difficult in life without learning anything… You must come to school immediately!" She called us to her place, gave us tea and candies, and told us:

"Starting tomorrow, you will come to school! I will give you notebooks and books, and you will begin studying."

We said that we did not speak Russian, and she said that we would get used to it because we were children and we would learn. But we had to be placed two years behind since we did not know Russian. We had already lost two years because we did not go to school. We had already grown quite a bit.

This is how we began second grade. We learned the Cyrillic alphabet - I actually knew it from Moldova. We learned well. Sometimes, she even told the Russian children:

"Look, these children came here and do not know the language, but they read better than you and they study, and they also solve the mathematical problems!"

I had very good memory. I could read a poem once or twice, and whenever I would go to the farm to help *mămica* with the calves, I seemed to see the letters before my eyes and I would recite the poem while walking on the road. The next day

I already knew it by heart. But to what use?... In the spring, they told us that they would take us again and move us some other place. They did not tell us where.

Digging ditches in Blagovescensk

Those who were there before us, the people from the Baltic States, the Latvians, who were learned and also had a radio and listened to foreign stations, knew what would happen. They told us that we would be taken to big cities to work in constructions. They took us from this small settlement to the city of Blagovescensk, on the shore of river Amur.

When they took us from there, the Russians cried after us. Even the chief of the *sovkhoz* became sad because such hard working people were taken from there! When they took us, they also took the Latvians and the Ukrainians. They took all of us from the settlement and took us to the construction sites, and so no people left to work for him. Their people worked as well, but not like our people. They cried after us and told us:

"Write us, tell us about your fate, what happens to you!"

Our parents had to go twice a month to the Police station to sign that we were all there and that nobody had run away. We the children were getting closer to being 15-16 years old, and they had to make papers for us as well. We prayed to God and talked among ourselves: "How nice it would be if we didn't have to go to the Police when we receive our papers! How nice it would be to be free!"

So they took us. They loaded us again in trucks. We were good workers, so we had already gathered some things, some chickens, a rooster, a little pig... They allowed us to take everything we had. We took these things with us, and they brought us to the city of Blagovescensk, on Amur.

This city was on the border with China. If you looked over the water, over Amur, you could see a city in China. It was very cold, and we were poorly dressed, with some paddy coats. After a while, we managed to get some felt boots. The first winter when we arrived in Siberia, the soles of our feet would freeze, and we could no longer take our feet out of our shoes. While we stayed in that settlement, the locals also helped us a bit. They threw us some warmer shoes, and later we could buy felt boots. But it was very cold at the beginning.

There, in the center of the city, there was a string of stores. They[176] gave orders to empty the stores and the warehouses where the stores kept their merchandise. They brought their bunk beds and placed them in rows. The warehouse was very large. But it was cold and dark, with small barred windows. They gave a space to each family. We spent the winter there. It was very cold. They gave us some electrical hobs, but you had to wait in line just to cook something. You waited in line everywhere, for the hob, for the restroom. It was very difficult. They began organizing brigades for work, deciding where to send everyone. It was either to dig the earth, to build, or whatever each person got. They did not pay attention to whether you were a woman or a child. "You are a slave, so make sure that you accomplish what you are told!" They made us work as well. *Mămica* had to dig ditches. My sister worked in construction, as a painter.

I would help *mămica*, but the earth was frozen because it was winter. They gave us small pieces of coal and wood to make the fire. *Mămica* made signs for the width of the trench that had to be dug. We knew that the depth had to be three meters. We dug a bit and made the fire there. The coal burned, then the wood on the coal, and so the earth defrosted a bit. Not much, perhaps half a meter, not more. We then took the fire with embers, coal, and wood, everything, and moved it a bit further. While it was defrosting there, we dug this little spot. This is how we dug.

We had to make trenches for water pipes, for the sewerage of the city. It was not stony, but it was frozen like bone. The whole city was dug by these deportees because there was no equipment back then for digging. It was us; we dug it with our hands. Of course, when the land defrosted, it did not defrost only half a meter width, as we needed to dig. The sides defrosted as well, so when we reached two, two and a half

---

[176] We have again the very impersonal but powerful "they." "They" represents the government.

meters in depth, the banks would fall on people. Some managed to escape, but others would suffocate and die there in those deep trenches. This is how we dug, with the picker and the spade, and I helped *mămica*.

They did not call us to school there either. However, the second autumn when we were in that city, we went to school. The teacher found out that we were deportees, and she hated us. I was also taking care of my nephew, so I was late for lessons at times. The school was not far from where we lived, so I went home during breaks to see how my nephew was; when the class started, I was late again. One time, for an exam, I asked for a notebook because we had to write on a new notebook. But that teacher answered meanly:

"I do not have a notebook for your excellence."

I burst into tears and left the class. I ran from there, and I never went back to school. This is how I ended up with no school. They moved us from the first warehouse to other warehouses. When we washed the floors, the water immediately froze, and we, the children, slid around. We were barefoot, and we hurt ourselves... It was something terrible.

We did not have money to return home

In 1953, when Stalin died, we all rejoiced. Perhaps it is a sin that we rejoiced, but each one of us, the deportees, came out in the street. Men threw the hats in the air, and the women cried with joy, saying:

"Glory to the Lord! We finally got rid of the tyrant! Perhaps something will change in our lives!"

Well, something changed, but it changed with much difficulty. Indeed, they gave orders to give amnesty to all the deportees, to retry them - but this was done gradually. They began to free people gradually, not all at the same time. They also allowed us to leave, sometime in 1956. But we did not have money for the trip home. When they took us to Siberia, they brought us in cars for cattle, but if you wanted to go back, you had to pay!

We worked for almost two years, day and night - we worked during the day in constructions, and in the evening we went to work on a contract, to make some money, so that we could go back home. In 1957, at the end of August, we returned to our native land. When we entered the Bessarabian land, we could hear Romanian everywhere. We could not believe it. *Mama* and we, the children, were embracing each other, crying… Finally, we were on our land!

Niet! There is no work!

When we returned home, some people received us well. They came to see us, and they had joy. Others looked at us with different eyes. I knew who turned in *tăticu* and who put us on the list for deportations. I went to that man's house and told him:

"What did you think? That we would die? Look, God was on our side, and we returned home!"

I do not know why God allowed that we went through this trial and these sufferings.

Tăticu was very faithful. *Mămica* sang in the holy church. We were all faithful, but perhaps this is what God wanted, that we would go through this dark period… However, with the Lord's help, we managed to return home. But *tăticu* remained there, and we do not know where he is.

Nothing good waited for us home. The house had been confiscated, and they did not return it to us. They made a kindergarten out of it.

We went to my sister Pelaghiţa. It was very difficult. It was hard to get a job. In the district of Floreşti, the Soviets made a sugar factory because there was plenty of room. Many people worked there from our village. After we returned from Siberia, I stayed for a week, and then I went to get a job because you must work. Young girls and boys from our village worked there, people of all ages. They told me:

"Come to the sugar factory; they will take you too!"

I was young, almost 19 years old, and I was strong and healthy; I could work. I went there, to that factory, and when the watchman saw me, he told me:

"They will take you immediately!"

I went to the window where they were hiring, and I told

them I wanted to work there. They asked for my papers. I gave them the papers, they looked at them, and they saw that my passport was from Amur. They answered harshly:

"Niet! There is no work!"

I said:

"How come there is no work? Many from our village work here! And the watchman told me that there is work!"

"I told you that there is no work!" And she closed the window in my face.

That was it. I came out from there in tears, and I went back home. This is how they mocked us, so that we could not find work. So I looked for work again. You could only find little things, working for people, so that they could pay you something. But it was very difficult.

We received the house, but nothing from our wealth...

We lived like this for a year. I do not know how she did it, but *mămica* managed to get hired in our own house, where there was now a kindergarten. She worked there, making food for the children. The woman who had done it before had retired. *Mama* cooked well, so the children were content... But one day, *mămica* told the kolkhoz brigadier:

"You want it or not, but I will get this house from you somehow! I will take it back because it is my house, made by me, with my own hands!"

He fired her on the spot. But *mama* found a lawyer in the city of Bălți, who was retired and did not worry about losing his job if he helped us. For two years, we wrote to Moscow and asked for our right. They returned the house to us only in 1961. We received the house back, but nothing from our wealth because they said that they did not find anything when they confiscated the house and sent us to Siberia.

I have the paperwork they gave me in Florești, made when they confiscated our house, and it says that they found only five objects: a bed, a table, a trough, a barrel, and something else. And it says that all this was worth only 8 rubles. This is how they valued everything we left there, 8 rubles!

We lost everything when they took us to Siberia! So we received back our house, but the house was destroyed. Before returning it to us, they took out the shutters and even the floor in some rooms. When they returned the house, they even took out the hob because they said they put it in.

When communism fell, I rejoiced very much! There was no meeting in the city, no demonstration to which I would not go! I was always in the first lines. One of my nephews even said: "I see my aunt rather on TV, at demonstrations, than in reality!" I fought against communism with all my heart.

After I returned from Siberia, I worked and I got married. At the beginning, I worked in the village. I was a day laborer, and then I managed to get in the sugar factory and later into a brigade for constructions. I moved to Chişinău in 1964. I was controlling tickets at the State Philharmonic, and later at the Opera Theater.

I regretted that I could not go to school. I went to school here, in Bessarabia; I did seven years with evening courses. I learned well, but it was difficult, and I could not continue. I was married with two children, and it was difficult, but I still went to evening courses. The teachers always praised me and said to some of my colleagues, children, who did not learn:

"This woman has two children, works, has a house to manage, and she learns well; you, young ones, with no cares, why can't you learn?!..."

This is how we have encountered and still encounter difficulties until this day. We were humiliated; it was difficult; we were truly slaves in Siberia.

Chişinău, Bessarabia, 22 of June, 2011

Alone Among Foreigners

Tamara Oală Pleşca

The night of deportation

My name is Tamara Pleşca, maiden name Oală. I am from
the village of Sofia, next to Drochia, in Bessarabia. I was born
in July 1935. I am from a family with six children. We were
three boys and three girls. Three were younger than me: two
brothers and a sister. Our parents were peasants. They had a
beautiful household because they were hard-working people and
had everything they needed.

Our family was deported in the night between the 12th and
the 13th of June 1940. That evening, I went to one of my sisters,
who was married. I had done it before since I loved her very
much. Her house was very close to ours, and I ran to sleep
there. But at 2:00 in the night, I missed *mama* so much that I
woke everyone up, telling them that I wanted to go home! I
went to my sister often, but that night I could not be convinced
otherwise:

"I want to go to *mama*, I want to go to *mama!*"

What could they do? Something pulled me home. My sister
and my brother-in-law got dressed and took me home. When we
got close to the house, we heard a powerful yell, and the dogs
were barking so loudly that your hair stood up on your head out
of fear. What could have happened? We did not know that some
people were taken right then for deportation. My sister began to
tremble. We crossed the road and arrived home. *Mama* heard
us, and she told us to come in because the door was not locked.

"What happened to you?" she asked.

"She began yelling that she wanted to go home, and we
could not do anything about it."

Mama gave me a couple of spanks on my back and scolded
me:

"Why didn't you leave your sister alone so that she could
get some sleep?"

Then my sister asked her:

"But why aren't you sleeping?"

"I do not know why we can't sleep... I don't know what is wrong with us; we have a heavy heart!"

I was awake, and I heard how *mama* and *tata* were saying this. They talked a bit, and then they left. Not long after, we heard the dogs barking again, and then one carriage. They were coming toward us.

Someone was kicking at the door. I remember what dad said when they knocked on the door:

"Who else may God be bringing us?"

Mama said:

"Perhaps our daughter and son-in-law have returned?"

"No; there are several people; you can hear voices," dad said. "Come in; it is not locked!"

When they rushed in, they were seven people or so. They filled the house. I was awake and, like any child, I was curious. I saw everything. When they came in, one of them started to speak in Russian with dad. I did not understand, but dad knew Russian because there were many Russians in our village and dad knew the language. I do not know what they told him. I only know that there were other people from our village there, and dad asked one of them:

"Why would they look for guns here? From where would I have taken them? How could I have any gold?... I just had two weddings (my brother and my sister had both married). How could I have such things?..."

To tell you the truth, we were deported in someone else's place, someone Istrate. He was on the list with the deportees that came from Bălţi. However, he was getting along well with the authorities, and they changed his name and took us in his place. They told us to get ready because they would take us.

My older brother and my sister-in-law, his wife, were there as well. During the day, they were hoeing the fields, and they stayed over to sleep at our place. There was also dad's mother, an old woman with no teeth. We went out, all of us. Our house was only one year old. My parents had demolished the old one and made this new one. My brother who was sleeping at our place was also on the list, so they took him too. They took all of us out. Two carriages were pulled in the courtyard. It was summer, and you could already see, even if it was four in the morning. *Mama* pulled her hair and bellowed like a wounded cow:

"How do I leave everything here, everything that I have worked for? For what? What is our crime?"

In that moment of fear, what could we take with us? We did not even have much to take, since dad had recently had two weddings. We still had corn meal, a barrel with cheese, but we did not think about taking them. They loaded us in the carriage and, when we were about to come out of the gate, my sister and my brother-in-law came over. Someone had told them that we would be taken. When I saw her, I jumped from the carriage to go to her. But a soldier caught me and put me back into the carriage.

It may have been better if I remained with my sister because then I would not have suffered as much as I did... Well, this is how my fate turned out; this is what God wanted...

When they took us, we were *mama, tata, bunica,* my brother with my sister-in-law, my younger sister, a younger brother, and a really small brother, who actually died on the journey. He was one year old. So we were nine people. They took us in the priest's courtyard. He had run to Romania in 1940, when the Soviets came. Now, they gathered all carts there, and we left from the village from the priest's yard.

On the road, we arrived at one of our lands, where we had six hectares. I feel like crying anytime I remember it. Dad came down from the cart and kneeled. He took some dirt and put it in his pocket. He kissed the land and made the sign of the cross. The wheat was ripe, so he took some grains in his hand, rubbed it in his palms, and put it in his pocket. He came back in the carriage, and we went further.

On the road to Siberia

We arrived at the Pământeni station, in Bălți. It was so sunny and so hot... And there were carriages everywhere. We had not taken bread with us, so we did not have anything to eat. We had not made bread at home that day. *Mama* was supposed to bake some bread in the morning. Men were sobbing. Children and women too. The entire scene... God forbid! We were in the sun, no food. They took the carriage to the train car, and all seven families from our village were loaded in the car. The man in whose place we were deported took us to the train station with his own carriage, and he later told me that he saw, after we were in the train car, that it said on it that we would be moved to Ukraine.

There, in the car, there was nothing to sit on. We put our luggage on the floor and we sat on it. The cars were not big. And we left. We went on with the noise of train wheels for some days.

All of a sudden, we heard sounds of bombing. I do not remember in which city we were, but I saw on the little window two planes flying very, very low. Our car was in the middle of the train, and, when we were in the curve, I could see that the train was very long and how some people tried to escape. They were coming out through that little window, jumping off the train, and I could see them rolling down. Many ran like this, even from our village. The planes passed over one side, then the other. I could see them close, staying with my head against that little window. Dad yelled:

"Make signs with your white head kerchiefs!"

Together with my other sister, we took our white head kerchiefs and started to make signs. We found out afterwards that two cars at the end of the train had been bombed.

We went by train farther. I cannot tell you how long, but then we stopped all of a sudden and they allowed us to walk, to come out of the train. They told us:

"Two men should take two buckets and go with the soldiers."

They returned with soup, but no bread.

While we stayed at Bălți, *mama*'s brother and an aunt, dad's sister, brought us bread. They were large loaves, as you make in the country, and we ate from them during the trip. The train stopped in various stations on the way, but they did not allow us to come out. For our necessities, there was a hole in the corner of the car, and we went there. The women had hung up a blanket, and we went there.

One time, the soldiers came and took the men, but they did not take dad. Dad had told us to grab onto his neck, to cry, and to cling onto him. So they did not take him. While we were in the train, dad taught me Russian. He told me Russian words, how you say this, how you say that, because he had understood what would happen to us. He said that it would be good to know at least some Russian words. The train stopped in stations from time to time, but most of the time we went nonstop, day and night. Continuing like this, we arrived in Siberia. We arrived in Novosibirsk. Someone came and said:

"The men are going to take a bath outside; the women will go in another place."

We washed, came back, and went into the train. I was more curious, and I looked everywhere. All of a sudden, my brother came with a soldier. My brother had left with dad, but now he came back alone, white as a sheet. He said:

"*Mama*, they are loading the men in another train; they are taking them. They allowed me to leave because dad told them I was too small, that I do not have the required age, and they didn't take me."

After a while, dad came back as well, with two soldiers. He asked for some bread from *mama*, for his boots, his coat, and his hat, and he only said this to *mama*:

"Zenovio, take care of the children. I was tried on the spot by a special troika and condemned to six years. This is what they decided. I will return to the children."

I looked at the window of a train that was leaving, and I saw dad at the window. But there were bars at his window. I can still see him today. I did not really hear what he said because there was great noise. This is the only thing I could hear: "Tamara, Tamara!" At the beginning, I did not really know from where the yelling came. I was the last one who saw dad. We do not know what happened to him.

We remained a few days in the train. Then, someone came and told us:

"Take everything you have; we are going on the ship. We'll take you on the other side of the river."

We went on the ship. It was some sort of ferry that had to take us over the river Obi. This is what they had told us, that we would cross over to the other side, but we went on the river for more than a weak, until the ship broke. Four-five other ships that were with us continued on their way, but ours broke. It went to the shore, and we sat down there. There were forests. The people from villages came and brought us milk.

I was going with *mama* to buy milk for my little brother. But other people went before us, and they had made holes in the ground and prepared the food in cauldrons. Walking behind *mama*, I fell into one of those holes, where there were embers. I got in to my knees, and I could not get out because it was narrow. I yelled, and *mama* came to take me out from there. I was hurting so much, and *mama* did not know what to do to me!...

While we stayed there, until they repaired the ship, my little brother died of hunger and perhaps of heat.

I don't remember how it was, whether they repaired the ship or brought another one, but we finally left. We came out of the river Obi and entered on one of its tributary rivers. We went and went... They disembarked us in one place, and people from the villages came to look for people for work at the kolkhoz, at the farms. Nobody took us: *mama* was with four children and a crone. They took my brother and sister-in-law and took them to a larger village. My brother went into the village, took a cart, and came and picked us up as well. I remember we were in the cart, and it was snowing and the land was frozen in August. *Mama* covered us, the little ones, with a blanket, as we were crowded into each other. We arrived in a village.

A wretched life

It was a settlement of fifteen, twenty houses... There were beam houses. We were placed in a home with a Russian woman. This woman had three girls, but after a while they left to work in factories. They put some straws on the floor, and that's where we sat. All of us: *mama, bunica*, my brothers... We had to live in the same room with our host, and this woman had a Russian oven and slept on it. She had a board right under the ceiling, and she thus created a small place where you could barely enter. That's where she would sleep because it was warmer. It was very cold during winter, -40 and -50 degrees Celsius. There were small houses there, and everyone slept like this, someplace higher up, because heat rises.

We were placed there. But what could you eat? We had no food. Their potatoes were frozen because of the cold. The potatoes froze in the field; they did not even get to gather them, so they had nothing to eat either. It was different in other years, for the frost did not always come so quick, but the potatoes froze that year, so they had nothing to eat either. What could they give us? Even the people who lived there had nothing to eat. They had nothing. What could you eat? We had nothing to eat.

My sister-in-law got some work at a farm, where they prepared milk. My sister-in-law did not live with us. After getting some woolen thick socks and galoshes, my brother and *mama* went to cut wood in the forest. This is where they received work. The snow was waist high, and they were dressed for summer because they took us from home when it was warm outside. Later, my brother had a tree fall on his leg. His leg got swollen, and he could no longer work.

Our host, the woman, had left with two of her girls, and only one of the girls had remained with us. This girl was as evil as the devil. She would not even consider giving us the little pan in which she made food. Since my brother and *mama* were working, we received a little rye flour. *Mama* wanted to boil something, but she had no way to do it because that girl, the host, hid the pot in which she made food. *Mama* finally found some tins, and she boiled the food in them. Later, my brother stopped working in the forest because he was no longer able to do it, and they made him weave some thick ropes because there was much flax. They dried it, beat it, broke it, and then made ropes out of it. We received a little bit of flour because he worked.

I had a dream back then that I remember even today, and I think I will remember it until the day I die. We seemed to all have been in that cart that brought us to the village from the ship. We were going, and then all of a sudden there was a large sea. There was only water all around us, as far as the eye could see. In the dream, the cart was overturned, and we all fell in the water. Only my sister-in-law and I escaped. Then, it seemed that my sister-in-law tried to push me under the water anytime I tried to come up, trying to drown me. When I managed to bring my head to the surface, I saw a man with a large, white beard, who seemed to walk on water, wearing a robe with long sleeves, dressed all in white. That man seemed to stretch his hand, grabbed me by my collar, took me out of the water, and put me on the land. When I woke up, I told *mama* my dream. I was yelling during the dream, and *mama* heard it. *Mama* did not say anything. She talked to *bunica* and she cried.

The dear ones die one after the other

After a while, we moved in a different place, in a small house. We had nothing to eat in this house either. We only drank water with salt. We were dying of hunger, all of us! As I said, the potatoes froze in the land, so the locals did not get to take them out. I used to go to gather some of those frozen potatoes. I could find some things, even fruit of the forest, so I ate things like that. I was looking for arrach or nettle. *Mama* used to grind it, prepare it, and make some sort of cake out of it. *Mama* gave us the little food we had, not keeping anything for herself.

I remember that she used to give all of us a loaf of rice bread on Saturdays. For all of us there, as many souls as we were, she had this loaf of bread. One per week. For six souls, one loaf per week! All the other times, there was only arrach and nettle. *Mama* made some sort of small cake out of arrach, potato peels, and whatever else we could find there. *Bunica* no longer had any teeth, and she used to say:

"I cannot eat this wooden board, this arrach cake."

One evening, my brother came with bread. Such a beautiful smell... We were all dying of hunger. My feet were swollen, and I could not walk. When we saw that bread, as we were hungry, we looked long at it... But my brother tied it with some string in the attic. This was on Saturday. We used to eat this bread only on Sundays. We ate on Sundays so that we would have that taste in our mouths for the entire week.

Bunica began crying, and she implored my brother:

"Vasile, give me a piece of bread! I cannot eat this cake. It is as tough as a board. My stomach cannot take it. I don't have any teeth."

But my brother told *bunica*:

"*Mămuca,* dear *bunica*, you raised us with these hands of yours! You saw many things, and you endured much! Please suffer it until morning. What would I do with these children, who have their eyes fixed on this loaf of bread? If I give you any of it, they are children and will want to have it too. You are older and understand. Please, endure a bit longer!"

Overnight, we did not close one eye. We lay down and looked up to the loaf of bread. We waited, hoping that one piece, one little piece would fall and we could put it in our mouths. Well, when morning came, *bunica* was no longer. She had cried and cried. She had rivers of tears on her face, and she died. In the morning, she was stiff. But now the question was how to bury her. Where? My brother went to dig her tomb. He was in a worse condition than us. Being a man, he needed more food. He dug down perhaps half a meter, but there was ice, and some water sprang out. He put *bunica* there, in water. After *bunica* died, the youngest brother passed away as well. He would constantly say, "papa, papa, papa..."[177] But what could *mama* give him, what could she give him for food? And my brother said, "papa, papa..." until he died. He died asking for food. We found him stiffen as well. My brother took him and placed him next to *bunica*. He put two crosses there. He made a small hole that filled immediately with water, he put him in that water, and then he covered him with dirt.

When brother Vasile got very bad, he died as well. Now, there was no one to bring us that loaf of bread that he used to bring. The people from the kolkhoz saw how we lived and told my sister-in-law, "Go and take care of them!" She never came to us. My sister-in-law lived in the same settlement. But she

---

[177] "Papa" is the word used by toddlers for food.

was at the barrack, with the cattle. She milked them and took them to pasture.

Now, that my brother died, who could take him to the grave? We had nothing, no coffin, nothing. In the end, some people, some of our Moldavians who worked there, came and placed him on a carpet and took him out of the house.

Mama made some food from weeds, whatever she could find. When the people took my brother out of the house, *mama* gave them a spoon from that food. This was like a wake for the soul of my brother; we had nothing else to give as alms.[178]

Mama could no longer move because of hunger. After my brother died, she was crying and shouting so much, all the time. My sister was weak as well. She was two years younger than me and could not go out to gather weed. I still used to go out and look for food. One evening, *mama* told us:

"Come, go to bed, because I have a little flour, and I will bake you something tomorrow. There is a great feast tomorrow, and we will eat!"

I do not know what feast it was. We went to bed hungry. What could we do? We only ate some fresh weeds because *mama* could not even boil them any longer. We both ate and went to sleep. When I woke up in the morning... my sister was dead. Other people came, and they took my sister next to the others. There were four crosses now.

Lord, take Tamara, too!...

After my sister died, *mama* prayed like this: "Lord, please, take Tamara to You as well! Take her from this world because she remains alone and in pains. Take Tamara and then take me too, Lord..." But I heard her, and I came close to her and told her:

"*Mama*, why do you pray that I would die?"

"You, if you remain alone," *mama* said, "if you remain

---

[178] In Romania, the relatives of the deceased organize a wake where the guests are invited to participate in a memorial meal for the soul of the departed. They also share the belongings of that person with everyone else and give alms.

with your sister-in-law, she will torment you, cripple you, and make you non-human. Jesus Christ was not as tormented as she will torment you!"

This is what she said - and it truly was this way.

The people where my sister-in-law worked told her, "Go and take care of that woman" - that is my mother. They told her to help us, but my sister-in-law said that I should be sent into another village to work there, and that only *mama* should stay. They eventually took me, but the people from the kolkhoz told my sister-in-law that she should have brought food to *mama*. She never went there.

They took me to another village, four or five kilometers away from where *mama* was. I had to take care of people's children. The people were working at the farm, and I took care of their children. It was like a kindergarten. I had to wash them, care for them, and feed them. I stayed there, but then I began missing *mama*, and I began crying and saying that I wanted to go to *mama*. Someone took me on a horse, and this is how I got back to *mama*.

Mama could not walk, and there was no one to give her a glass of water. She could stand for her necessities, but no more than this. Her legs were swollen, and she was all swollen as well. She saw me, called me to her, put my head on her arms, and began to clean my hair. I was not combed, and my hair was entangled, filled with lice. She began cleaning me and crying. She was crying, and her tears were falling on my face. She was crying and praying, "Lord, I implore you, take Tamara from this world!" I wanted to stay with her, but a strong storm started... Mama told the man who had brought me: "Take her back!"

If I had remained, I would have saved *mama* because I could gather weeds or look for other things... I was a fighter, and I would have helped her. But he took me on the horse by force and took me to the village where I took care of children.

After a while, my sister-in-law visited me, and I asked her, "How is *mama* doing? I want to be with *mama*!"

But she did not say anything, just spat in my face, and left.

Mama had sent her. She told her, "Go and bring Tamara, so I could see her. And bring me a piece of bread and a little milk."

I know these things from a Moldavian woman, who was there at *mama*'s. She took care of *mama*, washed her, and prepared her when she died. She was there when *mama* spoke to my sister-in-law and sent her after me.

She also told me that she was with *mama* when my sister-in-law came back. *Mama* was lying on one side and waited for her to bring me. When she came in, *mama* asked her:

"Where is Tamara?"

"She did not want to come; she ran away!"

She lied to *mama*, telling her I did not want to go. *Mama* began crying:

"You did not bring me a piece of bread!"

"You'll die even without it..." my sister-in-law said.

Mama sighed and gave up her soul. I did not know that *mama* had died. I found out much later. And she was buried in the same place, with *bunica* and my brothers.

With my sister-in-law

I do not know how she did it, but my sister-in-law managed to buy a small house together with another woman. After a while, that woman was taken into a concentration camp. My sister-in-law remained alone in that house. Winter came. I no longer had work in the village because people did not take their children to the kindergarten during winter. When winter came, I thought I would go to her because she was my sister-in-law and she had a house, and perhaps I could stay with her.

I will tell you what I suffered there... It would have been better to die than go through what I went through. She used to beat me so hard so that I thought I would die. She would beat me because I would not die! But was it my fault that I could survive?...

I remember another very painful moment that had happened before all this, when *mama* and *bunica* were still alive in the house where we stayed at the beginning. *Mama* received a letter. I do not know what was written there, but I know that she and *bunica* were crying. It was something about dad, I do not know... If he died or what happened... *Bunica* was crying, *mama* was crying, but I do not know exactly why. They were crying, and we were crying.

Let me go back to when I was living with the sister-in-law. She used to beat me, so then I ran away. But then she used to go to neighbors and complain:

"Haven't you seen this child, 'cause she ran away; she is bad; she does not want to listen and runs from home..."

But how could I have stayed with her if this is what she was doing to me? But I still went back because it was -40, -50 degrees there during winter.

One day, she took me and undressed me, tied my hands and legs behind me, and put me on the oven. I was thin - I did not have anything to eat! She put me on the oven, my hands tied in the back. I could not move to get down because I had my hands tied in the back, and the oven was high...

She left me there alone, with no fire. I stayed on the oven for three days and three nights, alone, in that frost. I was ready to die. I do not know why God did not take me then. When she came back, I was still alive. I was frozen. She took me down, went outside, picked up a rope, wet it, left it to freeze, and then tied me with this rope. In Russia, the ovens were high, placed on some legs. There was enough space beneath them to raise a chicken... She put me there, under the oven. I just prayed and wanted to die! I just wanted the Lord to take me, as *mama* said! Someone from the kolkhoz came, the chief or someone who had something with her, and he heard how I was moaning with pain, tied as I was... When he heard that moan, he told her:

"If that child is under the oven, take her out; I'll kick you out from here if not!"

He took me out from there as I was, covered in wounds, weak, just bones. I did not have skin where I was tied, not even blood. He took me out in the frost.

Not far from my sister-in-law, there was an old man who had some sheep, and I do not know how God helped me to crawl to that old man. I went where he had the sheep, and I took out some hay and wanted to hide there, to find some refuge there. But there was no light during winter in those places. In the summer, there is always light, and in the winter darkness, and you cannot see. When he came, he heard me moaning and took me inside. He knew how my sister-in-law behaved with me, how she beat me and how she had evil thoughts for me. The old man took me in the house, covered me, and oiled me with fat. I don't remember anything else because I lost consciousness.

My sister-in-law came to him and asked him:

"Did you happen to see the girl? I don't know where she left."

"I didn't see her; I don't know what happened to her!" the old man said.

"I think the wolves ate her!" she said.

The old man told me this, when I recovered. He made me some *opinci*[179] from birch, from tree crusts. He put in a lot of hay, cut some material from his padded coats, so that I could wrap my feet, dressed me, put a hat on my head, and told me:

"Do you see this path? Go on it as far as you can, until you find a road. The sleigh that brings milk into the village comes on that road. Go with that man; if you stay here and your sister-in-law catches you, she'll kill you."

He fed me and gave me some potatoes for the road, and I ate fast and left, so she would not catch me. I went for a long time because I was already better and my wounds were getting smaller.

Wandering in the world

I went like this for a while, and then I arrived at a place where they were making alcohol. They put a very large bowl on the fire, as they make the *rachiu*[180] at home. When I saw this scene (the fire was on and they only had to put on the lid), I thought, "This is where I will die." I went up on a ladder to jump in that boiling liquid. But the man who was there saw me and caught me:

"What? Should I have sins because of you? Because you want to kill yourself? Leave, dear girl, go away!"

---

[179] Traditional shoes.
[180] *Rachiu* is a strong Romanian drink, perhaps similar to brandy. The bowl the author mentions here was as large as a big bucket.

And I left. And I was well. I was not hungry, I was not cold, and I had no desire to eat because I was freezing.

There was no real road there. I could barely see the trail from a sleigh that had passed through the village. When the man came back from the village, he took me with him to another village. He was the first one who liberated me. I do not remember the name of the village, but there were some people who took care of me. The old women came with potatoes boiled in their skin because this is what they ate; they gave me a few pieces from time to time and rubbed me with alcohol. They kept me there until spring came, when I came to my senses. It was hard for me to stay there, and I asked them how to go toward Bessarabia - I did not know back then about Moldova.[181] Some women knew about it and told me:

"You have to walk and walk until you arrive to Tomsk. There is a train from there. You get in the train. The train goes to Moscow, and you will arrive there because you know Russian; you will not die."

And I left. I walked from village to village, but I arrived in a place where there were deportees, just like us, brought there by the ships that brought us. They had made some little houses on the bank of the water. When they saw me, the women kept me with them. During this time, my sister-in-law was interrogated:

"What did you do with that child? What did you do with her?"

In 1944, Bessarabia was occupied by the Russians. My sister-in-law wrote even home, in Moldova: "Everyone is dead; only Tamara remained, but nobody knows whether she is dead or alive. If I do not find her, if I don't know anything about her, they will prosecute me." She came to look for me even where I was. When I saw her, I began to shake and I hid away. The women that kept me jumped on her and yelled at her:

"How could you torture that girl like that? Yes, she passed

---

[181] Moldova was the name of the Soviet Republic of Moldova after it was annexed by the Soviet Union. Before the war, this province was called Bessarabia. Historically, it is part of the larger Moldova province.

by, but she's no longer here; she left. What do you need?"

They were so tough with her that she left immediately. After this, I was afraid to stay there. I said, "I will no longer stay here; if I do, she'll find me, and this will be my end!"

So I left, going from village to village again. But the villages were far from one another. During the night, when I could no longer walk, I climbed a tree, tied myself there with some straps from willow barks, and I stayed there so that the wolves would not get me. If I could not get in a tree, then I made a hole in the snow, huddling there to protect me from the wind. It snowed over me. The people were good, very kind-hearted. They took me in and gave me a potato, if they had one; but it also happened that I would be caught by night between villages.

If I could no longer walk when I was between villages, then I stayed there, in the snow, what could I have done? If I had strength, I would climb a tree. What did I have to eat? I gnawed tree bark - this was my food. How could you not have stomach aches? How could you not be sick?

I walked and walked, and I arrived at the outskirts of a village. I had lice, and all my clothes were torn. I stopped at the first house, and I fainted at the gate. The woman who was there took me in, saw that I was a child, undressed me, and washed me. I don't remember all of this because I had lost consciousness.

When I woke up, I was dressed with her clothes. She cut my hair because she could not do anything with so many lice. She told me that the lice stayed there one next to another, stuck in my skin. She washed me and she wanted to adopt me because she had no children and her husband was on the front. I agreed. She found out that I was an orphan, that I was deported - I told her everything; I did not hide anything. You must say the truth because it will be found out anyway. I began helping that woman: I went to the forest, took the cow to the pasture, and brought water from the small river - I would do all kinds of things. I also milked the cow.

One day, she received a letter to go see her man in a hospital in some town, I do not know where. She left me there with the cow, the pig. It was right during this time that they gave an order to gather all orphans and take them to the orphanage. They took me as well. One neighbor told them to leave me alone me because I was staying with that woman. But the order was to take all children to the orphanage. They gathered all of us and took us on a barge. It was very difficult on that barge; it was only one palm length above the water. I cried after that woman the whole way on the barge.

We were 12-13 children on that barge, of all kinds: older, deported ones, or orphans. At one moment, the barge went to the shore to get some wood. The engine needed firewood. What came to my mind? I ran from there, from the barge, to go back to that woman. I got lost, and the torment began again. I did not know where to go. So I went again from village to village - I would try to help here, there…

It was already summer. They had gathered us during the summer because the water was no longer frozen and the barges could go - the barges and the ships could only be on the waters in June. Before June, everything was frozen, and as it thawed large pieces of ice would float down the river to the sea. After the water was cleaned of these ice floes, the transport began. I was going again from one village to another. I would help, working where I could, with potatoes or other things…

I could not remain anywhere. I worked to be fed, to receive a piece of food. Even when I was with that woman, at whose gate I fainted, when I recovered a bit I asked her to give me some work. When I came to my senses, she brought me a glass of milk and some bread, so I told her:

"No! Let me work first, and then you feed me."

She crossed herself and said:

"You want to work, and you're so weak? Take and eat!"

I took and ate, but it was even worse because I had not eaten for so long. She then took care of me and put me back on my feet. This is why I wanted to stay there, but they took me to the orphanage. Now, where could I go? I went from village to village to get to Tomsk. This is what I believed, that I would get to Tomsk. But it was a long way, hundreds, perhaps thousands of kilometers, and I could not get there on foot.

Winter came back. Winter begins in August there, and the great frosts in September, October. Where could I have stayed, what could I do? The snow was big, and I slept under the snow from time to time. I walked and walked, and I fell on the road. I was at the point of freezing and dying.

I was saved by a soldier who was coming home to see his parents. This soldier had a broken hand and broken ribs, and, walking, he saw a little pile. When he kicked it with his foot, he saw that it was a child! He looked at me and checked if I was still breathing. "She's not dead yet; her heart is ticking! She's a child..." He took me, put me inside his coat, and began walking. He told me afterward what he thought: "I would at least bury her, so that the dogs, the wolves, and the animals would not eat her if she died."

After a while, he saw a little light. He feared that it was a wolf, but it was a little house. There were some little houses for the hunters. He went to one of those houses. There was a man inside. The soldier was not healthy either; he had recently returned from the hospital. He took me in, and the man inside rubbed me with the fat he had. He fed us, he saw that we were coming to our senses, and he sent us on a sleigh in the village where the soldier's parents were.

At the orphanage

I got sick again when I arrived. I told them my name was Tamara Oală. But they could not pronounce "Oală." In Russian, they cannot pronounce with the letter "o." They called me "Alla," and they registered me with "a": "Alla Baghina." The soldier recovered and left for the front again. I stayed with his parents. The man took care of the horses, of the house, and the old woman cooked. They took me to the orphanage and registered me there. They fed us well enough at this orphanage, and they gave us work because they had cows and horses, so that they could feed us. There were many children, over two thousand.

In our village, in Moldova, the man who put us on the list in Istrate's place worked at the post office. The first thing he received at the office was the letter that my sister-in-law had sent to her mother. My sister - at whose place I slept on the night of deportation - had remained in the village. My sister heard that my sister-in-law's mother received the letter. The old woman did not want to give her the letter, but the letter finally got to my sister. But my sister did not know to read. She went to that man, at the post office, who had been a secretary when they took us. He read the letter and saw that my sister-in-law said that she did not know whether I was still alive. He said:

"I put them on the list when they were deported; I will bring the girl back if she is still alive."

He began writing to all of the orphanages to look for me. He wrote my name as Tamara Oală, but I was registered as Alla Baghina, as the soldier wrote my name. This is how they called me, and this is how I answered.

There was a Jewish woman at the orphanage. During the war, when the Jews were persecuted, she ran to Siberia and she worked at the orphanage. When they wrote everywhere from the post office, to all orphanages, the director called me a few times to ask me where I was from. But someone had made a joke with me; we were around seven children from Moldova, and he told us that we should no longer say that we were Moldavians because they would shoot us. So, when the director asked me where I was from, I did not tell him I was Moldavian.

I had even forgotten Moldavian. I spoke perfect Russian, and all people thought I was Russian. But my sister wrote by the mailman that Tamara had a sign on her hand, like a raspberry. *Mama* had told me that she stole a raspberry when she was pregnant with me. She told me that this was why I had that sign.

So the director called me and asked me where I was from, and I did not tell him. One time, they took us to wash us, and they undressed us. They washed and greased us every ten days, so that we would not have itching or lice. They saw it there: "Look, she has the sign on her hand; look, the raspberry!" The war was over. Many came to take their children, those without parents or those whose fathers were on the front. I cried that I had nobody and that no one was taking me. They took me to the director, and he told me:

"Do you know where you are from? If we knew, we would send you home." He took me like this, gently.

I then told them I was from Bessarabia. I had forgotten that they were supposed to shoot me.

"Bessarabia! Do you remember anyone there?"

I told them I had a sister.

"Do you remember her name?"

I did not remember. I used to call her *leliţa*, but I could not remember her name. I no longer knew the family name, nor my sister's name after her husband. He asked me:

"Do you want to go home? If you want, tell the truth about who you are and where you are from."

So I told them.

The soldier who had saved me and found me when I almost froze on the road was back from the front, and he worked at the orphanage. He said, "Glory be to God! I am so glad I found her, I am so glad I saved her!" He wanted to adopt me. But when they announced from the orphanage that they found me, a letter came from Bessarabia.

What a letter! A long letter in which all the relatives wrote something for me, in Moldavian. The Jewish woman who knew Moldavian read what my relatives from Bessarabia wrote. She read about some, about others. I then received another letter, but there was no one to read for me. The war had finished, and the Jewish woman went back. There was nobody to read to me, and they sent me from the orphanage to the sanatorium, in Tomsk, because I had holes in my lungs. I stayed there a winter, a summer, and then they sent me back.

When they sent me back from the sanatorium to the orphanage with the boat, the river froze. We had no option. We were blocked, so we came down on the bank of the river with the children. There was also an older girl, 18-20 years old. Some of us were children from the orphanage, and we went around and found a little house for hunters. There was firewood and something to eat…

We stayed there. One time in the night, a pack of wolves started to howl. They were howling and rattling about so much… We were lucky that there were some older boys, and they could make a fire. We were afraid, even if we were in the house, but what could that small door do when a pack of wolves were howling outside? We were afraid that they would come after us. But the children were making the fire, and the wolves are afraid of fire. When day came, they were still outside rattling about.

The older girl was all pale with fear. We were afraid and were crying; we did not need food or sleep. We prayed to escape. Even if we were from the orphanage, we knew some prayers[182]... We prayed even when we were at the orphanage, but not aloud, so that no one could hear us, but we put together our little hands and prayed to God. When the people from the ship came to the cart with guns, they started to shoot so that we could hear them and answer; the wolves ran away. But we did not come out because we were afraid - what if the wolves were close by? Eventually, the people from the ship found us and took us on the cart. We were so scared there!

They took us back to the orphanage. We were taken to gather blackberries, mushrooms, and other things that grew during the summer. The fruit was for the hospitals, to make juices and teas. One day, we filled baskets with blackberries. We also gathered raspberries... but then we got lost. We thought we were close by, but we actually went far away. When we looked around, it was only us: a girl, a boy, and I. The others yelled after us, but the voices were resounding, and we thought they were coming from in front of us.

So we continued to go toward the marshes. When we saw that the swamp was large, we began crying and we crowded under a tree. We ate the blackberries, and we left the baskets there because we no longer needed them. We fell asleep. We woke up because we were cold, and we thought we should eat something. We ate raspberries. As I was eating raspberries, I suddenly saw a bear in front of me, standing upright. I got scared and I fainted. I was weak - I had suffered so much - so I fell. The children, the girl and the boy, went up onto the tree, and they told me afterward that the bear came toward me and I

---

[182] Religion was forbidden by the Bolsheviks.

fell face forward. The bear smelled me and turned me on my back with his paw. He smelled me, but apparently he was full and didn't need me. And he left. But I did not come back to my senses. When I came back, the hunters were already looking for us. They barely carried me, as I was very scared and very weak. They sent me to the sanatorium again.

I did not go back to the orphanage because I found two very nice female doctors at the sanatorium. I will remember them till the day I die... They asked me where I was from, and they found out I was from Bessarabia. It was called Moldova by that time because it was 1946 already. There was a drought in Bessarabia, but it rained every day in Siberia.

I remained at the sanatorium for the entire year of 1947. I left only in 1948. The two doctors looked for ways to send me to Bessarabia, but they said, "We won't send her now because there is famine and drought there. We'll keep her here." They made a request to Moscow and they obtained the rehabilitation for me.[183] Those papers said that I was rehabilitated and that I should get back everything that they had confiscated. But I did not know this. As I was the only one who was still alive in the family, I was supposed to get back all this.

On the way to Bessarabia

They did everything so that I could go back home; they wrote to my brother-in-law, my sister's husband, who had returned from the army. They wrote him asking him to meet me in Moscow. This is what they decided. So they sent me with a woman from Tomsk to Moscow, to an orphanage, until my brother-in-law would come to take me. They gave me clothes and shoes. When I arrived in Moscow, they took my clothes and gave me some bad ones from there. They were very thin, and the shoes were large and always came out of my feet, so I was barefoot most of the time. Someone came in and shouted my name, but they mispronounced it, they did not say Oală. They shouted once, twice. I was at the window, watching the train. They shouted a third time, but, since they said my name wrong,

---

[183] Even children were considered the "enemies of the people."

I did not answer. Then they asked:

"Is there someone from Bessarabia? Who is from Moldova? They came after her."

As I was there, at the window, I jumped over a few chairs, barefoot as I was. I did not look for shoes, but I ran to meet who came after me! When I entered the room, my brother-in-law was there. He was dressed as a soldier, how he was when he came from the army. They asked him, pointing at me:

"Is this the one?"

He did not remember me - I had grown and I had changed. He looked at me and nodded:

"I think this is the one."

They asked me too:

"Is this your brother-in-law? Is he your relative?"

I said:

"I don't remember him, but, if he came - I was afraid that they would send me to another orphanage - if he came, I'll go with him."

They saw that it was him, so they allowed us to leave.

He came to me and began to speak to me in Moldavian and he kissed me on my forehead. I got scared. Who has kissed me, who has caressed me before? Nobody. I was scared, so I stepped out the door and started running. Barefoot as I was, I was running through Moscow. He followed me. He left his luggage there, and he ran after me. I got scared when he kissed me, thinking that it was something else, fearing that he had different intentions. He was a soldier... I did not understand. He finally caught me, took me by hand, and began speaking with me in Russian.

"Why are you running? I am married with your sister."

And he explained to me in Russian.

"But why did you have to kiss me?" I said.

"What do you mean? We are relatives!"

He took me calmly, and I left with him.

He bought me shoes because I no longer had shoes. I had small feet. But when he saw me so tall, he bought me big shoes. They were falling from my feet. I could not wear them. I was tall, but I wore children shoes. He looked at my feet, saw, and said:

"So tall but with feet so small!"

He eventually bought me some nice small shoes; he also bought me a head kerchief, and that was it. He was slow and calm with me:

"Let's go to the bath."

This is how it was there. If you went on the train for a longer trip, you had to take a bath first. Then, with a ticket from the bath, you could go buy your train ticket, as we had to take one from Moscow to Kiev. He left me there with the sac, with his luggage, with whatever else he may have bought, and, being a child, I left to look around.

When he came back, he no longer found me. He was scared because he did not know what to do. What would he tell my sister? But I saw him looking for me, and I went to him, telling him that I did not run away, that I was there. We then went to buy tickets. It was a long line. People were speaking in Moldavian. I asked for money from my brother-in-law, I went through people's legs, I made it to the ticket office, and I began speaking in Russian and asking for the tickets. I took the tickets and I left. We then went in the train that went to Kiev. In Kiev, you had to change trains, to take the one that went toward Moldova.

In the train, I heard people speaking in Moldavian. I said:

"What language do these people speak?"

He told me:

"You will speak the same way."

"But my sister speaks the same way? Like these people?"

"Yes!"

I no longer wanted to eat. I was scared - how could I speak with my sister? I have not seen her for so long, she did not speak Russian, and I no longer knew to speak like her, in Moldavian. So I started crying. I no longer ate anything, and my brother-in-law no longer ate anything. I listened how people spoke among themselves. Some were saying that they bought "perdele."[184] But in Russian "perdele" means when you eat and

---

[184] "Perdele" is the Romanian word for "curtains."

then you have gas. I asked my brother-in-law:

"What do they say about *perdele*? Aren't they ashamed to speak about this?"

He explained it to me. Eventually, I accepted the situation and I calmed down.

Home again

When we arrived at the train station in our village, there was so much mud and slime, and you could not see anything. I was with those small shoes. In the station, where we came down, I saw a sister of my sister-in-law; she looked so much like my sister-in-law from Siberia. When I heard she had her voice, I got really scared. There was a stove, and I hid between that stove and the wall, so that she could not see me. I was afraid that I did not escape from her even there. "This is it," I thought, "the torment will begin again and she will beat me." But this sister of my sister-in-law went into the train and left, so I remained with my brother-in-law. He said:

"Come out! Why did you get scared?"

I cried and told him:

"She is my sister-in-law!"

He said:

"No, it's her sister."

So I calmed down and wanted to come out. But I could no longer do it. I do not know how I got in, but I could no longer come out from behind the stove. I moved one way, I moved the other, he pulled me, and I finally got out. Everything hurt, but I came out.

But how could you walk? It was dark, there was mud... How could I have walked with those small shoes? My brother-in-law took me under his arm and carried me. When we arrived on the hill, next to our house, I recognized the house. I recognized the house, the barn, the fence, and I started trembling. I said:

"Is this our house? Is there someone from our family living here?"

My brother-in-law said:

"Your sister and I. And the children, your nephews."

My sister was waiting, knowing that my brother-in-law would bring me. He knocked on the door, and I saw my sister and my nephews coming out, uncombed from sleep, in their sleeping shirts. But my sister did not see me because I was under his arm. She said:

"My God, he did not bring her!"

She thought he did not bring me, and she fainted; she fell down. I was under my brother-in-law's arm, and I turned my head to see her. But I could not see much because it was dark. He put me down, we went into the house, and shortly everyone heard that I came back. The relatives started to come. They came, looked at me, turned me around on all sides, and said to my brother-in-law:

"What did you bring here? A Russian?"

Painful reconnection

In 1956, my sister-in-law returned to the village as well. She had married in Siberia with someone who was from our village, a Moldavian. My sister-in-law gave birth to three children there. When we heard that she came home, my sister told me:

"Let's go to her place to see her. Let's go. We know how much you suffered, but let's go to her to see her."

So we went. After we went into the room, I saw her, with a child on each side and with another in her arms. When I saw her, my heart started to beat fast and my temples throbbed, and I thought I would fall down that very moment. I had the child in my arms. I almost let the little boy fall. My sister jumped and took him, and my sister-in-law said:

"How beautiful you are! I thought you were paralyzed and your jaw was dislocated."

"If you had done anything good to me, I may have forgotten, but the evil you did... You beat me with a rope that you had wet and put in ice, you crushed me, you hit my head with the rope, broke my jaw..." She had moved my jaw from its place; the old man put it back; I was lucky with him. "And don't say lies, say the truth, because you made me less than a human with all your beatings."

When I began crying and saying all these things, she put her head down and said nothing else.

"I remember everything you did to me."

And I went out crying. My sister stayed. Then, being good at heart, I went home and took a sac with corn meal, one with flour, and some potatoes, and I asked someone:

"Take them and give them to her; she needs them. Her mother is poor, and she has three children, and they are not guilty. I suffered enough of hunger, and I do not want others to suffer as well; the children are not guilty; she is."

He took those things to her. Then, all were amazed, even her mother, and my sister-in-law said to everyone:

"Look how many things I did to her and how much I tormented her, but she sent me things to feed my children now."

This was the story of my troubles in Siberia.

The village Sofia, Bessarabia, July 10, 2011

I Came Out of Prison without Being Bitter and Vengeful

Nicolae Istrate

The beginnings

My name is Nicolae Istrate, and I was born on February 27, 1926, in the district Lăpuşna, when Bessarabia was part of the Romanian state. I am, then, Romanian by origin. My parents are also Bessarabians. My father, born in 1886, was in the army when Bessarabia was part of the Tsarist Empire. He was decorated with four St. George Crosses, and he was a full knight of the St. George order. In Bessarabia, only two people had this military distinction, the highest one for soldiers.

During those times, before the communists, people were better, much more faithful. The church was always full, and young people came to services as well. The derailments from morality that one finds today did not exist. Life was peaceful. All people were used to work, from the youngest to the oldest. They helped each other, and everyone had his own purpose and helped in various things.

Only lazy people did not work - this is how it has been from the beginning of the world. The working people lived well; they had been given land, five hectares each, and they worked this land. The lazy ones sold it. When the Russians came, the lazy people, who did not have land, were the first who took advantage of it and were placed in command.

We were five children, three boys and two girls. The peasants did not really send their children to school back then, but my father wanted to see his children in school. *Mama* was also very faithful, and she wanted to make two of her children priests. This is how one of my brothers and I went to the Theological Seminary.[185]

At the Seminary, we had very good teachers. I remember that the bishop visited us when we were in eighth grade, and he

---

[185] The seminary was at the level of high school.

asked us who wanted to become a priest. Before that time, if you went to the Seminary, you were obligated to become a priest. But it was no longer so in my time. Those who said to the bishop that they wanted to become priests could no longer go to study something else in the university. Those who did not want to become priests could go to other departments after the baccalaureate.

When the Russians came in 1940, the building of the Theological Seminary was deteriorated. They did not destroy the painting in the chapel, but they put a star on the heads of all saints.

In 1940, the Theological Seminary was already moved to Romania, so I moved there as well. But during the war, a colleague from Bessarabia came to me and said:

"Istrate, let's go back to Bessarabia to take something from there before the Russians come!"

So we went. Our idea was to come back and remain in Romania. But the Russians caught us there, we fell in the surrounding of Chişinău-Iaşi, so we were forced to remain in Bessarabia. When I arrived to the river Prut, to cross over to Romania, I could no longer return. When they arrested me, I was in the uniform of the Theological Seminary.

I tore my number[186] from my clothes because I was afraid. I had heard what had happened in Russia, with the persecution against faith. I knew that priests, theologians, and seminarians were watched. A woman who knew Russian told them that I was not German, but a student at the Theological Seminary. Then, the Russian soldier patted me on my shoulder and said:

"Well, Stalin allows faith now, allows the Church! You'll be a priest. You can go home!"

This is how I returned home and I remained in Bessarabia...

The first arrest

In 1944, when the Russians came, they did not have school-teachers. The teachers had left for Romania. Now, they wanted

---

[186] Students had a number on their uniforms.

to open the schools, so they were trying to find people who would be made teachers. This is how some people who only had four or seven elementary classes became teachers. I was supposed to be mobilized in the army, on the front, because the war had not finished. Someone from the department of education came to me and asked me:

"What would you like to do? Go on the front or take some courses and become a teacher?"

Of course I accepted, and I became a teacher. I went to some courses for a month, where I learned the Cyrillic alphabet because by then everything was done in Cyrillic, in Russian. After this, they made me school principal in a village. I worked there for more than one year, from 1944 to 1945.

In that village, there was an old priest who had a daughter. Of course, when I arrived there, I introduced myself to the priest; the parochial house was just over the fence from school. This priest had a son with whom I used to be colleagues at the Seminary; the priest also had six daughters. Five of them were in Romania; they had managed to take refuge, but the youngest one remained home. The priest used to invite me to eat with them, and there was another teacher that would often accompany me. He had been assigned to the school where I was principal. He was a young man who said that he had deserted from the Romanian army and that he was a partisan. He was a vicious man. He began courting the priest's girl, but the priest noticed the kind of man he was, and he was opposed to it.

The young man believed that I was creating problems for him. He went to the *Securitate* and told them I had written an epigram, something terrible, an epigram about Stalin. When they translated it to me, I don't know how I did not die from fear. It was written in Romanian. They read it to me as well. When he heard it, the KGB officer who interrogated me poured out all of his hatred against me. He disfigured me and broke my teeth and my skull. Ten years later, when I was in a concentration camp, I met the author of the epigram. Here is the text:

Stalin, we wish a mărţişor[187]
To be around your neck,
To be weaved from silk
And well greased with soup made at home.
We would hang on it a millstone
And throw you in the sea.

You can imagine: when Stalin was considered the liberator of Europe, the vanquisher of fascism, a Moldavian could write something like this! Of course, the KGB officer began to beat me and crush me so that I would admit that I had written it. He beat me and tortured me terribly. He broke my arms and crushed my jaw. I could no longer speak, so they left me in the cell; when I came back to my senses, they took me back to interrogation. I had sworn that I would only say what I saw and what I suffered. I held up for sixteen nights for the interrogation - they only called me during night.

The one who tortured me was a solid, robust man. He used to handcuff me, but not with my hands in front, but in the back. This is how he beat me, and I fell, not having any means to protect myself when he hit me. I fell and groaned. He asked me ironically, "What, are you weak?" He would pistol-whip me, and I could not wipe away the blood that was flowing on my face. My mouth was disfigured, crooked, opened so that I could take some air, but I could not answer him. Then he used to take me and put my head into a bucket with water; the blood would wash away, and the beating started again.

I have to say that I felt God's help. I knew I would be beaten and tortured, and it no longer hurt as much as the first time. He hit me in my jaw, my teeth came out, there were cases when I even swallowed my tooth, but I held up; he could not get anything from me. Sixteen nights I held up.

After this, they took me for execution. They took me into a basement, put me with my back on the wall, and took out a pistol. They showed me that the pistol was loaded, how they put

---

[187] The *mărţişor* is small decoration that has white and red strings. On March 1st, friends exchange these "*mărţişor*" that are then pinned on their clothes. It is one of the most delightful celebrations of spring.

in the cartridges, and they started to threaten me in Russian. As I was crushed, I realized that it was no joke and they would shoot me. I did not know how to tell them in Russian that I wanted to sign, that I would accept what they wanted, but I made a gesture, as if I wanted to sign. They took me, and I signed the declaration they wrote.

The second day, as crushed as I was, they took me to Chișinău. I stayed in the building of the Securitate. Even today, when I pass by this building, I get nervous. In the Tsarist times, they had cellars in this building where they kept wine bottles. They were made like an oven, without a window, with nothing. When the Bolsheviks came, they put in doors and they made cells there. Everything was made of cement; there were no beds, nothing, and they gave you a wooden board during the night. I was lucky to be with a professor in that prison, and he asked me why they tortured me so much to bring me to that state. I told him everything. He asked me:

"Did you write it? Here, they take graphological proofs. If you wrote it, there is no way to deny it. If you did not, then you can say that you signed the declaration because you were tortured."

They kept me there for a week, to recover and be able to talk. My tongue was bitten, and I was completely destroyed, deformed. My nose moved both ways. Then, when I could speak, they took writing proofs, with my left hand, right hand, capital letters, small letters... They made me write that text dozens of times.

This is how I learned it by heart. However, even if they realized that it was not written by me, they gave me 10 years because this is how it was: once you were in, you would not come out not guilty! They would give you some years of detention immediately.

On the way to Siberia

I was arrested in 1945, and the trial took place in January 1946. I was tried in Chișinău, by the Military Court, and I received 10 years of detention in prison. They sent me to Siberia, in the region of Chelyabinsk, beyond the Urals. They

theological notions since I had been at the Seminary, and I tried to find him during the day, when we were free; we guarded the barracks during the night. I found him. I told him I went to the Theological Seminary and that I was from Chişinău.

He asked me:

"Who were your teachers at the Seminary?"

I told him. He then asked me with whom I studied French for a year. And I told him:

"With a priest, Seraphim."

This priest whom I encountered at the morgue was father Seraphim! When the war began, he volunteered as a missionary and went behind the front lines to give religious services, to Christianize the paganized population from the Soviet Union. Then he was arrested. I do not know what happened to him because I no longer met him after I was liberated.

In the meantime, my parents, who had taken refuge in Romania, were brought back to Bessarabia. Dad found a lawyer and since it was proven that I had not written that epigram, I was liberated. As I was condemned for provoking agitation too, they transferred the accusation, claiming that I talked to the priest and I created havoc. For creating agitation against the regime you would get ten years. But the lawyer proved that the war had ended and that for agitation when there is no war you only get three years. This is how I could get out, and I returned home after three years in Siberia. They took me in 1945 and I returned in 1948.

The second arrest

In those times, the kolkhozes had not been created, and my folks had all sorts of things; in a short amount of time, with good nutrition, I recovered. But nobody gave me work; I could not find anything. My younger brother told me:

"If you want to disappear, I have some friends who went to the Theatrical Institute in Leningrad. You can sign up and go there. You take an exam, get in, and they lose your trace."

I did not want to do this. What kind of an artist could I be? But in order to do something in my life, because nobody accepted me back home, I finally went. I managed to be accepted. In Leningrad, together with some colleagues, we began discussing against the regime. People found out, and we were all arrested and accused of wanting to make a political party. They brought us to Chişinău, and the trial began. We were a large lot, 27 persons. They no longer beat us during interrogations, no longer tortured us. Now they gave us pills, drogues, and we signed whatever they wanted.

The interrogation took eleven months for the second arrest. They were done only during the night, and they did not allow you to sleep during the day. You had to stay there in the cell and be awake. We tried to sleep, but they looked in the peepholes and knocked on the door immediately. In our lot, the sentence was like this: six condemned to death, among whom one was pardoned, and five were shot. My brother was among them. He was in a neighboring cell. We were not allowed to talk, but when I was passing in the hall, I used to call him, and he answered. The guard was mean to me, but I still called him. It was like this for several days. After a while, he no longer answered... I realized he had been executed. They were shot here, in Chişinău, on Grenoble Street. We tried to make a triptych there. We, the others from the lot, received many years.

At the coal mine

After the trial, they loaded us and took us to Krasnoyarsk, on Enisei. From there, they took us up to the Polar Circle. When we got to Norilsk, at the mine, it was terrible. They unloaded us from the train cars in that tundra, and you could see nothing, no trees; there were only some lichens, and the snow was black from the coal dust. You could also see the aurora borealis; for almost half a year it was only day, and you no longer knew if it was day or night. The sun would set for just a bit, and then it was up again. You did not know the date; it was very difficult. Everything discouraged me very much, especially since I was condemned to 25 years. I thought, "Well, I won't make it here for 25 years..."

After we arrived, they sent us to work in the mine. There also was a psychological limit. When you entered the mine, you went from one world to another, and it was very difficult. A part of the older prisoners laughed at us, especially when they saw how scared we were. They were mean; they told us various terrible things with people who had died, with accidents, just to laugh at us:

"Well, we don't know whether the ceiling may fall on us before evening!"

In the mine, when you work and clean the coal, there are some props to hold the ceiling, and you can always hear some cracks in it, and coal sand falling down. Not anybody can make it there. You are always tense, and you can get crazy in a week. You do not resist mentally.

But there were also people who explained things to us, spoke nicely, and made us understand. Eventually, little by little, you got used to it, but the first time I was there I was certain that I would not make it for 25 years. But I overcame this limit. When I began communicating with those who were there before us, with the teachers who were condemned as we were, I calmed down a bit. They encouraged me:

"Well, you won't stay for 25 years... Many things change in 25 years! Either Stalin will die, or something else will happen. You will not stay for 25 years, you'll see. You are young, and you'll escape." They encouraged me this way.

I could divide the prisoners into three categories. The first group was composed of those who had fallen in some kind of depression. They were pessimistic, everything was dark, and they could not care about what happened; they had no hope. Others became bitter and accused themselves: "Why didn't I take the ax when they came to pick me up, to hit them in the head and run into the forest?" They judged and accused themselves. The third category realized that salvation is only in God. You could distinguish these people from the others by their behavior, even if they did not speak about God, even if they did not preach. But one could see they were different. I do not know why they did not tell others, too. Perhaps they were afraid that they would not convince them and then they would be worse. But they were different from the others. From these three categories I mentioned, the faithful were the fewest in number, and this was mainly because the Soviet Union had fought quite a lot against faith and, among those who arrived there, many were already without God.

The black wind

Then, there was the frost. In Norilsk, the lowest temperature I experienced was -63 degrees Celsius. There were terrible winds. It was called the black wind, and it destroyed anything, people and machines, everything. When you walked, you had to hold on to some cables, so the wind would not take you. And you had to have your face covered because you would get frostbite. Your eyes would freeze open. When this wind came, the people at the surface had to lie on the ground. If you rose up, it would take you as if you were a blade of grass. The problem was that our gloves were made out of some fluffy material and were oily, and we could not hold onto that rope.

One time, a student who was behind me let the rope go, and the wind took him. He took me, and the wind threw us into the wall of a boiler house. Our face covers fell, so our faces got frostbite, of course. They found us there and took us immediately to the hospital. We were fortunate that the hospital director was a doctor who had been deported there in 1937. He was part of Gorki's trial. When he saw us, he forbid people to treat us with warm water or alcohol. He placed each one of us between two warm bodies, and so, slowly, we started to unfreeze with this human warmth. When our faces began to thaw out, in the place of the frostbite we had something like a bladder filled with water, as if we were scalded.

The doctor gave the order that no one should take this liquid out, so we walked around for ten days with this pouch on our faces, until the derma from beneath scarred up a bit. Then, he came with a large syringe and took the liquid out. That pouch remained hanging on our faces. He again gave the order that no one should take this skin off, so that our faces would scar up some more. We remained there and, in time, this layer of skin fell off, and our faces remained red, as if it was just flesh. The doctor came to us and told us in Russian:

"Young men, you will no longer be prince charming, but I saved your noses and your faces. Be careful, and when there is too much sun, when there is wind, put some cream on to protect yourself. Otherwise, you will get red."

I put him on my prayer list, to thank him. If it were not for him, we would have been completely disfigured. This was the most difficult trial for me.

Back into the mine

After this, we went back to work. We had some perforators to make holes, then we put in trotyl, and this made an explosion. After that, we started a machine that had some claws with which we gathered everything that had exploded. However, because there were some larger pieces of coal after the explosions, we were sent to the transporting band, each one of us with a sledgehammer, and whenever a larger piece came, we hit it and crushed it. This was our duty. When we came out of the mines and went to the barracks, they controlled us so that we would not take coal to make more heat. We had to come to the surface with our pockets out, to show that we did not hide anything in them. It was a very severe regime. We were around 150,000 political detainees in Norilsk, at those coal mines. We stayed in some wooden barracks, and there was slag in the middle. We had three rows of beds inside, on three levels. We had no changing clothes, so we slept with whatever we had on us. We slept with the same clothes with which we worked. They did not give us absolutely anything. We did not have even sheets.

After Stalin and Beria died, they began to give us some things. I used to sleep with my hat on. In the morning, when I woke up, the hat was frozen and glued to the wall, and I could not even detach it from there. In the evening, they locked us in the barrack, and we had a bucket inside where we did our necessities.

We worked in shifts. We worked for 10, even 12 hours. Those who worked on the surface - because there were exploitations on the surface as well - worked until the cold reached -50 degrees. When the temperature went below -50 degrees, they were no longer forced to work. In the mine, at 700 meters under the earth, you worked regardless of the temperature outside. The people at the surface had diverse jobs, because in a coal mine there also is an entire factory on the surface.

There were also civilian employees working with us, but they were helped by the detainees. For example, the accountant was a civilian, a free man, but his work was done by an economist from Moscow. The economist was content as well because he was not forced to work underground, since there were always accidents in the mine. There were accidents from the marsh gas that emanated; anytime there was a spark, there was also an explosion.

There was one accident where 27 people died, and they took them out in pieces and tried to reconstitute them. They were especially interested in their hands, for the fingerprint. After they took them out, they calculated how many there were, who they were, and then they communicated the information to the central administration of the gulag.

Then, there were also people who had been deported and, after they finished their punishment, remained there to work, and they were paid for whatever they did.

Food was very bad, but we ate it with so much appetite - we were very hungry! - and our bodies apparently could assimilate it all. When I was not working, I was always in a state of somnolence, very drowsy. I was always dreaming about how dad used to make food for the cattle, how he boiled the mangel-wurzel, how we put in potatoes, and I was thinking: "If these things were here now!" We were given some sort of soup there. In Russian, it was called *balanda*; there were a few potatoes in this soup; we also had some kind of mush as second dish.

They noticed that we were getting *tânga*. This was a disease, in which the gums get soft, and the teeth no longer hold onto the jaws and they begin to move in the mouth. When they saw this, they took some shrubs, boiled them, and gave us a can of this bitter soup. This strengthened our gums so we could keep our teeth. But what really put us back on our feet was the fish. There were many lakes filled with fish in that taiga. This fish saved us.

I met special people...

I stayed there for eight years. I met special people, very intelligent, who had been deported even since 1937, people who had been teachers at the Lomonosov University. There were also engineers, doctors at the Energy Institute from Moscow. Being older, they no longer worked in the mine, but did lighter jobs: they cleaned or made the fire. When they saw that I was not interested in other people's activities in the barrack - the others used to play domino - they each came to me and told me:

"Young man, I know many, many things. Do you want to talk?"

They told me who they were - one was the dean at the Department of Literature. In this way, with me and with other six or seven persons, they made a group and began to give lectures according to a program. They had no books, nothing, so they made these lectures from memory. They used to tell us:

"You will find out things that even those who study at the Institute do not find out because they are censored."

I had a professor of literature from Moscow who told us about Esenin, Tolstoy, and Dostoevsky, the classics of literature. He had a lecture series, and we stayed and listened. By then, I knew Russian. At the beginning, I learned only the jargon in Russian, the bad words, because this was the situation there. But then I also learned the literary language. After I took this course in literature, I also followed a course in nuclear physics with a professor who knew to explain everything to me in very simple terms. He spoke to me so simply, and I could understand everything; he started with me from zero.

I encountered Romanians from Moldova, Japanese, Chinese, all the nationalities from the Soviet Union. Among the Moldavian detainees, I had some sort of authority because I was recidivist, I was arrested the second time, and I knew the rules of the camp. I tried to help people to maintain their morale. I helped them to not fall into despair. I used to tell them just what others had told me:

"We cannot stay here for 25 years! Either Stalin dies, or something changes!"

I encouraged them in this way. They used to come to me

and confess:

"Look, I am so sorry that I did not get along with my wife and I offended her. If I could be with her now, I would know to appreciate her..."

I talked to them and encouraged them:

"Look, let's make a pledge: if you get out of here, you will behave nicely with her!"

They told me about their problems, their family lives, but I did not know how it was because I was not married. When they arrested me, I had yet to kiss a girl.

I also encountered people who suffered without any fault. There was an old man in Norilsk, named Telepan. Let me tell you how he was arrested: his son was engaged with a girl from the village. He found out only after some time that the girl was a komsomolist,[188] UTC-ist.[189] Eventually, the girl broke up with his son, but while they were together, the old man said these words while the girl was present:

"Well, if I could become a fly, I would get into Stalin's office, then I would transform back into human form, and ask him why he destroyed our religion..."

That was it. The girl denounced him, and for these words he was condemned under the accusation of attempted murder against the leader of the international proletariat. 25 years, just for that! I laughed, and he laughed. For what reason could a man stay in prison...

I will also tell you a story from the gulag when I saved a woman, actually her and her husband. I was no longer working in the mine, but on the surface. I was working at calculating the coal that had to be loaded and sent by wagons. My boss was a civilian woman, a Russian; she was not condemned. I told you that there were also some civilians for certain positions. Her husband was also a civilian, and he worked in the mine.

One time, they brought into the camp around five hundred

---

[188] The Komsomol was the youth organization of the Communist Party in the Soviet Union.

[189] The UTC (Uniunea Tineretului Comunist—the Union of Communist Youth) was the youth organization of the Communist Party in Romania.

prisoners who were very cruel, condemned for political banditry, so people who may have killed a komsomolist, a communist, or other deeds like this. They were a special category: they were included among the political detainees, but for breaking common law. They were very well organized. They asked for and received separate barracks, just for them.

Their leader, Nicolae, tried to make sure that he did easier jobs, since they were taken out for work as well. This is how he found out that there was some sort of train station where the coal was loaded into wagons. He came to this station where I was working and got work there. Before him, there was a History professor from the University in Odessa. Nicolae, the bandit, came to the professor and told him:

"You will no longer come back here starting tomorrow. Ask for work some other place; if not, we'll hang you."

The professor was afraid, so he asked to be moved, and Nicolae came in his place. But he was not able to calculate the volume there, to do what he was asked, so someone else had to work for him. When he saw this woman who worked with us, he thought he could seduce her, but she was not that kind of woman and did not want to reciprocate. At the end of the workday, in the evening, her husband used to come to take her, and they went home together.

If he saw that she refused him, Nicolae got angry and wanted to punish her. When he told me what he wanted to do to her and her husband, I was terrified. I had not believed until that moment that such people could exist in this world. How does God bear them?... They were building a large boiler house. He told me that he wanted to catch her and her husband, take them to the boiler house with six of his people, and first force him to get naked. They wanted to rape the woman on his waistcoat, all seven of them, and to force the man to sing naked the whole time. He even invited me to be part of it.

God forbid such savagery! When I heard this, I thought about how I could save the woman. I told her everything I knew, and she did not return to work the second day. I was terrified; these people were very cruel, very aggressive, and terribly barbarous. Whenever many of them gathered together, they persecuted others and took their bread. They gave you the middle and took the other parts if they were better baked.

Whenever someone died in the barrack, if it was night, we could not take him out since we were locked in. You can imagine - we knew we were there with the dead, and we could no longer sleep. We were in a very tense psychological state, and we could relax only after one-two days, when they took him out. It was the same when I was a guardian at the morgue, when I saw how they threw out the bodies... I was barely breathing too, almost dead. Some people even said that there were cases where people injured in the mine, still breathing, not dead yet, were taken to the morgue. They even asked them:

"What are you doing? Where are you taking me?"

They could see they were being taken away. And then, with their final powers, they shouted:

"Brothers, I am still alive!"

The guards replied:

"Shut up! The doctor knows better."

So they took the man and threw him there, and of course he died immediately. I did not see this, but other people told me of these cases.

It was especially hard when someone we knew died after an accident in the mine. He could be broken into pieces, with his legs amputated, and each one of us thought that we could have been in his place. Whether you wanted or not, the people who worked in the mine were different than those working at the surface because the former did not know when they could be injured, and their lives were always in God's hands. They were more faithful, friendlier, and they helped each other. They were all very good people and did not fight; they were an example for the others.

The roughest prison in which I stayed was the one in Tobolsk, someplace on a cliff. It was lugubrious. The prison existed from the time of Catherine II. It had three rows of walls, and the hallways were paved with felt, so that you could not hear when the guards were walking. I met an old man there who told me that Emperor Nicolas was first brought there, in Tobolsk, with his entire family, when the Bolsheviks arrested him. The old man who told me this was from Tobolsk, and he said that they allowed the emperor to go to church. One time, when the emperor went to the service, a soldier lost his mind, dropped the gun, and ran away. They caught him and asked him why he ran away. He replied that while the emperor and his family were in the church, he saw an angel above the emperor who told him, "endure it, son, to the end!" The soldier was scared and ran away. This is what the old man whom I met at the Tobolsk prison told me.

I have a habit from prison. When someone died, as it was very cold, if he did not die with his hands on his chest but rather having them somehow at his side, he froze this way and nothing could be done. They broke his hands to be able to carry him from there. I got used to sleeping with my hands on my chest because I was afraid I would die with them on the side and they would break them too. Even after I came back from the gulag, at home, I was still sleeping like this because I got used to it.

Also, because of the cold, I used to move my toes all the time during night so that I would not get frostbite. I got so used to it that I moved them even during sleep. Later, when I came back from the camp, I kept this habit for a long time. I moved my toes even when I was home. I would sleep next to my wife and she would get scared when I touched her while moving my toes. Well, after Stalin died and after they shot Beria, I told all of them:

"You must know that now, on earth, after these two died, we cannot say that the world has lost two humans. These were not humans."

After their death, when Khrushchev came into power, they began forming committees to retry the trials of the detainees. But before that, the detainees had a strike and stopped all the coal mines. They asked for a representative from Moscow to speak to them because they did not trust the local authorities. However, the local leadership was afraid to tell Moscow. So they came in disguise and claimed they were from Moscow. The problem was that there were important people among the detainees, who knew the people in Moscow and so realized their trick immediately.

Eventually they sent a committee from Moscow, from the Supreme Soviet, from the Prosecution, and from the Central Committee. They called every detainee, to reanalyze the causes for which he was condemned. They called me as well, and I told them the truth, that I was not in the army; I told them everything that happened to me. But they did not liberate me. They only wrote on my file that Istrate continued to be an enemy of the Soviet Union. They liberated the others, but they left me there, to continue my condemnation of 25 years.

From our trial, only three of us remained in prison. I remained there until they took us for re-investigations in Chişinău. But they still did not liberate me. However, they did not send me back to Naransk, but to Mordovia, on the shore of Volga, where I stayed one more year. I did not want to write any complaint because I knew that if I wrote one and asked for clemency, I would be recognizing my guilt.

In Mordovia, I stayed at a camp, in Iavas, in camp number 2. I was sick and I could not eat, so they left me in a camp for disabled people. There were many detainees there, even from 1937. Eventually, they liberated us in 1960, unexpectedly.

The liberation

When I came back from my second prison, I looked for my papers. My papers remained at the Theatrical Institute in Leningrad when they arrested me. I went to the KGB, in Chişinău.

I was no longer afraid of the Securitate, because this is what they say: the first 10 years are hard, but then you get used to it. I was no longer afraid of them, and I went there to ask for my papers. I told them:

"Look, I was liberated; I need my papers to continue my studies."

The one with whom I spoke at the Securitate showed me an envelope in which it was written in Russian: "Top secret." They were kept forever, so they were not returned. This man told me:

"Whatever fell in here, alleluia, you will no longer get them! Go and write to Leningrad where you studied!"

I lost one year looking for my papers. I wrote everywhere,

even to Bucharest. As I told you, I had followed the seminary in refuge to Romania, but I did not receive anything that could prove this. Indignant as I was, I eventually went to the Ministry of Education and told them:

"How is this possible? If you want, if you don't believe me, examine me!"

Those people told me:

"It is no longer possible. Go and follow the evening courses for a winter; tell them you have nine years of schooling, and you sign up for the tenth year" - back then you did ten years in school - "you will receive a certificate, and then you can go to whatever major you want. If not, you will lose more time searching for these papers."

I thought about it and it seemed right. So I signed up for evening courses. I took again all the courses, I studied, and I finished with very good grades; I was first in my class. Then I went to the University and took only one exam. I passed it with the maximum points, so I was accepted. I signed up for History and finished it, even if I realized I had an inclination toward technical fields. But since I stayed in prison with world-class historians, I learned many things from them. I thought that the truth about our nation could be found in History.

I wanted to study the Romanians and our history more in depth, to see who we are, since when we existed. I wanted to find out the whole truth, not only what I knew from Trajan's Column, from Tacitus' *Annals*, from Stefan's defense castles, from the *doinas*,[190] the ballades, and so many other things that show that here, in these lands, we are Romanians and our ancestors were Romanians.

The Russian historians also began to study the history of these lands. They speak about it starting with 1300 and, the larger majority of them, from 1812, when the Russians occupied Bessarabia. For them, this is it; this is when history began. But we, the Romanians, we are from here, we have not come from other places. They are the ones who came. This is why we are

---

[190] The *doinas* are folk songs that express a mixture of feelings—desire, love, revolt. They usually take the form of a lament.

much oppressed, because the Russians wanted to assimilate us. They succeeded to separate us from our mother country, but they could not assimilate us, and we must resist.

I consider these things to be sacred, and this is why I speak about what happened to me, so that our descendants know who was here before them. During communism, the Russians were poisoned with this ideology. They believe that they are the older brother, and when they look at Moldavians or others whom they occupied, they think, "Who is this guy? We are masters here."

In general, wherever the Russian boots fell, they no longer left willingly. The Russian believes he is entitled, and this is what happens in many other places, not only in Moldova. What connection does the Russian have with the Baltic States? With Moldova? Nothing, but wherever they land, they are very aggressive.

The power of faith

I want to tell you about faith, about the power that faith has when we are truly honest. I am convinced to my last cell, to my last fiber, that I would not have resisted without faith in God. During my first arrest, when I worked in those trenches and was dystrophic, we had to go from the camp to the zone where we had to work. It was two-three kilometers long. Winter, summer, we had to go in formation, five in a line. If you made one step to the left or to the right of the convoy, it was considered an escape attempt, and the guards would shoot you without warning.

During winter, we were followed by a sleigh that carried the sick. But if anyone fell, the dogs were the first who came over him; then, they would put him on the sleigh to take him from there. Before the sleigh came, you were either shot by the guards or killed by the dogs. I was dystrophic, and I could not walk. I prayed to God to get through the march. If the people next to me had not supported me, I would have fallen. The entire time, in the morning, marching from the camp to the zone where we had to work, I closed my eyes and said the prayers I knew. I used to say all of them: the Creed, Birthgiver of God, Our Father, everything I knew.

After I finished them, I said them again, and this is how I walked the whole way, saying prayers. I repeated them, and when I arrived, I could breathe relieved: "I arrived; I am saved here!" In the evening, going back, I said the same prayers. "Look, I am saved, one other day passed!" This was repeated not only one or two days, but many days. I got used to this. Whenever I was going and coming back, this was my preoccupation, to pray, but with extraordinary honesty! I realized that, indeed, if man understands faith and addresses God, God helps him immediately, gives him the power to fight, to go on, regardless of the difficulties. This stayed with me my entire life. I am convinced that only prayer saved me because I would not have been able to go on this road otherwise, and I would have fallen. The guards would have shot me or the dogs would have killed me.

One other time, when I was working at the conveyor where the coal was taken out, I fell into a bunker that I thought was covered. It was ten meters deep, in a pyramid form, with the base at the surface. I was fortunate that there was some small coal inside. I began shouting, but it was like in hell, I could hear nothing. I shouted for nothing. I tried to get up, but I could not. I found wires from when they detonated this bunker, so I tried to hold onto them to go up. I got up a bit, and then fell again. I tried again and again. All of a sudden, I heard that this bunker was the next one to be filled with coal - I knew that if they filled the bunker next to mine, this one would be next. They did not know I was in there. All of sudden, I don't know where I found so much strength to grab the wires and get to the top. I managed to get almost to the top, but I could not find something to hold onto and get out. I finally found something, grabbed it, and, little by little, I managed to get up to the surface.

I have another story from the camp. I was on a construction team that worked on painting some houses. I had to carry the water used for painting. I went some place outside to get water from a hole made for canalization. It was a deep hole, and I put a board on top of it. During the day, the ice that was holding up the board melted, and I fell in that deep hole filled with water. I was very scared. I was alone, and it was very difficult to get out of there. I made an extraordinary effort. I felt God's help there because the greatest athlete could not have come out of the hole by himself, without help. I fell into the water, to the bottom of the hole. I could not grab anything; the board was on the brink. However, I managed to come out alone.

When I returned and the workers saw me all wet, they did not know what to do with me. It was evening, and it was getting cold, so all the clothes froze on me. It was as if I was made out of a tin plate. It was very difficult to get back to the camp. I went to the infirmary. They took my temperature, but I did not have fever, so they did not give me any pills. They only gave me pills the second day. I was so scared when I fell into that hole! I prayed to God then as well. No one was there to help me, and I felt God's power. I am convinced now, at the end of my life, that true faith does not consist in spontaneity, to pray to God only when you need it. It is good to pray then, but you must pray all the time, to think of God permanently and to pray.

There was something else. When I was arrested the second time, after the condemnation, when I was in my cell, before they took us to Siberia, I had a dream during the night. The Mother of the Lord came to me and told me: "What you have suffered until now, in the first prison, is nothing; suffering is from now on. Suffering awaits you, so prepare for suffering!"

When I returned home, I was dystrophic. I was 1.80 meters tall, and I had 40-45 kilograms. I was only skin and bones. When I got out of the train, I had 10 kilometers from the station to home, and it took me half a day. I could not walk; I had to take breaks constantly, to get some rest. When I arrived home, my mom did not even recognize me. She thought I was a beggar. I had to tell her:

"*Mama*, it's me, Nicolae!"

She then recognized me and took me in her arms, but I told her:

"*Mama*, let me go bow to Him."

I went and I kneeled. I kneeled, I made the sign of the cross, and I thanked God that he brought me back alive.

Now, I am joyful for one thing: I came out of the gulag and these prisons without being bitter and vengeful. I even met the one who tortured me badly, and I did not tell him anything. I did not reproach him at all. I thought about my sins, and I remembered how many times God saved me. So I thought I have to forgive as well, and I tried to find excuses for him: this is how the times were... I tried to put myself in his place, and I managed to forgive him. I used to meet with many of the survivors who stayed in prison with me. We used to talk. They were surprised that I could forgive, because not all forgave. I used to tell them even when we were in prison:

"We must forgive, so that we don't come out from here with this hatred, so that we do not go to get revenge."

It was not difficult for me to forgive those who wronged me, but it was very difficult to convince my comrades, those who were together with me. After they came back, they thought about revenge with hatred. They really considered getting revenge. There are so many methods; we could get revenge and no one would have found out. But I did not agree to it, and they began to blame me and wonder whether I was a traitor. They were amazed:

"How can you pray for these people who did so much evil?"

I explained to them that I pray for those people so that God would illuminate their minds and they would see that they were doing evil. If they had understood, they would have immediately stopped doing evil, torturing so much. This is what we have to do; otherwise, we would remain bitter, and evil is formed within our souls and attacks us first of all. This stain of sin is developed within the soul. This is what I told them.

Later, when some of my comrades from prison began to die, I told those who were still alive that they have to prepare so that they would not leave this world being bitter, but rather peaceful. I used to tell them that we had to prepare to have a peaceful death. You must conquer this peaceful death; otherwise, evilness harms us badly. I am glad I could do this, and I did not find any of them to leave this world in a bitter state. If I look back, I can say that the prison helped me get closer to God. All the tortures and atrocities made me understand that I had no other escape but in God. How much they wanted to destroy me, to murder me during the interrogations! But God helped me and I survived. I went through all this, and I was freed from prison. Who helped me? Nobody helped me in the gulag; God helped me.

I do not regret that I went through this experience of the prison. If I did not go through it, I may have been a totally different man. I may have become a communist, or who knows what other things I may have done. How can I know what I could have done... Who knows what may have happened to me if I did not go to prison? If I think about my situation before the first prison, when I was a school principal, I may have gotten married, joined the party...

When I came back, I found all my colleagues who were like me, teachers, professors, those of the same age with me who had not been to prison - they were all party chiefs. They were already heroes of the socialist work, had cars and all kinds of things. I may have been the same way if I did not go to prison. Now, see, God helped me; I am healthy and I can help anyone. I thank God for the help He gave me. Each evening, before going to sleep, I pray to God and ask Him for forgiveness for every evil I may have done, and I forgive all who wronged me.

Chişinău, Bessarabia, June 24, 2011

Photos from the lives of the narrators

Margareta Cemârtan-Spânu

There was only one girl among those at the orphanage with whom I felt closer, Zoia Panamariova.

Bunica was our support the whole time, and we were saved from many things because of her. She was a very good, very faithful, and very wise woman. She raised me until I was ten years old, and she was like a mother to me.

Bunica died with a candle, confessed and communed. They buried her beautifully, with three priests, a memorial service, alms, and everything as is the custom. This is how her prayer, that she had said every day and night in Siberia, was fulfilled.

An orphan child is only a bitter tear, an unfulfilled desire,
a bird without wings…

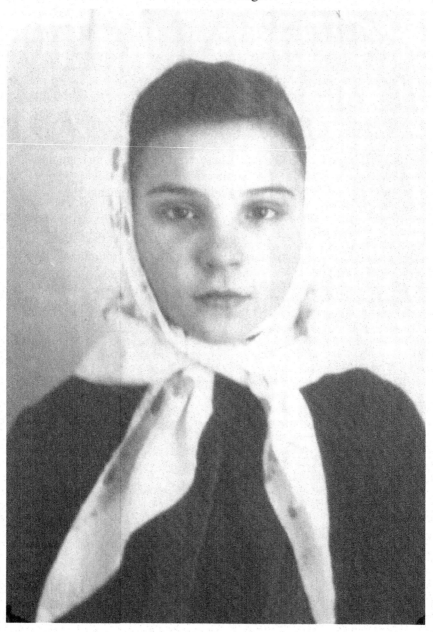

Margareta Spânu at 13 years old.

I got a job as a nanny.

Dad bought me some fabric, and I sewed a dress. I even took a picture with it, and I wore it for a long time, until it broke. This was my first experience with sewing.

I got married when I was sixteen, and my life as a child ended.

I was at ease only with dad. With him I was happy and open.

Ion Moraru

Bunelul, Pintilie Oloinic, was the pillar of wisdom that supported me my whole life.

My *mama*, my dear holy *măicuţă*, please forgive me for all the pain that I brought upon you.

Lealea, the first girl with whom I fell in love…

There are millions like me in this devilish and crazy country, and someone must raise the Sword of Justice sometime…

Profira and I became husband and wife from that day forward. I was 28 years old, and she was three years my junior. She was so small and thin, but with a soul as great as a mountain. We then began to build our house and to get settled. Adeluța came to the world, and after seven years Inuța, my younger daughter, also arrived. The two of us were teachers at the school in the village, and life flowed slowly.

Galina Baranovski Shapovalova

Mama loved *tata* until her last breath.

So I remained alone, and you/ Could help me not in wilderness/ To feed my children, powerless…

Mama was my model and my encouragement.

You, children, must be honorable successors of your parents.

The narrators telling their stories

Margareta Cemârtan-Spânu   Ion Moraru

Galina Baranovschi Şapovalova   Teodosia Cosmin

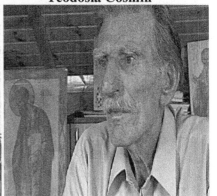

Tamara Oală Pleşca   Nicolae Istrate

CPSIA information can be obtained
at www.ICGtesting.com
Printed in the USA
LVOW03s0313090517

533708LV00029B/878/P